Computer Architecture for Scientists

The dramatic increase in computer performance has been extraordinary, but not for all computations: it has key limits and structure. Software architects, developers, and even data scientists need to understand how to exploit the fundamental structure of computer performance to harness it for future applications.

Using a principled approach, *Computer Architecture for Scientists* covers the four key pillars of computer performance and imparts a high-level basis for reasoning with and understanding these concepts. These principles and models provide approachable high-level insights and quantitative modeling without distracting low-level detail. The pillars include:

- Small is fast: how size scaling drives performance.
- Hidden parallelism: how a sequential program can be executed faster with parallelism.
- Dynamic locality: skirting physical limits, by arranging data in a smaller space.
- Explicit parallelism: increasing performance with teams of workers.

Finally, the text covers the GPU and machine-learning accelerators that have become important for more and more mainstream applications. Ideal for upper-level undergraduates.

Andrew A. Chien is the William Eckhardt Professor at the University of Chicago, Director of the CERES Center for Unstoppable Computing, and a Senior Scientist at Argonne National Laboratory. Since 2017, he has served as Editor-in-Chief of the Communications of the ACM. Chien is a global research leader in parallel computing, computer architecture, clusters, and cloud computing, and has received numerous awards for his research. In 1994 he was named an National Science Foundation Young Investigator. Dr. Chien served as Vice President of Research at Intel Corporation from 2005 to 2010, and on advisory boards for the National Science Foundation, Department of Energy, Japan RWCP, and distinguished universities such as Stanford, UC Berkeley, EPFL, and the University of Washington. From 1998 to 2005, he was the SAIC Chair Professor at UCSD, and prior to that a professor at the University of Illinois. Dr. Chien is a Fellow of the ACM, Fellow of the IEEE, and Fellow of the AAAS, and earned his PhD, MS, and BS from the Massachusetts Institute of Technology.

Computer Architecture for Scientists

Principles and Performance

ANDREW A. CHIEN
University of Chicago

CAMBRIDGE
UNIVERSITY PRESS

University Printing House, Cambridge CB2 8BS, United Kingdom

One Liberty Plaza, 20th Floor, New York, NY 10006, USA

477 Williamstown Road, Port Melbourne, VIC 3207, Australia

314–321, 3rd Floor, Plot 3, Splendor Forum, Jasola District Centre, New Delhi – 110025, India

103 Penang Road, #05–06/07, Visioncrest Commercial, Singapore 238467

Cambridge University Press is part of the University of Cambridge.

It furthers the University's mission by disseminating knowledge in the pursuit of education, learning, and research at the highest international levels of excellence.

www.cambridge.org
Information on this title: www.cambridge.org/highereducation/isbn/9781316518533
DOI: 10.1017/9781009000598

First published 2022

Printed in the United Kingdom by TJ Books Limited, Padstow, Cornwall, 2022

A catalogue record for this publication is available from the British Library.

ISBN 978-1-316-51853-3 Hardback

Additional resources for this publication at www.cambridge.org/chien

For my father, who inspired a deep love of science, technology, and teaching, and for my mother, who inspired a deep joy of life

Contents

Preface

Because of computing's history, the pedagogy of computer architecture has been aimed at future computer designers and engineers. However, a growing number of data scientists, engineers who are not computer engineers, and even the majority of computer scientists (i.e. artificial intelligence and more) see computing as an intellectual tool. These scientists and engineers need an understanding of computer architecture for insights into how hardware enables, shapes, and limits performance. They need an understanding of computer architecture that allows them to reason about performance today and scaling into the future. It is for them that I have undertaken this book.

In fall 2011 I joined the University of Chicago faculty and taught undergraduate computer architecture. As the quarter progressed, it became clear that my students had different backgrounds, motivations, and interests – a marked contrast to the engineering students I taught at the University of Illinois and University of California, San Diego. Over the course of several quarters, I realized that the traditional bottom-up approach to teaching computer architecture (from gates to sequential circuits, from instruction sets to pipelines and caches – with an emphasis on how it works and how to optimize it) was not reaching these students. This traditional pedagogy is designed for computer engineering students, and increasingly even many computer science students do not find it compelling.

The University of Chicago students were interested in the "scientific principles" of computer architecture, principles that would enable them to reason about hardware performance for higher-level ends. Their view of computation was as an intellectual multiplier, and they were interested in a top-down view of capabilities, scaling, and limits – not mechanisms. Their point of view reflects computing's broad expansion, most recently manifest in artificial intelligence and data science, that has shifted computer science's center of mass upward and its boundary outward – into a wide variety of sciences (physical, biological, and social) as well as nearly every aspect of society, commerce, and even government.

For these data science, artificial intelligence, and applied machine learning students, a foundation in computer architecture should provide scientific understanding of how the remarkable power of computing is possible, and what limits that power – and, as we look forward to the future, how the continued progress in technology will increase computing capabilities. This book provides such a principles-based grounding in the current and future capabilities of computing hardware. It is designed for several different curricula and settings:

- A quarter-long course in a Computer Science program in a liberal arts college or Data Science program: Chapters 1–3, 5, and 7. Depending on the curricular fit, perhaps add parts of microarchitecture (Chapter 4), framing CPUs as practically universal (Chapter 6), and accelerators (Chapter 8).
- A semester-long course in a Computer Science program in a liberal arts or Data Science program: Chapters 1–5, 7, and 9. If there is time, perhaps add back the hot topic of accelerators (Chapter 8).
- A semester-long course in a Math–Computer Science or Data Science program at an institution with a deep engineering culture: Chapters 1–9. This includes the full text.

I would like to thank the students in my "Computer Architecture for Scientists" course at the University of Chicago for their contributions – their thoughtful questions and responses were critical to increasing the clarity of the text, lectures, and exercises.

Finally, a heartfelt thanks to my family, including my wife, Ellen, and my two daughters, Jennifer and Athena. For their steadfast support for my writing this book and my absence on many late nights, I am grateful. Without your patience, tolerance, and encouragement, it would have been impossible. Thank you!

I am indebted to the University of Chicago, whose spirit of innovative scholarship and pedagogy has been both an inspiration and support for this book!

1 Computing and the Transformation of Society

This book is for the growing community of scientists and even engineers who use computing and need a scientific understanding of computer architecture – those who view computation as an intellectual multiplier, and consequently are interested in capabilities, scaling, and limits, not mechanisms. That is, the *scientific principles* behind computer architecture, and how to reason about hardware performance for higher-level ends. With the dramatic rise of both data analytics and artificial intelligence, there has been a rapid growth in interest and progress in data science. There has also been a shift in the center of mass of computer science upward and outward, into a wide variety of sciences (physical, biological, and social), as well as nearly every aspect of society.

For these audiences, the book provides an understanding and the scientific principles that describe the unique scaling that enabled computing to improve over a billion-fold in performance, cost, and size. It frames the fundamental characteristics of computing performance today, and how it can be tapped for applications. Further, it provides insights into the constraints that limit further improvement of computing, and likely directions for future advances. In short, it frames where computing hardware is going in the coming decades.

In this chapter, we survey the broad and pervasive impact of computing on society, and discuss computing's unique characteristics that have driven its proliferation. We describe the four pillars that account for the remarkable improvement of computers, and discuss expectations for readers as well as specifics of the book's organization.

1.1 Computing Transforms Society and Economy

It is no exaggeration to say computers are endemic, present in a staggering breadth of human-made devices, and used to deliver many of the new innovations and capabilities that drive our society and economy forward. Through the 1980s and 1990s it became common for professionals in the developed world to have *personal computers*. In the past decade, since the introduction of the smartphone by Apple in 2007, it has become common for not only professionals, but all adults and even children to have *smartphones*. These device categories represent 250 million, and one billion units sold per year, respectively. The cloud, for all its glamour, is a relatively small number of processors, accounting for tens of millions of server sales each year. However, these evident computers, while important, are but a small fraction of computing in the world today.

Embedded computers have long accounted for the largest numbers of computers in the world. For decades these computers have been used to implement fixed functions (thermostats, engine timing, factory machines, point of sale terminals, etc.), doing so in a cost-effective and compact fashion for the need at hand. These systems use computers to implement control systems, communication protocols, and in some cases user interfaces. Since 2010, as embedded computers with integrated networking and storage have become quite inexpensive, driven by the explosive growth of the smartphone ecosystem, momentum has built behind the vision of the "Internet of Things" (IoT). The IoT can be more precisely described as embedded networked computers [69] and is expected to grow to 40 billion devices in 2025. These devices combine low-cost computing in everyday devices such as motion detectors, video cameras, doorbells, smoke detectors, hotel door locks, automobile keys, stereo speakers, holiday lights, smart TVs, public trash cans, and more with network access that enables intelligent data processing, smart group analytics, and in-field upgrades. Together, these form a potent combination for new services, and acceleration of the data economy.

To get a sense of how pervasive computing is, here we consider several dimensions of its ubiquity.

1.1.1   Home

When personal computers became cheap enough in the late 1980s for individuals to afford them, affluent families began to buy home computers. As laptops, a standard package of computer, display, and Wi-Fi networking, became widely available in the early 2000s families might have had several computers. In today's home, a collection of smartphones, tablets, laptops, and more is typical. As for embedded computers, a modern collection might include smart keys, thermostats, smart TVs, intelligent voice assistants, wireless routers, smart appliances, security cameras, and smart locks, just to name a few. Each of these devices includes computing, storage, and networking – for amplified capability through the cloud. Today, a family of four might have 50 or more such computing devices in their home.

1.1.2   Automobiles and Transportation

Similarly, the automobile has progressed through phases of computing adoption. Early uses included engine timing control and anti-lock brakes (traction control), both applications of high-speed monitoring and response. From there, applications exploded into a broad range of areas ranging from cabin heating and cooling, lighting, turn signals, windshield washers, wireless locking, and more recently USB power, as well as entertainment and navigation systems. An automobile generally depends on more than 50 computers, and the recent addition of wireless connectivity has created new "networked" features such as LoJack, Onstar, and Tesla's software updates. For more than two decades computing systems have accounted for the vast majority of new features in cars, and despite the low cost of electronics, a growing fraction of the vehicle cost.

With the advent of electrically powered cars, the adoption of computing in cars is deepening and accelerating. Per-car navigation and efficient dispatch has given rise to ridesharing companies such as Uber, Didi, and Lyft, which dispatch millions of drivers for billions of rides each month! With public-transit tracking and sensors on buses and trains combined with cloud-based aggregation/integration, commuters who choose not to drive can optimize their trips. These moving sensors allow cloud services to infer dynamic traffic maps, and they are used by drivers and logistics companies to optimize delivery, pickup, and more. The dream of self-driving vehicles is built on the integration of sensors, artificial intelligence (AI), and large quantities of computation (>100 tera-operations/second computing power) in cars and trucks. This growth has been remarkable, and we're likely to see more and more!

1.1.3 Commerce

There are many examples where computing has revolutionized commerce, ranging from finance to retail to logistics to manufacturing. Let's describe retail as a relatable example – everyone shops. Computing has totally transformed the retail process. We depict elements of computing in retail and more in Figure 1.1. Here's one slice through it!

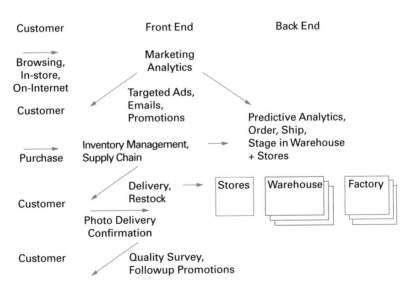

Figure 1.1 Examples of computing applied to retail, supply chain, and manufacturing. Each box includes both computation and extensive sensing (location, scans), as well as large-scale data collection and analytics.

- **Marketing:** Products are extensively advertised through social media, web ads, and emails. In virtually every online activity we have become accustomed to the idea that ads will be placed next to whatever we are doing. These ads are clickable and transition directly to web pages to buy the product.
- **Purchasing:** Buying products online, once an oddity, is now a mainstream method of shopping. With online shopping comes delivery, from services such as Amazon Prime, Instacart, Grubhub, and Walmart Delivery surpassing 10 percent of all retail in 2019. The online purchasing process is made possible by computing and the Internet.
- **Tracking:** Both before purchase (stock-check) and while in transit, buyers can track the location of their purchase, following it from the warehouse, to their city, and then en route to their home. These capabilities expose information from the store's inventory system and the delivery service's internal logistics system – both complex computing applications. And the end result is continued engagement, anticipation, and diagnosis of any mix-ups all the way to your door.
- **Delivery:** The hardest step is often to find the customer's front door, and delivery services employ global-positioning service (GPS) tracking, per-address notes, and time-of-day customized logistics, all implemented as computing systems, to not only get the purchase to the customer, but to report the package's delivery with a photo – sent to your smartphone. This ensures your immediate awareness, and also documents the delivery of the product to you.

While we have focused on the consumer retail process, many other dimensions of commerce, such as supply chains, billing, and finance, have been equally transformed. Each e-commerce purchase transaction triggers a collection of follow-on activities, all of which are enabled by the low cost and extraordinary speed of computing.

For example, a purchase triggers artificial intelligence (AI) applications. A purchase updates customer classifiers, and these classifiers drive predictors used to target advertising. Many e-commerce sites also host customer reviews singing the praises (or excoriating the flaws) of products. One way to think of this is as computerized and online "word of mouth." We can easily search for reviews of a particular product – and its competitors – as well as find the most positive and negative reviews – out of a sea of thousands. All of this is provided courtesy of fast, inexpensive computing.

Another dimension of the purchasing process is payment. With credit/debit cards and even electronic payment apps on smartphones, customers can pay "with a tap," or in the case of e-commerce "with a click." Charges are customized for local taxes, shipping, and personalized reward programs before they are charged against a credit account or directly removed from our bank account. Purchase histories are tabulated against complex loyalty programs, from total use (membership miles) to customized promotions (2 percent off on gasoline or grocery stores), and even temporary promotions (2 percent off on clothing this month only). This dizzying array is beyond the ability of most consumers to keep straight, and the retailers can only manage with complex computer applications that seek to optimize revenue and profit against products, inventory, and customers! One more important dimension is the supply chain, which triggers manufacture and retailer purchase of items in response to a sale. That supply chain may include multiple parties, span 15,000 kilometers, and weeks of latency.

1.2   Computing Transforms Science and Discovery

Science and discovery are about the creation of new knowledge and understanding, so they are fueled by tools that speed information access, analysis, and propagation. Consequently, computing has transformed them, and it's now unthinkable to pursue discovery without computing as a fundamental tool. We outline several specific dimensions below:

- **Finding information:** The growth of the Internet and the power of text-based search enables scientists to find relevant information and recent discoveries from around the world. Increasingly sophisticated indexing enables automated filtering and notification of potentially relevant advances.
- **Disseminating knowledge:** Electronic publication combined with rapidly expanding open-access publications and innovations such as arXiv, and digital libraries allow new insights to rapidly spread around the world. With growing government-led requirements for open access to government-funded scientific research fueling growing global access, new discoveries are propagated both faster and more widely than ever before.
- **Scientific modeling:** Some of the earliest computers modeled the flight of projectiles. Another major task was fluid dynamics – flows and explosions – and soon thereafter, nuclear physics. Today, computational modeling at the molecular level underlies drug design, materials design, nanotechnology, advanced electronics, and more. Climate change, epidemiology, and ecology are all studied with computational models. Increasingly, computational modeling is used for human behavior, modeling psychology, economics, and more.
- **Analytics:** Computer simulations are used extensively for scientific and engineering modeling. The explosion of data from internet usage, rich sensors, video, smartphones, and the IoT enables "digital twins" that track the real world. With terabytes of data, large-scale computing is required for analysis, including precise analysis to extract even small signals. For example, analysis to understand the spread of the virus that causes COVID-19, and the effectiveness of antivirals and vaccines, or the health impacts of the widespread economic disruption caused by it. Bioinformatics and clinical data are used to understand its evolution and spread (analysis of its lineage).

Despite the broadly transformative impact of computing on society, economy, science, and discovery, few people understand why such a transformation has been possible. This book explains the science behind why it has been possible, how it came to pass, and where it is going!

1.3   Extraordinary Characteristics of Computing

How has this radical transformation been possible? The proliferation of computing into every sector of society and economy has been enabled by the central importance of information – for intelligent behavior, control, and organization. Access to up-to-date and detailed information is well understood to be a prerequisite for success in an increasingly fast-paced, competitive, and global environment. So industry has been a key driver for ambitious use of computing, but recent developments have demonstrated that individuals are equally interested in up-to-date and detailed information to drive their personal connection, enjoyment, and even social status.

Computing technology has made remarkable advances over the past 75 years since the pioneering digital electronic computer, ENIAC, in 1945 [104], delivering dramatic improvements in cost, size, power, and performance. These advances are explained below:

- **Cost:** The original ENIAC system cost $487,000 (about $7 million in 2019 dollars), in contrast to today's ARM Cortex-M3 microprocessor, which costs a few cents. Adjusted for inflation, today's cost of computing is 1/350,000,000 that of 75 years ago, not even taking into account the much higher performance of the modern processor. This cost reduction is primarily due to miniaturization and high volumes of computers sold.
- **Size:** The original ENIAC system occupied 2,350 cubic feet (65 m^3) of space, filling a 50-foot long basement room. In contrast, a small microprocessor today occupies the area of 0.11 mm^2 (silicon) and is 1.1×10^{-9} m^3 in volume. This area corresponds to the cross-section of about 10 human hairs. Thus, today's microprocessor occupies a space approximately 1/60,000,000,000 of the ENIAC system.
- **Power:** The original ENIAC system consumed 150 kW of power; in contrast, the Cortex-M3 processor is dramatically more energy efficient, consuming less than 5×10^{-6} watts. This means that today's processor has a power requirement less than 1/30,000,000,000 that of the original ENIAC 75 years ago.
- **Performance:** The original ENIAC system could complete approximately 5,000 operations per second, whereas the Cortex-M3 is approximately 50,000 times faster in computation. Today's fastest microprocessors achieve single-thread performance of about 10 billion instructions/second, which translates to a performance increase of nearly 2 million times compared to 75 years ago.

Overall, the performance of a single computer – at first a collection of racks but now down to a single silicon chip – has increase by a factor of a trillion, 10^{12}, as illustrated in Figure 1.2. These remarkable advances have enabled the widespread adoption of computers and computation to replace and improve the capabilities of our modern products and systems. These million- and billion-fold improvements have allowed computing systems to acquire new functionalities (features!) and a staggering complexity of software systems (hundreds of millions of lines of code across iOS and

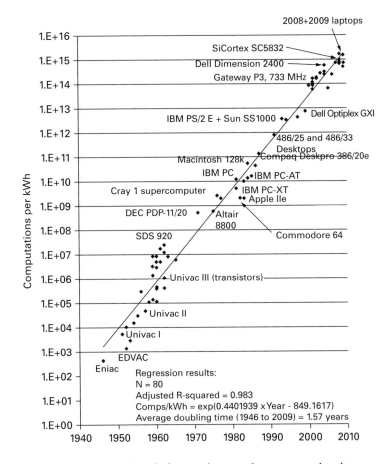

Figure 1.2 Increase in the power/speed of computing over the past seven decades.

Android). These codebases depend on the modern advanced hardware capabilities to deliver interactive applications and new features in mobile and IoT devices.

The decreased cost of computers has also led to the rise of cloud computing, where millions of processors are combined to do global-scale computations. These large assemblies of computers enable applications of unthinkable scale, such as internet search and global social networks. Further, their ability to efficiently share resources among applications allows a further drop in the cost of computing.

Beyond enabling large, complex systems, the falling cost of computing, combined with its widespread availability, has driven the growth of a vibrant, international computer science community. That community of hundreds of thousands of researchers and millions of computing professionals has driven a broad advance in fundamental topics such as theory and algorithms, programming languages and compilers, software systems as we have mentioned, and a dizzying variety of applications of computing. For example, there are currently over three million software applications available in the iOS and Android mobile application stores. And these advances also fuel growing excitement in AI and statistical machine learning.

1.4   What is Computer Architecture?

Computer architecture is the science and engineering that underpins the design of computer hardware. It is both the design of the software–hardware interface that defines portability and correct execution for software, and also the organizational understanding for hardware that effectively exploits advancing microelectronics technology for increased computing performance. For this reason, computer organization is another term used for computer architecture. These forces are depicted in Figure 1.3.

Because computers are rendered useful by software programs, the flexible support of software applications, and thereby well-developed uses of computing, is critical. As a result, existing software (applications and operating systems) acts as a conservative force on computer architecture, constraining its rate of change and limiting advancement of its performance. One manifestation of this is that computer architectures typically provide **binary compatibility**, the ability to run programs written for older versions of the architecture. On the other hand, new applications often demand new computing structures and efficiencies, driving higher rates of change, and in some cases radical incompatibility. A good example of this is the new computing paradigm created by deep learning (aka deep neural networks, or more broadly AI and machine learning), in which arithmetic operation density and efficiency is favored over flexible data structures and control. A 2019 article noted over 100 venture-funded AI hardware startups – all pursuing approaches incompatible with traditional CPU software [93].

Beneath these tensions for software portability, legacy software, new applications, and new software, all computer performance depends on organizing the work of executing software programs, and the corresponding blocks of hardware to achieve high performance. This gives rise to the basic structure of computers, covered in Chapter 2. But beyond a basic organizational understanding, computer architecture is driven forward by the rapid advance of hardware microelectronics technology that has provided

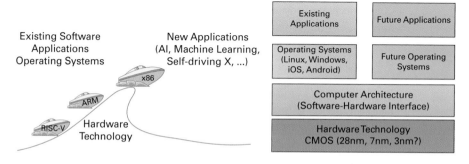

Figure 1.3 Computer architecture supports existing and future applications by providing a stable interface for software and increasing performance. Performance is driven by advances in hardware technology and in computer architecture understanding of how to organize systems, notionally (left) and formally (right). Beneficiaries of these advances are future applications – and you!

dramatically faster devices, larger numbers of devices, and lower-cost devices over the past seven decades. When building blocks change in these three dimensions by factors of one thousand, one million, and in some cases one billion, qualitative changes in computer organization become not only possible, but profitable in terms of performance. Thus, computer architecture also involves the invention of new algorithmic techniques (implemented in hardware), as well as new organizational elements that shape computer organization. We will discuss the basic trends and most important insights that enable programmers of today to efficiently exploit billions of transistors with the ease of a high-level Python or JavaScript program.

Principle 1.1: The Role of Computer Architecture

Computer architecture enables software portability and determines the performance properties of software applications.

1.5 Four Pillars of Computer Performance: Miniaturization, Hidden Parallelism, Dynamic Locality, and Explicit Parallelism

The development of computing technology has created advances in computing performance of ten billion billion-fold (10^{19} times) over the past seven decades. This unprecedented increase has been achieved based on four major pillars and thousands of smaller innovations (see Figure 1.4). These four pillars are:

- **Miniaturization:** Riding the rapid shrinking of electronics to smaller sizes, computers benefited in speed, power, cost, and size.
- **Hidden parallelism:** An important technique used to manage complexity in computer software the sequential abstraction (computing operations are ordered). Employing growing numbers of inexpensive transistors, computer architects invented techniques that execute a program's instructions in parallel while preserving software's key tool for reasoning – sequential abstraction. These hidden parallelism techniques significantly increase performance.

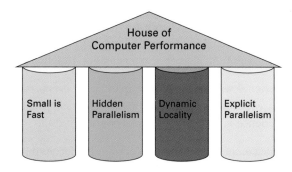

Figure 1.4 The four pillars that provide the extraordinary performance of computers are miniaturization, hidden parallelism, dynamic locality, and explicit parallelism.

- **Dynamic locality:** Software applications' growing complexity demands memory capacity increases, but large memories can only be accessed at low speed. Computers finesse this paradox by exploiting dynamic locality, making small, transient sets of data accessible at high speed, and efficiently guessing which are most important to the application.
- **Explicit parallelism:** Beyond the limits of a single processor (core), growing computing requirements are met by employing millions of cores in both supercomputers and the cloud. The primary drawback of explicit parallelism is the loss of the sequential interface to reason about computing correctness and performance. However, software has developed new application-structuring techniques to stretch the use of sequential reasoning and make ever-larger applications possible.

These pillars reflect the most important dimensions to understand how computers have accomplished their extraordinary advances in both performance and efficiency. We use these four pillars as the organizing structure for the book.

1.6   Expected Background

This book is intended for three growing communities, all of whom share an interest in understanding how computing's unique capabilities arose, including its real limitations and likely vectors of change in the future. First, there are the computer scientists pursuing careers in high-level software, large-scale applications, and even mobile and interactive systems. Second is the growing community of data scientists who use computing and the growing sea of data to analyze scientific phenomena, economies, human individual or social behavior, and every aspect of business to understand, shape, and optimize it. Third is anyone who uses computing to empower their creativity, business, or life who seeks a deeper understanding of how computing's remarkable capability came about – and insights into how it continues to evolve.

We present computer architecture concepts, not engineering, with a scientific approach. The focus is on principles and concepts that feed understanding and can be used for extrapolation. We use programs as examples of computing structure and common industry products as hardware examples. We explain material with analogies and illustrations, often tying computing's capabilities or limitations to fundamental scientific principles from physics or mathematics. Helpful background for readers includes:

- experience with scientific principles and concepts (high school or college physics);
- basic exposure to code – able to read code snippets that describe computation; and
- experience in computing for analysis, applications, or more.

While computer architecture necessarily touches on hardware technology, we have assumed no technology or hardware design background. Further, the approach takes a principled scientific approach, avoiding the need for engineering hardware knowledge and terminology.

1.7   Organization of the Book

In this textbook, you will gain an understanding of the scientific principles that under-lie the remarkable advances in computing capabilities, how the nature of these scientific principles limits the scaling of systems and software applications you may design and build, and how they are likely to evolve in the future. Each chapter covers a coherent group of topics, summarized with a highlighted set of key **principles**. Each chapter concludes with a **digging deeper** section, providing resources for students who wish to explore in-depth in several directions. The organization of the book across chapters is as follows:

- **Instruction Sets, Software, and Instruction Execution** (Chapter 2) reviews foundational concepts of instruction sets – the software–hardware interface. These include the critical elements of every instruction set – compute, load/store memory, conditional control flow, and procedure call instructions. We discuss how these key concepts relate to the high-level constructs – data structures and procedures – found in all modern programming languages. It illustrates the connections between software and hardware. The chapter closes by examining the elements of instruction execution, and the two major conceptual approaches for building fast computers.
- **Processors: Small is Fast and Scaling** (Chapter 3) outlines the basic scaling phenomena of microelectronics that has extended for 50 years from 1965 to 2015, and is colloquially known as Moore's Law, and increasing energy efficiency under Dennard scaling. This chapter explains the process of miniaturization – the scaling to smaller size that enables the high speed of computers, their tiny size, and their energy efficiency. In short, this chapter explains where the largest portion of computer performance has come from.
- **Sequential Abstraction, but Parallel Implementation** (Chapter 4) begins with discussion of the idea of sequence, in which one compute operation happens after another, with distinct machine states in between. This abstraction has enabled complex, large-scale software and hardware systems, organization, construction, and debugging. We then cover how the sequential abstraction can be preserved, while cheating underneath for higher performance. The computer architecture notion of an instruction-set architecture implements sequential abstraction, powering correct sequential programs. But beneath that abstraction, we describe how the hardware can exploit large amounts of parallelism, using cheap transistors provided by Moore's Law. Techniques explored include pipelining, out-of-order execution, branch prediction, and speculative execution.
- **Memories: Exploiting Dynamic Locality** (Chapter 5): Modern computer applications (software) demand vast quantities of memory capacity, but large size in computers makes them slow. We describe the idea of filters (caches), how processors exploit dynamic locality, and why it is present in the behavior of many computers. This capability is essential for the robust, high performance of all computers. For users of computing, we provide a model to understand dynamic

locality and performance that is portable. This software and application-oriented method enables quantifying dynamic locality and guiding application tuning for high performance.

- **The General-Purpose Computer** (Chapter 6): Why do nearly the same computers appear in nearly every car, smart toy, smartphone, and internet service – essentially all products and services? It is because the foundation of all of these things is information, but more importantly, it's because computers are universal information processors. We examine practical notions of general-purpose computing systems. These systems share a basic model that is consistent across the industry – spawning rich programming languages, software development environments, tools, and frameworks. We relate this notion to the computer science theory of computability and complexity, which considers a mathematical notion of universality.

- **Beyond Sequential: Parallelism in Multicore and the Cloud** (Chapter 7): We discuss explicit parallelism. In the past 20 twenty years, as we have reached the limits of performance for single computing engines (a core that executes a single stream of instructions), we have met the ever-increasing demand for larger and faster computing systems through parallelism. This scaling of performance through replicating hardware has been pursued by internet-scale systems since the late 1990's, and even by single-chip microprocessors since 2005. Explicit parallelism requires new software approaches for programming. We first describe a parallel multicore CPU – the building block used for the backbone of the Internet. Then we explore how the tiny, powerful building blocks that computers have become can be combined into large, powerful computing ensembles that realize both multicore CPUs and cloud computing datacenters. We survey the major approaches for building explicitly parallel applications for multicore chips: OpenMP and pthreads. We also survey major approaches for building large-scale cloud applications. Both types of explicit parallelism require careful software design to achieve good performance, and we cover basic performance models for efficient parallelism.

- **Accelerators: Customized Architectures for Performance** (Chapter 8): We describe the graphics processing unit (GPU), which is a new class of parallel accelerator that attains new levels of performance for data-parallel applications. Next, we expand on the idea of accelerated computing and describe a scalable machine learning accelerator called the tensor processing unit (TPU). While often more difficult to program, these customized architectures are emerging as an important complement to traditional processors in narrower domains such as data-parallel and machine learning computations. Acceleration requires careful software design to achieve good performance, and we cover basic performance models for efficient acceleration.

- **Computing Performance: Past, Present, and Future** (Chapter 9): We discuss future technology trends and opportunities in computer architecture. Computing hardware has passed through several phases – building-sized computers, then Dennard scaling of single-chip CPUs, and more recently scaling system throughput with massive quantities of parallelism. At each stage, the great driver was the availability of cheaper transistors, integrated in greater density provided by Moore's Law scaling of microelectronics. We explore how computing may evolve in the coming decades, discussing both challenges and limits. With Moore's Law fading, the challenge to continue the exponential increase of computing performance (at decreasing cost) is daunting indeed. Even more challenging, the major promising approaches require significant reinvention of software – abstractions, algorithms, and perhaps even fundamental paradigms. With accelerators, quantum computing, and neuromorphic computing on the horizon, these are exciting times indeed!

1.8   Summary

Computing has had an extraordinary and growing impact on nearly every aspect of society, and after seven decades it is a ubiquitous presence. It underpins communication (email, texting, social media), commerce (online shopping, business-to-business, and more), sophisticated products (automobiles, airplanes, smartphones, intelligent assistants), logistics (delivery, inventory), webcam surveillance and photo optimization, and product design. This pervasive use is enabled by its extraordinary flexibility and decreasing cost (prices, size, energy). These are enabled by software programming and technology advances in the four pillars of miniaturization, hidden parallelism, dynamic locality, and explicit parallelism. In the coming chapters, we will explore how these pillars have enabled computing's revolution.

1.9   Problems

1.1   In this exercise, you will think about how computing has been added to many devices that you use in your daily life.
(a) Enumerate five devices in your daily life that have computers inside today, but didn't 20 years ago.
(b) For each, explain why computing benefits the user in terms of features, capabilities, and services.
(c) For each, explain why adding computing benefits the company who sold it. Does it affect the costs? The ability to collect data about its customers?

1.2   Automobiles now have dozens of microprocessors, mostly providing invisible functions such as anti-lock braking, mileage tracking, and even running the lighting systems. However, recently cars by Tesla and General Motors have been pioneering new capabilities enabled by computing, such as self-driving. Do some research and write a paragraph on how computing is enabling self-driving cars.

1.3   The integration of computing and networking have accelerated many activities in society; e-commerce is one example.

(a) Analyze the steps to identify and purchase an article of clothing in a world without the Internet, smartphones, and e-commerce.

(b) Analyze the steps in the modern world.

(c) Compare them and explain how the latency to receive the desired article has changed.

(d) Explain how the time investment required of you to find and buy an article has changed.

(e) Speculate how these changes affect your shopping and buying habits.

1.4 In the 1700s news traveled via horseback messengers and ships, often taking days or months to travel from city to city. Clever traders and stockmarket participants exploited information asymmetry (early news) to profit in markets. Example, include Telegraph Hill in San Francisco to warn of incoming trading ships, and a low-latency microwave link between the New York Stock Exchange and the Mercantile Exchange in Chicago. Today, information transiting the global Internet drives high-frequency (low-latency) trading. Describe and analyze how computing increases the speed of analogous actions today.

1.5 The 2020–2021 COVID-19 pandemic caused a large-scale shift to "work-from-home," with teaching, meetings, and even family gatherings going online. This highlights computing as a communication tool. What role does computing play in a video call? A multi-way video-conference? In sharing a screen image?

1.6 Another pervasive communication use of computing is social media.

(a) Describe several features of how you create a social media post. How is computing used for richness of communication (multimedia) and creativity?

(b) Think about consuming social media. How is computing used to describe what gets into your feed? What shows up next when you swipe or scroll?

(c) What pays for the running of a social media network such as Facebook or Snapchat? How is computing used to target these communication services?

1.7 The extraordinarily small size and efficiency of computing has enabled computing systems that scavenge enough energy from the ambient environment (light, radio-frequency radiation, etc.) to operate. To learn more about what low power and scavenged power enables in terms of capabilities, find the smallest available surveillance video camera that can be bought and describe its capabilities. In particular, how long can it operate? How is it powered? What computing does it do? How frequently?

1.8 Perhaps medical devices are more interesting to you. In this problem, you will learn more about what low power and scavenged power enables in terms of capabilities.

(a) Find the smallest available medical device implant and describe its capabilities (hearing aid, insulin dispenser, heart-rate monitor).

(b) Where does it get its energy and how long can it last?

(c) How does the energy efficiency of the computing in the medical device affect its medical effectiveness?

1.9 Internet search engines catalog petabytes of web pages, and deliver responses to web searches with average latencies of one second. To compute these searches so quickly, the search companies compute an index on the petabytes of data. How many operations would it take to index two eight-character words? And if we wanted to create a new index each month, what computing rate would we have to achieve? Each day? Each hour?

1.10 The growth of single-computer performance over the past seven decades has been tremendous, increasing from 5,000 operations per second in ENIAC to over 10 trillion in NVIDIA's A100 GPU. This one-billion-times increase is remarkable. For example, the US government budget deficit in 2019 was $984 billion dollars, a billion times larger than the cost of a high-end laptop computer. Identify three additional hypothetical analogies to this large increase in computing capabilities, and explain how remarkably things would change if they came to pass.

1.11 The largest computing facilities in the world are now hyperscale cloud data-centers such as those built and operated by Amazon, Google, and Microsoft. Many of these exceed 200 megawatts today, with many 1 gigawatt datacenters under design.
(a) If your laptop can perform 12 billion operations/second using about 24 watts, what is the projected computing capability of a 200 megawatt datacenter?
(b) What is the projected computing performance of a 1 gigawatt datacenter?

Credits

Figure 1.2 J.G. Koomey, S. Berard, M, Sanchez and H. Wong (2010) Implications of historical trends in the electrical efficiency of computing. *IEEE Annals of the History of Computing* 33(3):46–54.

2 Instructions Sets, Software, and Instruction Execution

Each computer can perform a set of instructions (basic operations) to move and transform data. To support software, which evolves at a different pace, instructions are a critical interface for compatibility. For the hardware, the instruction set is the specification that must be implemented correctly, and as fast and cheaply as possible. To illustrate these concepts and give a practical understanding, we describe the elements of an instruction set using an emerging open-source instruction set, the RISC-V. This concrete example illustrates how an instruction set supports basic software constructs, and the challenges of implementation.

2.1 Computer Instruction Sets

Computer instruction sets (aka **instruction set architecture**, or ISA) form the interface between software and hardware in computing systems. While the application software provides the novel functions and services that drive the expanding uses of computing, in contrast the hardware provides both dramatic increases in performance and reductions in cost that enable them. Application software demands flexibility while the need for speed and low cost in hardware drives simplicity and regular structure that can be sold in high volumes (millions to billions of processors). These tensions are illustrated in Figure 2.1. Computer ISAs reflect these tensions, and evolve in response to them over time. As a standard interface, ISAs are the basis of software portability, distribution, and sale. Thus, they are an important technical concept as well as a business/ecosystem concept.

If a computer instruction set is successful, computers that implement it give rise to application software that depend on the ISA for portability to each new, improved processor implementation. This **instruction set compatibility** allows users to simply buy a new computer, move their applications and data to it, and reap the performance benefits of the improved hardware (technology and architecture). In 2020, leading computer ISAs include the "x86" family (supported by Intel and AMD) and the "ARM" family (supported by ARM, Qualcomm, Samsung, Apple, and Mediatek). An emerging instruction set is the "RISC-V" (an open-source ISA). The x86 family is the foundation of PCs, laptops, and cloud servers, and dominates large-scale cloud infrastructure. The ARM family is managed by a single company, but licensed to

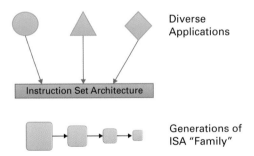

Figure 2.1 The demands of diverse applications influence computer ISA. The architecture defines software portability, easing software costs and enabling application software and computer hardware implementation to advance separately. The succession of computer hardware products is often called a family, and are different hardware implementations of the same interface (ISA).

hundreds of chip design companies, underlying smartphones and the billions of "smart things" or "Internet of Things" (IoT) devices being deployed each year.

Because the ISA forms a stable interface for software, it can be thought of as a software interface (data abstraction, object interface) that allows programs that are users of the interface to run portably across many computers. Each of these computers in one family is a different implementation of the same interface (the ISA). These interface implementations are each a different hardware design, not software. The reasons for the varied implementations are improved performance, lower cost, and lower power consumption, among others.

2.2   Computer Systems Architecture

Let's begin with a high-level view of the basic elements of a computer system. This abstract view captures the structure used in systems from a smartphone, laptop, and cloud server. It even captures IoT systems such as smart speakers and security cameras.

As shown in Figure 2.2, there are three key elements to a computer system. First, the processor that executes the instructions that transform data. These instructions are what we call programs or applications, and they deliver the fundamental capability of computing. Second, there is the memory. The memory contains data for the short term (generally minutes or hours) while the processor is computing on it. It might seem a simple function, but application demands for large capacity and processor demands for extreme speed make this a challenging part of a computer. Third, input/output (I/O)-devices provide long-term data storage (hours to years), and connect computing systems to the world. This ability to interact with the world is a major source of their usefulness. Input/output devices include microphones, speakers, and networking (e.g. Wi-Fi, Bluetooth) in a smart speaker, and a touchpad/screen and display in smartphones and laptops. In contrast, cloud servers lack these human-interface

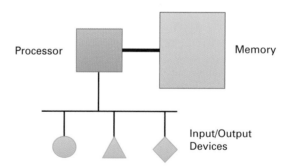

Figure 2.2 Basic elements of a computer system include a processor, memory, and I/O devices. The I/O devices are the most varied, customized to the setting for the computer system.

devices, but instead connect 100 gigabit-per-second (Gb/s) networks, accelerators, and 100 terabyte storage arrays. Instruction set architectures include instructions for the processor, memory, and even for doing I/O operations. However, over the years, processors and memory have become much faster than most external devices, so ISA has focused around controlling processors and memory efficiently. We will focus on those elements of ISA that address computing and memory.

> Principle 2.1: Elements of a Computer
>
> *The basic elements of a computer include a processor, memory, and I/O system (cameras, storage, networking, and more). Instruction set architecture must efficiently control all of these parts of the system.*

2.3   Instruction Set Architecture: RISC-V Example

Every ISA has several key elements that are required for a computer system that supports a full range of functions. These groups of instructions provide first the ability to do general-purpose computation,[1] and to control all parts of the computer system, as shown in Figure 2.3. These elements are summarized below:

- **Computation instructions** include a rich set of arithmetic and logic instructions that transform data types of various sizes. They also include operations for conditional control flow and procedure calls, giving them the full power of a programmable computer.
- **Memory instructions** compute addresses for the memory and bring data to/from the processor. These instructions support addressing modes for arrays and structures. They also support various data sizes, enabling flexible computing.

---

[1] They are Turing complete [30], meaning they can compute all computable functions.

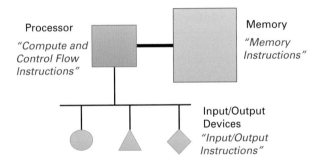

Figure 2.3 Basic elements and instructions to control them.

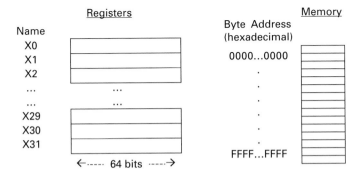

Figure 2.4 Computer instructions operate on a fixed number of registers and a larger byte-addressed memory.

- **Input/output instructions** perform operations on I/O device registers, enabling a program to read input from a user or sensor, fetch data over a network, display images or video on a display, and more.

These instructions operate on the processor state, which includes a fixed number of registers, and a large, byte-addressable memory, as shown in Figure 2.4. The RISC-V includes a set of 32 registers, which are typically 64 bits each. The memory is expandable, limited only by the number of bytes that can be addressed by a computer word of 64 bits (2^{64} bytes, or 16 billion billion bytes).

Nearly all of the work done in programs is done with computation and memory instructions, so we focus on them for the remainder of the book. We use a simple subset of the RISC-V instruction set. RISC-V's regularity afforded by its recent design makes it suitable for pedagogy. In short, we can avoid explaining the legacy complexity that arises as instruction sets mature and evolve over decades.

2.3.1 Computation Instructions

All modern computer architectures use a notion of fast, local state called **registers**. These registers are used to contain working values for the computation, and because

Table 2.1. Arithmetic and logic instructions.

Instruction	Function	Description	Datatype
add r3, r1, r2	r3 ← r1 + r2	add word	32-bit integers
addi r3, r1, #imm	r3 ← r1 + imm[12b]	add immediate	32-bit integers
sub r3, r1, r2	r3 ← r1 − r2	subtract word	32-bit integers
and r3, r1, r2	r3 ← r1 & r2 (bitwise)	bitwise and	32-bit integers
or r3, r1, r2	r3 ← r1 ‖ r2 (bitwise)	bitwise or	32-bit integers
add r3, r1, r2	r3 ← r1 + r2	add word	64-bit integers
addi r3, r1, #imm	r3 ← r1 + imm[12b]	add immediate	64-bit integers
sub r3, r1, r2	r3 ← r1 − r2	subtract word	64-bit integers
mul r3, r1, r2	r3 ← [r1 * r2] mod 2^{64}	multiply word	64-bit integers
and r3, r1, r2	r3 ← r1 & r2 (bitwise)	bitwise and	64-bit integers
or r3, r1, r2	r3 ← r1 ‖ r2 (bitwise)	bitwise or	64-bit integers
xor r3, r1, r2	r3 ← r1 ∧ r2 (bitwise)	bitwise xor	64-bit integers
slt r3, r1, r2	r3 ← (if (r1<r2) then 1 else 0)	set if less than	64-bit integers
sltu r3, r1, r2	r3 ← (if (r1<r2) then 1 else 0)	set if less than unsigned	64-bit integers
sll r3, r1, r2	r3 ← r1 << r2	shift left logical	64-bit integers
slli r3, r1, #imm	r3 ← r1 << imm[12b]	shift left logical immediate	64-bit integers

there are only a few of them, they can be specified with a few bits of instruction and accessed quickly in the hardware implementation.

The computation instructions in Table 2.1 all use registers to specify their operands (the values on which they compute) and their target (where they put the results of their computation). This style of architecture is called "register-to-register." Consider the arithmetic and logic instructions in Table 2.1.

Note that the first set of instructions operates on 32-bit integers. The second set of similar operations applies to 64-bit integers. The *imm* (immediate) fields are limited to 12 bits by a 32-bit fixed-width instruction encoding. While conceptually the same computation, their precise transformation of bits in a computer is quite different. Obviously, the latter set all read 64 bits and produce 64 bits. This type of duplication over datatype sizes (1, 2, 4, 8 bytes) is a significant reason for large numbers of instructions in ISAs. A handy reference for the RISC-V instruction set is provided in the Appendix.

2.3.2   Conditional Control and Procedure Linkage Instructions

Another important set of computation instructions are for control flow, supporting both conditional execution and procedure calls. Without control flow instructions, a program would start and execute straight through – this is basic instruction execution. A program with *X* instructions would execute each of them exactly once, producing a fixed-length computation. Now we know from programming as well as from algorithms and even computational complexity classes that the capabilities of a program are limited by how long it runs. Adding control flow instructions enables programs to

Table 2.2. Control flow and procedure linkage instructions.

Instruction	Function	Description	Datatype
j offset (jump)	PC ← offset	unconditional jump	64-bit word
beq r1, r2, offset	if r1==r2 then PC ←PC+offset	branch if equal	64-bit word
bne r1, r2, offset	if r1 ne r2 then PC ←PC+offset	branch not equal	64-bit word
blt r1, r2, offset	if r1 < r2 then PC ←PC+offset	branch less than	64-bit word
jal r1, offset	r1 ←PC+4; PC←PC+offset	jump and link	64-bit word
jr r1	PC ← r1	jump register	64-bit word

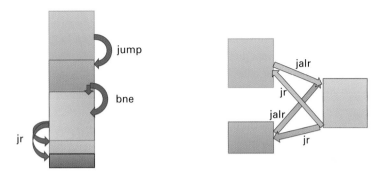

Figure 2.5 Control flow instructions connect different parts of the program (left) and create dynamic return links for procedures (right).

run for much longer – in loops or even recursive calls that terminate based on program computed values. This enables computers to capture the full class of what theorists call **computable functions**, which is considered to be all useful computations. The problem that control flow introduces is that it now becomes possible to write an infinite program – that is, one that will run forever until you kill it. Let's look at the three key types of control flow instructions (Table 2.2).

The first type of control flow instruction is **jump**, which changes the course of instruction execution, switching from a straight line to the one specified by **PC+offset**. This effectively stitches the current program instructions to those at the target address (see Figure 2.5). The second type of control flow instruction includes **beq, bne**, and **blt**, which do switching conditionally. They check whether their operands are equal, not equal, or less than, and if the condition is satisfied they switch the current program instruction to the target address. For all of jump, beq, bne, and blt, the target address is specified relative to the current instruction. With these three instructions for control flow, a full complement of algorithms, including loops, and various convergent terminations can be expressed. In fact, all of the computable functions can be performed with just this set of control operations.

The third type of control flow operations are used for procedure calls. Procedures are a different type of flow control, where the target of a procedure return depends on the history of the procedure – who called it – not on any static property of the program. As a result, we need an instruction that can jump to a dynamically computed target (see Figure 2.5). **jr**, or jump register, provides that capability, and is used to implement returns from procedure calls. Its partner, **jal**, aka jump and link, does the calling part of a procedure. jal jumps to the procedure beginning, and then stores the address of the instruction that should be executed after the procedure is complete. This address, sometimes called the return link or dynamic pointer, after being captured by jal in a register, is typically saved to the stack. jr is implemented with jalr (see the Appendix); jr is a pseudo instruction.

2.3.3   Memory Instructions

Memory instructions allow programs to operate on a larger amount of data than can be held in registers. For example, a machine with 32 registers, each 64 bits, can only hold 256 bytes of data. Today's applications often demand gigabytes or even terabytes of memory. With computation instructions designed to use operands in registers, the natural structure for memory instructions is to move data between the memory (very large) and the registers (small). This type of instruction set design cleanly separates computation and memory instructions, and is called a **load-store** ISA. A subset of the memory instructions for RISC-V are shown in Table 2.3.

The memory instructions illustrate the basic operations of bringing data from memory **ld**, or load doubleword (64 bits), and shifting it to memory **sd**, or store doubleword. The instructions use registers to specify the locations in memory, as the large capacity of memory requires long addresses (typically 64 bits). Memory values are loaded into registers for further computation, or computation values can be stored to memory for later use.

As with computation instructions, one complicating factor for instruction sets is the need to move different size data elements. The most common size moved is a machine **word**, which is typically 64 bits (8 bytes), and matches the size of a register. In some older machines, this word size can be 32 bits (4 bytes). However, in all types of machines, there is a need to manipulate smaller data items, all the way down to individual bytes. The **lb**, or load byte, and **sb**, or store byte, instructions move only a single byte, leaving the rest of the register or memory unchanged. Remarkably, this

Table 2.3. Memory instructions.

Instruction	Function	Description	Datatype
ld r1, I(r2) sd r1, I(r2) (store word)	r1 ← memory[I+r2] memory[I+r2] ← [r1]	load doubleword store doubleword	64-bit word 64-bit word
lb r1, I(r2) (load byte) sb r1, I(r2) (store byte)	r1 ← memory[I+r2] memory[I+r2] ← [r1]	load byte store byte	8-bit (byte) 8-bit (byte)

simple set of computation, control flow, and memory operations is sufficient to write many programs – the entire set of examples in this chapter and most of the book. But if you find an example where it's not sufficient, refer to the full instruction set definition for the core of the RISC-V ISA in the Appendix and in [103].

2.4 Machine Instructions and Basic Software Structures

To show how these instructions can be used together, we consider some simple examples. By showing how such a small set of instructions can implement rich high-level program features, one can begin to see where the full range of computing's breadth of applications and power come from. A little closer, one can see how computer instruction set designers were able to satisfy the diverse needs of applications with a single instruction set. And the instruction set, specifying small computation operations precisely, can effectively control the computer hardware. Using these basic instructions, we illustrate how the key features of modern programming languages such as Python, Java, JavaScript, C++, and more are implemented. While we will use examples with the RISC-V instruction set, essentially the same correspondence exists for other architectures such as Intel's x86 and the ARM processor families.

2.4.1 Implementing Basic Expressions

We first begin with basic expressions, data structures, and arrays. Basic expressions in a higher-level program can be complex collections of operations, nested several levels deep. Basic expressions are compiled into a sequence of machine instructions, typically using the registers to store inputs, intermediate values, and results. Thus, the corresponding assembly language programs for the three `result` expressions are as shown in Figure 2.6.

In the examples in Figure 2.6, the initial values of x, y, and z are presumed to be in registers x12, x13, and x14 when the execution of the code begins. The program snippets use registers x16 and x17 as locations for intermediate values, and present the expression values as indicated. A few instruction names (operation codes or opcodes) are a little obscure. **sll** is shift-left, logical, **sltu** is set-if-less-than, unsigned, and the program for `res4` implements the C++ notion of Boolean values, and thus need to return exactly "1" or "0" and no other bit values.

2.4.2 Implementing Data Structures: Structs and Objects

Much of the power of programming arises from the ability to construct and manipulate complex data structures. Programming languages typically support two kinds of fundamental aggregators that can be used to build larger data structures. These are aggregations of heterogeneous types – `structs` and `objects` – and of homogeneous

```
int x,y,z;                      ~
int res1=(x+y)-z;               res1:
                                    add x15, x12, x13
                                    sub x16, x15, x14
                                    // res1 is in x16

int res2=((x+y)<<4)+z;          res2:
                                    add x15, x12, x13
                                    sll x16, x15, #4
                                    add x17, x16, x14
                                    // res2 is in x17

int res3=(x^y+23)&z;            res3:
                                    xor x15, x12, x13
                                    add x16, x15, #23
                                    and x17, x16, x14 // bitwise
                                    // res3 is in x17

int res4=(x>0)||y;              res4:
                                    sub x15, x12, x0 // x0 always==0
                                    or x16, x15, x13
                                    sltu x17,x0, x16
 ~                                  // res4 is in x17
```

       (a) Struct definition   (b) Assembly code

Figure 2.6 Basic expressions in RISC-V assembly code; initial values for x, y, and z are in registers x12, x13, x14.

types – arrays. First, let us consider heterogeneous aggregations of types – structs or objects. Figure 2.7 shows two simple struct definitions:

```
struct Account {
    int UniqueID;
    char Owner[64];
    char Country[32];
    int Balance;};
```

```
struct SocialPost {
    int UniqueID;
    User* Author;
    int Likes;
    int Timestamp;};
```

These definitions are used by the code in Figure 2.7, where the left side is a C++ code example that accesses struct fields (object members). The machine instruction implementations of these C expressions for struct access are shown on the right.

We have several examples using the Account structs. The first example simply accesses the theID field. Because it's the first field in the Account struct, the offset used is 0. In the second example, RichPoor, offsets must be added for each of the

Account Mandy, Jose;
int theID = Mandy.UniqueID;

```
theID:
    ld  x16, 0(x12) // offset is 0
    //  theID is in x16
```

bool RichPoor =
    Mandy.Balance >100000;

```
RichPoor:
    addi  x16,x12,#8 // for UniqueID
    addi  x17,x16,#64 // Owner
    addi  x17,x17,#32 // Country
    ld  x17,x17
    //  RichPoor is in x17
```

char∗ theName = &(Jose.Owner);

```
theName:
    addi  x16,x13,#8 // for UniqueID
    //  theName is in x16
    //  its a char pointer (char∗)
```

SocialPost A, B;
int A_ID = A.UniqueID;

```
A_ID:
    ld  x16,x14
    //  A_ID is in x16
```

bool B_Popular =
    B.Likes >1000;

```
B_Popular:
    ld  x16,16(x15) // UniqueID, User∗
    slti  x17,x16,#1000
    //  B_Popular is in x17
```

// time in seconds
int NOW = gettimeofday();
bool B_Old =
    (NOW−B.Timestamp)>3600;
~

```
B_Old:
    ld  x16, 24(x15)
    sub  x17,x28,x16
    slti  x17,x17,#3600
    xori  x17,x17,#1
    //  B_old is in x17
```

(a) C++ struct expressions   (b) Assembly code

Figure 2.7 Struct (or object member) access in RISC-V assembly code; initial values for Mandy and Jose are in registers x12, x13; for A and B in x14 and x15. NOW is in register x28.

fields, as the reference to the struct points to the beginning of its representation in memory. The total offset needed is the sum of the field sizes, $(8 + 64 + 32) = 104$ in this case. We show them as separate instructions for clarity, but a compiler might combine them using a single addi instruction. Next, theName wants a pointer to the field, not its value. This is easy to compute by simply adding the appropriate offset (the size of the UniqueID field in bytes) to the address of the Jose struct.

Next we have several examples using the SocialPost structs. The first example, A_ID, simply accesses the first struct field. The second uses an offset to access the third field, combining the sizes of the first two fields. One is an int (8 bytes) and the other is a pointer (also 8 bytes). It then uses slt, set-if-less-than, to compute the Boolean test. The last example uses the time of day in seconds to figure out if a post is more than one hour old (3,600 seconds).

2.4.3   Implementing One- and Multi-dimensional Arrays

Arrays in most programming languages are homogeneous collections. With primitive types such as int or float, they are an ordered collection of values. But they can also be used to form homogeneous collections of structs or objects. This notion of a "homogeneous collection" of "heterogenous collections" is extraordinarily useful in programming, databases, and organizing many kinds of information. It is sometimes referred to as an "array-of-structs" (AOS). In Figure 2.8, we illustrate assembly programs to compute the memory address of the array element, and then fetch the desired value for the C++ expression. As before, we present C++ code on the left, and the corresponding assembly code on the right.

In the first example in Figure 2.8, the first element of a one-dimensional array has the same address as the pointer to the entire array. So, the first element of the array can be accessed by simply loading the memory location indicated by the array reference. In the second example, we have to compute the address of the tenth element using the element size of 8 bytes. This produces an offset of 72 bytes. In the third example, the resulting offset of the 500th element is $499 \times 8 = 3,992$. Two-dimensional arrays require a two-level structure of address computation. However, none of this is revealed in the `first_2D` example because the first element is easily accessible. For the `tenth_2D` example, we see the full complexity. We have to first calculate the address of the corresponding row (first index) and then the value within that row (column). We compute the address of the tenth row, using the row size of 64 elements $\times$ 8 bytes/element $= 512$. Then we compute the right element of the row, using the element size of 8 bytes. Only then can we load the desired value. In the last example, this plays out with a more extensive code sequence that computes 19 $\times$ (value), but does so avoiding use of the multiply instruction – which is expensive in both runtime and energy. Finally, we load the desired value. As you can see, the address computation for arrays can involve quite a few instructions. Next, we move on to the array-of-structs examples in Figure 2.9. As before, we have the C++ code on the left and the RISC-V assembly on the right.

For an AOS, we show several examples in Figure 2.9. When accessing an AOS, the program must first compute the address of the appropriate struct in the array, then the appropriate field within the struct. Our first example, `myAccount`, returns the address of the 18,452nd account. To do so, it must compute the address of the account, using the Account struct's size of 112 bytes ($8 + 64 + 32 + 8$), and that number times 18,451. We illustrate a sequence of assembly that avoids using the multiply instruction; instead, eight simple add-type operations are used. The code sequence returns the address of the requested account. Our second example, `myBalance`, first computes the address of the desired account. To simplify, we chose a more convenient account index. After computing the address of the account, the program adds the offset to the `Balance` field within the struct. This is just as in the earlier discussion of how to access struct fields. A load from that location returns the desired value. Finally, the last example returns the address of a different field from a struct within the array.

```
int OneD[2048];
int TwoD[64][64]

int first = OneD[0];


int tenth = OneD[9];



int five_hundredth=OneD[499];


int first_2D=TwoD[0][0];



int tenth_2D=TwoD[9][9];








int twentieth_2D=
        TwoD[19][19];
```

```
first:
    ld x16, 0(x12) // offset is 0
    // first is in x16

tenth:
    addi x16, x12, #72
    ld x17,x16
    // tenth is in x17

five_hundredth:
    ld x16, 3992(x12)
    // value is in x16

first_2D:
    ld x16, 0(x12) // offset is 0
    // first_2D is in x16

tenth_2D:
    addi x16, x0, #512 // 8*64
    slli x17, x16, #3
    addi x17, x17, x16 // 9*64*8
    addi x17, x17, #72 // 9*8
    add  x17, x17, x13 // add to base
    ld x28, x17
    // tenth_2D is in x28

twentieth_2D:
    addi x16, x0, #512
    slli x17, x16, #4
    add x17, x17, x16 // 17*64*8
    add x17, x17, x16 // 18*64*8
    add x17, x17, x16 // 19*64*8
    addi x17, x17, #152 // 19*8
    add  x17, x17, x13 // add to base
    ld x28, x17
    // twentieth_2D is in x28
```

~

      (a) C++ array expressions   (b) Assembly code

Figure 2.8 Array access in RISC-V assembly code; base pointers for OneD and TwoD arrays are in registers x12 and x13.

2.4.4   Implementing Conditional Iterative Constructs: Loops

Much of the power of programmable computers comes from the ability to execute code both conditionally and repeatedly. This allows computations to make choices based on the data values and, more generally, due to the power of iteration, solve problems much more complex than their program textual length. For example, a program with 1,000 instructions in it can in fact execute millions, billions, and more instructions when run. Let us first consider a simple conditional program, as shown in Figure 2.10.

```
Account ZBank[65536];

Account* myAccount=
        &(Zbank[18451]);                myAccount:
// Conveniently,                          addi  x13, x0, #112 // sizeof(Account)
//   18,451 = 16384+2048+16+3             slli  x14, x13, #16 // 16384*112
                                          slli  x15, x13, #11 // 2048*112
                                          slli  x16, x13, #4  // 16*112
                                          add   x14, x14, x15
                                          add   x14, x14, x16 // 18448*112
                                          add   x14, x14, x13
                                          add   x14, x14, x13
                                          add   x14, x14, x13 // 18451*112
                                          add   x15, x12, x14
                                          // myAccount is in x15

int myBalance=                          myBalance:
        Zbank[8].Balance;                 addi  x13, x0, #112 // sizeof(Account)
                                          slli  x14, x13, #3  // 8*112
                                          add   x15, x12, x14
                                          addi  x15, x15, #104
                                          ld    x16, x15
                                          // myBalance is in x16

char* myCountry=                        myCountry:
        &(Zbank[8].Country);              addi  x13, x0, #112 // sizeof(Account)
                                          slli  x14, x13, #3  // 8*112
                                          add   x15, x12, x14
                                          addi  x16, x15, #72 // 8+64
~                                         // myCountry is in x16
```

(a) C++ array expressions   (b) Assembly code

Figure 2.9 Array-of-structs access in RISC-V assembly code; the initial value of Zbank is in register x12.

```
                                        slt  x14, x12,x13
if (a<b){                               beq  x14, x0, elseclause
   b=0;}                                add  x12, x0, x0 // b=0
else {                                  j    done
   b=b+16;                            elseclause:
   }                                     addi  x12, x12, #16
                                      done:
~                                       // a is still in x12
```

(a) C++ conditional statement   (b) Assembly code

Figure 2.10 Conditional statement in C++ and RISC-V. Initial values of a and b are in registers x12 and x13.

```
//   c++ program
struct post {long int ID, likes; char[16] info;}
post HIST[100];
int sum = 0;
for (int i=0; i++;i<100){
  sum = sum + post[i].likes;
  };
```

Figure 2.11 Simple C++ loop that sums struct values in an array of structs.

```
                                     // init sum, i
                                     loadimm r5, x12
                                     add x13, x0, x0 // sum
                                     add x14, x0, x0 // i
    // init sum, i
    xor %ecx,%ecx
    xor %ebx, %ebx         loop:
loop:                                // compute effective address
    // load it                       slli x15, x14, #3
    movl 0x8(%edx,%ebx),%eax         add x16, x15, #8
    add %ecx,%eax,%ecx               add x16, x16, x12
    addi %ebx,#32,%ebx               // load it
    cmpi %ebx,#(100<<5)              load x17, x16 // post[i].likes
    ble   loop                       add x13, x13, x17
                                     addi x14,x14, #1
                                     // loop test
                                     slt x17,x14 #100
  ~                                  bne   x17, x0, loop
```

(a) x86 code, HIST value in %edx   (b) RISC-V code, HIST value in x12

Figure 2.12 Equivalent assembly code struct values in an array of structs in two different ISAs: x86 (left) and RISC-V (right).

The program shown in Figure 2.10 tests the relationship of two variables, a and b, and then modifies the value of b based on the result of the test. Its implementation in the RISC-V assembler is shown on the right. Next, we consider a simple looping program that brings in arrays and structs (Figure 2.11).

Consider a simple C/C++ program that loops over the elements of an array, summing the values (Figure 2.12). To make it a little more interesting, the array contains user-defined structs (or objects), and the field we are summing is likes. For example, this program might sum the total number of likes your Facebook posts have accumulated over the past year, where the array contains statistics for each of your posts, and the "likes" object member is the number of likes garnered.

The program uses the control flow instructions to loop over each element of the array, terminating when it has finished counting all 100 posts. Within each iteration, the program increments the loop index variable, sums the likes for that post, and continues if it's not done with all of the posts.

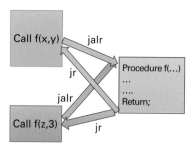

Figure 2.13 Procedure calls require a dynamic return link because they can be called from many procedure call sites, and each call needs to return to its own program continuation.

We will explain the RISC-V assembly code (see right of Figure 2.12), and for comparison the x86 assembly code for this program is also shown. The RISC-V program first initializes sum and i. Then it computes the effective address for post[i].likes, loads that value, and adds it to the running sum. Next, it increments the counter variable i, and performs the exit test. If i ≥ 100, then the test succeeds and the program exits. If the test fails, control returns to loop: for the next iteration.

To illustrate the differences between computer instruction sets, and the particular advantage of RISC-V for instruction, we present the x86 code for the same loop at the left of Figure 2.12. While the x86 code has fewer instructions, it contains a range of cryptic instruction and register names and mixes computation and memory operations in each x86 instruction. While execution may be of equal speed, we find it less clear for instruction.

2.4.5   Implementing Procedure Call and Return and the Stack

Procedures are a key element of all modern programming languages, and in fact the addition of recursive procedures and local variables (sometimes called **automatics**) was a signature feature of ALGOL-60 [2], which set the basic structure for all procedural programming languages such as C++, Python, and Java.[2]

Implementing procedures requires the use of a stack, and some special control flow instructions **jump-and-link (jal)** for procedure invocation, and **jump register (jr)** for return from a procedure. **jal** is critical to capture a return address for the procedure because when a procedure call completes, control returns to the statement after the procedure call. This is called the dynamic link or dynamic return link, and is illustrated in Figure 2.13. **jr** makes use of the captured return address to implement the return of control to the correct location. Other instructions for control transfer, such as beq, j, and more, are not able to provide this capability.

---

[2] Object-oriented ideas came along – both concurrently [20] and later [32, 61] – and are an important element of these languages as well.

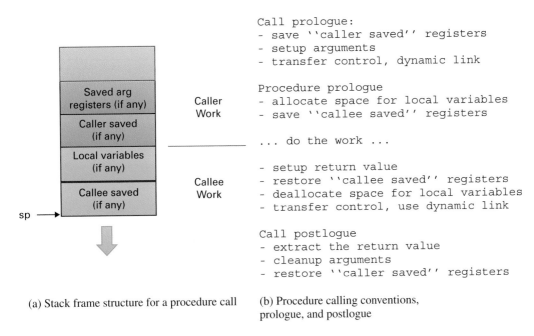

```
Call prologue:
- save ''caller saved'' registers
- setup arguments
- transfer control, dynamic link

Procedure prologue
- allocate space for local variables
- save ''callee saved'' registers

... do the work ...

- setup return value
- restore ''callee saved'' registers
- deallocate space for local variables
- transfer control, use dynamic link

Call postlogue
- extract the return value
- cleanup arguments
- restore ''caller saved'' registers
```

(a) Stack frame structure for a procedure call   (b) Procedure calling conventions, prologue, and postlogue

Figure 2.14 Procedure call requires conventions for stack structure and the responsibilities of caller and callee.

But implementing a procedure call requires more than just passing control to the procedure code and back. A procedure call requires us to pass arguments to the procedure, allocate space for local variables, perhaps call other procedures (recursive or co-recursive), and then finally return a value, cleaning up all of these changes in the process. There are many possible ways to accomplish this, and in the history of computing at different times and on different machines a significant range of diversity has been explored. However, within a single machine architecture (e.g. x86 or RISC-V) it's productive to standardize this procedure **calling convention**. This is because a standard calling convention enables procedures from different compilers, or even different languages, to interoperate – a significant value in this increasingly complex software world. The calling convention for the RISC-V processor is illustrated in Figure 2.14, showing where arguments, return address, and local variables are stored. Next to it, we illustrate procedure-call prologue and postlogue, as well as procedure prologue and cleanup. Modern machines have registers that are much faster than memory, so it's productive to use registers to pass values between procedures. Nearly all microprocessors have a register-usage calling convention that strictly defines the use of registers across procedure calls. The RISC-V register calling convention is included in Table 2.4, and our sample prologues, postlogues, etc. reflect the register-usage calling convention.

To realize the abstract calling convention in the RISC-V machine, specific sample code for the prologue, postlogue, etc. is shown in Figure 2.15. This code begins on the caller, setting up the arguments that are going to be sent to the callee, putting them in

Table 2.4. The RISC-V register usage calling convention defines caller and callee saved registers; these must be saved to the stack by the corresponding procedure call prologue and procedure prologue.

Register	ABI Name	Description	Saver
x0	zero	Hard-wired zero	—
x1	ra	Return address	Caller
x2	sp	Stack pointer	Callee
x3	gp	Global pointer	—
x4	tp	Thread pointer	—
x5–7	t0–2	Temporaries	Caller
x8	s0/fp	Saved register/frame pointer	Callee
x9	s1	Saved registers	Callee
x10–11	a0–1	Function arguments/return values	Caller
x12–17	a2–7	Function arguments	Caller
x18–27	s2–11	Saved registers	Callee
x28–31	t3–6	Temporaries	Caller
f0–7	ft0–7	FP temporaries	Caller
f8–9	fs0–1	FP saved registers	Callee
f10–11	fa0–1	FP arguments/return values	Caller
f12–17	fa2–7	FP arguments	Caller
f18–27	fs2–11	FP Saved registers	Callee
f28–31	ft8–11	FP temporaries	Caller

registers denoted a0, a1, etc. These are not new registers, but in fact just convenient synonyms that an assembly programmer can use to make sure they conform to the register calling convention shown in Table 2.4. Next, the caller allocates space on the stack and saved any relevant caller saved registers. These are the registers denoted "caller" in Table 2.4 for which the caller would like to keep the values safe from any modification by the procedures. Next, the caller uses **jal** to transfer control to the called procedure (callee), saving the dynamic return link in registers *ra (aka return address)*, again a symbolic name used for convenience.

In the callee, in Figure 2.15, we can see that the callee may allocate space on the stack to save callee saved registers or local variables. In this case, the callee makes space for two callee saved registers, s0 and s1, and one local variable. Note that **ra** is a callee saved register. It then proceeds to do its work. When it is done, it takes the function return value and puts it in a0, the return value register, and then restores the callee saved registers. Next, it cleans up the stack, returning it to the same level it was upon entry, and then returns control to the caller, using the dynamic return link, ra. After the procedure returns, the caller restores its caller saved registers and accepts the return value, and continues with its computation. Yes, this complex dance is really all required to make procedures work, and every time you run a program, this sequence happens perhaps millions of times per second.

Several times we have referred to the RISC-V register calling convention in Table 2.4. It is a little complicated, so let's walk through its structure. First, the calling convention sets aside several registers for special purposes, such as stack

```
                                        // Callee code
                                        //
    // Caller code                      CALLEE:
    //                                    addi sp, sp, 24 // make room
    add a0, ...  // setup args           sd s1,8(sp) // 2 callee saves +
    add a1, ...                          sd s0, 0(sp)// 1 local variable
    addi sp,sp,8 // make room
    sd t1,0(sp) // caller saves
    jal ra, CALLEE                       ... local work...
    //
    // procedure returns below
    //                                   add a0, a0, x0 // return value
    sd t1,0(sp) // caller restores       ld s0,0(sp) // callee restores
    addi sp,sp,-8 // clean stack         ld s1, 8(sp)
    add x,x,a0 // use return value       addi sp, sp, -24 // clean stack
                                         jr ra
```

(a) Caller code sequences   (b) Callee code sequences

Figure 2.15 RISC-V assembly code sequences for the procedure calling convention.

management and return address (x1–x4) and a constant zero (x0). This reduces the 32 general-purpose registers to 27. Of these, 13 are set aside as caller-saves (x5–x7, x12–x17, x28–31), and the remaining 14 registers (x8–x11, x18–x27) are callee saves. What's the reason for all of this complication? The whole objective is to avoid sending values to and from memory, keeping them in registers as much as possible. In modern computers, memory is as much as 500 times slower than instruction execution (see Chapter 5), so this avoidance is a critical performance goal. Dividing the registers into caller and callee saved groups allows calls of small procedures to avoid using the memory for arguments and return values, and even for large procedures a number of memory operations can be avoided each time. This brings us to the end of procedure calls in assembly language.

Principle 2.2: Elements of a Computer Instruction Set

The essential software interface to hardware is the ISA, defining both the function of the hardware and the means to optimize performance. Key elements of the ISA to make it general-purpose include arithmetic/logic operations, memory addressing modes, conditional branches, and procedure calling features.

2.5 Basic Instruction Execution and Implementation

Each instruction in a RISC-V assembly program is encoded in a 32-bit word. These encoded bits are the program that is executed by the hardware. The elements of instruction execution are the same on all modern stored-program computers, consisting of the following seven steps. We explain each of these steps in detail as follows:

1. **Fetch instruction:** Using the program counter, determine the bytes that represent the next machine instruction in memory. Each of the instructions in the RISC-V architecture is encoded into 32 bits. Load them from memory so they can be interpreted for execution. For variable-length instructions, fetch is more complicated.

2. **Decode instruction:** Take the instruction bytes, and decode them into detailed control for the hardware. Each 32-bit RISC-V instruction includes bits for the operation and to describe the values to be operated on (register values or memory addresses), and where the results should be placed. For more complicated legacy instruction sets, decoding may be interspersed with instruction fetch.

3. **Fetch operands** (includes compute effective address and get values): Based on the addressing modes, compute the effective address for each operand, and then fetch the needed operand data bytes from memory or register.

4. **Compute operation** (compute add, xor, memory effective address, etc.): Perform the specified operation on the operand values and memory effective-address computation.

5. **Memory read operation** (if needed): Read data from the memory.

6. **Write results** (to register or memory): Write the results to the register or memory address (may use a computed effective address).

7. **Update program counter** (+1 instruction, or branch address): If an ordinary instruction, increase program counter by the size of the instruction (i.e. PC = PC +4 if instructions are four bytes each); if a branch or jump is taken, set PC to the target address.

The fetch and decode instruction steps support the basic capability of software programmability, enabling the software to express computation as a sequence of instructions. The hardware fetches and decodes these instructions to understand the specified computation. Fetch, compute, memory read, and write results operations are all basic computation steps – obtaining the values to compute on and moving values between registers and memory. Finally, update of the program counter determines the next instruction to execute. While it could be a simple increment, it could also be a more complex computation. Control flow instructions are a critical machine capability, supporting high-level program structures such as conditionals, loops, and procedure calls. All of these are implemented by changing the program counter. Every modern computer does each of these steps for each instruction, as each contributes an essential capability of a stored-program (i.e. programmable) computer.

Together with the instruction set design, the ISA computer interface provides the ability to support software across the full spectrum of applications on a single hardware platform, which enables the creation of rich software libraries, programming languages, and development tools, as well as high-performance, low-cost hardware implementations. Consequently, this stored-program computer paradigm is the dominant model for computing. We will further expound on the universality of the stored-program model in Chapter 6.

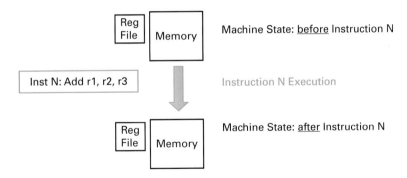

Figure 2.16 Machine state and sequential instructions that modifies it.

2.5.1 Sequential State and Instruction Execution

A critical element of program execution – the aggregate of instruction executions – is the notion of sequence. The state of the machine is defined by the program counter, registers, and state of memory between instruction executions. That is, each instruction reads and modifies a small amount of machine state, and a larger program execution reflects **an ordered sequence** of such modifications, as shown in Figure 2.16. This ordered sequence is visible to software via single-stepping (traps used in a debugger) or external asynchronous events (interrupts) that can stop the machine between instructions, making the register and memory state visible.

It's important to recognize that the instruction set is *the* interface between software and hardware. Because computers depend on software to deliver value to applications, as the interface, the instruction set *is the definition* of correct implementation of a computer. Beyond this functional correctness, there are only secondary attributes such as speed, power, size, etc.

2.5.2 Hardware Implementation of Instruction Execution

How do computers implement the steps for instruction execution in hardware? In the 1950s, when the first computers were being built, hardware was scarce and expensive, so hardware for each step was reused. Today, with many millions of transistors per processor, the approach is straightforward, using dedicated hardware for each step. A simple realization of the hardware for instruction execution is shown in Figure 2.17 which includes a hardware block for each function. This example shows the correspondence between instruction set features and hardware. Even with this simplified example, it is already possible to see that features in the ISA have a direct implication for hardware. This holds particularly true if you want fast execution (high performance) from the computer.

For a fetch instruction, we have an instruction memory and simply read the instruction indicated by the program counter. For instruction decode, we have a block of special logic that determines the type of instruction and generates control signals for the rest of the execution. For fetch operands, the processor reads the needed values

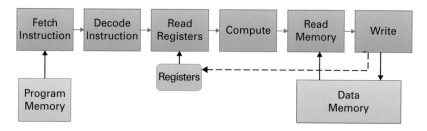

Figure 2.17 Hardware elements for simple instruction execution. Blue and green boxes are part of the processor; the gray boxes are memories that are physically much larger (see Chapter 5). The update-program-counter step is omitted.

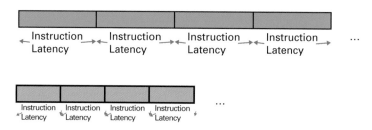

Figure 2.18 Reducing individual instruction latency improves program execution time.

from the register file. For compute operations, we have a datapath that implements all of the arithmetic and logic operations. Further, for memory instructions, the datapath may also compute the effective memory address. If necessary, read memory accesses the data memory. For write results, we simply write the computation or memory results back into the register file. If it is a store instruction, we write the results into the data memory. For the update-program counter we have a special program counter register and incrementer that advances to the next instruction. In the exceptional case of a jump or conditional branch instruction, we update the program counter before the next instruction fetch.

2.6   Speeding Up Instruction Execution and Program Performance

To implement a computer, we need to implement all of the steps of instruction processing. A basic approach is to think about all six steps that need to happen within a single clock cycle, and work to improve computer performance by speeding up that single clock cycle (instruction processing time). This approach preserves the sequential execution of instructions – one at a time. This idea is depicted in Figure 2.18.

There is a simple model for reasoning about the performance benefit of this approach. Improvements here are a multiplier for performance of all instructions, but the clock cycle is limited by the slowest instructions, as we'll see in Chapter 3.

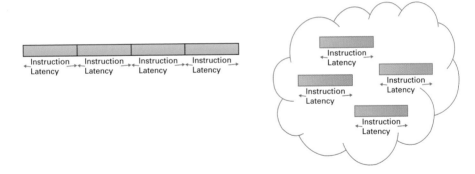

Figure 2.19 Reducing latency of a collection of instructions by overlapping them can improve program execution time.

A second approach illustrated in Figure 2.19 considers not only speeding up individual instructions, but also allows their execution to be overlapped. This views the execution of a program as a collection of instruction executions, and thus the challenge is to increase instruction throughput, which speeds up execution of the overall program. The challenge of this approach is how to maintain the sequential abstraction and the ability to trap/interrupt and thereby make visible the machine state betwixt any two instructions.

The performance model for this second approach is more complicated, The ability to overlap instructions depends on the availability of hardware, but more importantly on the relationship of their reads and updates of the machine state, which are themselves subject to conditional execution. This makes both achieving overlap and reasoning about the benefits of such approaches complex. This topic is the focus of Chapter 4.

Principle 2.3: Speeding Instruction Execution: Clock Rate and Instruction-level Parallelism (ILP)

Instruction execution can be sped up by increasing clock rate (reducing cycles to make each instruction faster) and by overlapping instructions for increased throughput. The latter approach is known as **instruction-level parallelism (ILP).**

2.7   Summary

We have reviewed the basics of computer instruction sets and program execution. Key insights here include that the generality of a stored-program computer has enabled hardware designs of incredible complexity and sophistication that achieve high performance and support a wide range of applications. These designs have high commercial volume that enables them to also be low cost. But a further importance of the general-purpose framework is that it enables the construction and sharing of rich sets of programming languages, software tools, and libraries that make complex application software creation possible.

We describe the role of a computer instruction set as the interface between software and hardware. It enables software portability and defines the specification for a correct hardware implementation. All computer instruction sets have four classes:

- arithmetic and logic;
- memory addressing and access;
- conditional control; and
- procedure call and return.

Together these instruction classes represent the fundamental features of every general-purpose computer. Collectively, they can support all programming languages and applications. In fact, with these, a computer can support general, Turing-complete programs (except the memory is finite). However, this basic support, while essential, is just the beginning of ISA, as computer companies add specialized instructions in a number of varieties as a key way to improve performance, and thereby outperform their competition.

With an instruction set defined, the key challenge is efficient execution of programs. As software has grown in complexity, programs have exceeded billions, trillions, and quadrillions of instructions. Thus, speed of instruction execution is an important goal. In the following chapters we will consider the scientific principles of how computers have achieved the extraordinary advances in performance that power our modern world. At the heart of these advances are approaches that overcome the limits of speed (physical size) and overlap (sequence), highlighted in this chapter.

2.8   Digging Deeper

There are numerous textbooks on basic instruction execution that elaborate the variety of operations, encoding styles, and more. However, all of these instruction set architectures include the key fundamental elements of computation, memory, and control flow instructions. In recent years, the most rapid source of new instructions has been wide word instructions, commonly called single-instruction-multiple-data (SIMD), that operate on as many as 512-bit wide operands to improve performance [77, 91]. Most recently, these instructions are being expanded to support deep neural networks (so-called DNNs or deep learning) more efficiently. For example, extensions to Intel's AVX2 include support for convolutional neural networks, variable word-size operations, and "brain" float (bfloat16) [48].

There are many references for the Intel x86 and ARM ISAs, detailing both their designs and their long evolutions. The RISC-V was barely 10 years old in 2020, and more information on this open-source ISA is available [74, 103].

In instruction set design, there is a long-running debate on whether instruction sets should be regular and orthogonal (so-called reduced instruction set computers, or RISC) or optimized with special structures to reduce instruction count (so-called complex instruction set computers, or CISC). Classical papers on this debate include Doug Clark's analysis of VAX vs. RISC [6], Bhandarkar's revisiting of the debate [5], and a more recent comparison of Power (a RISC architecture) and x86 that shows how complex ISAs can actually outperform RISCs [49]. In practice, the pendulum seems to swing back and forth between these design styles, with the short-term advantage depending on the current hardware technology and compiler balance. However, there is not much doubt that RISC instruction sets are easier to use for teaching.

2.9   Problems

2.1   Write a RISC-V assembly language program to perform the following tasks (64-bit version):
(a)   Set the value to 0 for registers X18-X25.
(b)   Put the first eight prime numbers (1, 2, 3, 5, 7, 11, 13, 17) into registers X18–X25.
(c)   Put the value 0x0 0FFF FFFF FFFF into X18.
(d)   Put the value 0x0 0101 010F FFFF into X18.
(e)   Put the value 0x0 0101 0101 0101 into X18.
(f)   Put the value 0x0 0123 4567 89AB into X18.
(g)   Put the value 0x0 0BA9 8765 4321 into X18.

2.2   Write a RISC-V assembly language program to perform the following tasks (32-bit version):
(a)   Set the value to 0 for registers X18–X25.
(b)   Put the first eight prime numbers (1, 2, 3, 5, 7, 11, 13, 17) into registers X18–X25.
(c)   Put the value 0x0 FFFF FFFF into X18.
(d)   Put the value 0x0 010F FFFF into X18.
(e)   Put the value 0x0 0101 0101 into X18.
(f)   Put the value 0x0 4567 89AB into X18.
(g)   Put the value 0x0 8765 4321 into X18.

2.3   Write a RISC-V assembly language program to perform the following tasks (64-bit version):
(a)   Load the value from address 0x0 0FFF FFFF FFFF into X20.
(b)   Store the value 13 as an 8-bit (byte) value into address 0x0 0FFF FFFF FFFF.
(c)   Store the value 13 as a 64-bit value into address 0x0 0FFF FFFF FFFF.
(d)   Load the value from address 0x0 0101 010F FFFF into X20.
(e)   Store the value 17 as a 64-bit value into address 0x0 0101 010F FFFF.
(f)   Load the value from address 0x0 0101 0101 0101 into X20.
(g)   Store the value 127 as a 64-bit value into address 0x0 0101 0101 0101.
(h)   Load the value from address 0x0 0123 4567 89AB into X20.
(i)   Store the value 27 as an 8-bit value (byte) into address 0x0 0123 4567 89AB.
(j)   Store the value 27 as a 64-bit value into address 0x0 0123 4567 89AB.
(k)   Load the value from address 0x0 0BA9 8765 4321 into X20.

2.4   Write a RISC-V assembly language program to perform the following tasks (32-bit version):
(a)   Load the value from address 0x0 0FFF FFFF into X20.
(b)   Store the value 13 as an 8-bit (byte) value into address 0x0 0FFF FFFF.
(c)   Store the value 13 as a 32-bit value into address 0x0 0FFF FFFF.
(d)   Load the value from address 0x0 0101 010F into X20.
(e)   Store the value 17 as a 32-bit value into address 0x0 0101 010F.
(f)   Load the value from address 0x0 0101 0101 into X20.
(g)   Store the value 127 as a 32-bit value into address 0x0 0101 0101.
(h)   Load the value from address 0x0 4567 89AB into X20.
(i)   Store the value 27 as an 8-bit value (byte) into address 0x0 4567 89AB.
(j)   Store the value 27 as a 32-bit value into address 0x0 4567 89AB.
(k)   Load the value from address 0x0 0BA9 8765 into X20.

2.5   Write a RISC-V assembly language program to perform the following tasks (64-bit version):
(a)   Put the value 0x0 0101 010F FFFF into X18, then compute its one's complement.
(b)   Put the value 0x0 0101 010F FFFF into X18, then compute its one's complement.
(c)   Put the value 0xFFFF FFFF FFFF FFFF into X18, with as few instructions as possible.

2.6   Write a RISC-V assembly language program to perform the following tasks (32-bit version):
(a)   Put the value 0x0 010F FFFF into X18, then compute its one's complement.
(b)   Put the value 0x0 010F FFFF into X18, then compute its one's complement.
(c)   Put the value 0x0 FFFF FFFF into X18, with as few instructions as possible.

2.7   Write a RISC-V assembly language program to evaluate the following C++ expressions.

```
struct House {
    int Number;
    int Residents;
    char* Name[32];
    int Cars;
}
House myBlock[16][16];
House yourStreet[128];
```

(a)   yourStreet[12].Number;
(b)   yourStreet[12].Cars;
(c)   myBlock[3][4].Cars;
(d)   &(myBlock[3][4].Name);
(e)   The sum of all of the residents on yourStreet.

(f) Suppose you live at myBlock[3][4]. Compute the sum of the residents that live in the same row of your block.

(g) Suppose you live at myBlock[3][4]. Compute the sum of the residents that live in the same column of your block.

2.8 Write the RISC-V assembly code that corresponds to the following loop:

```
int  j;
j  =  0xAAAA;
do  {
    j  =  j  <<  1;
}  while  (j >0);
```

(a) Explain your program; specifically, which parts correspond to each section of the C program?

(b) What is the mapping of program variables into registers and memory?

(c) What instructions implement the control structures?

2.9 Write the RISC-V assembly code that corresponds to the following loop:

```
int  j  =  3;
for  (int  i =0,  i ++,  i <10){
    j  =  j  *  3;
}
```

Think about how to make this code go fast. How few instructions can you use to implement each loop iteration?

2.10 Write the RISC-V assembly code that corresponds to the following loop. What is the function computed by this code?

```
int  j  =  16;
int  fig1  =  1;  fig2  =  1;
int  fig;
for  (int  i =0,  i ++,  i <j ){
    fig  =  fig2  +  fig1;
    fig2  =  fig;
    fig1  =  fig2
}
return  fig;
```

Explain your program. Which parts correspond to each section of the C++ program? What is the mapping of program variables into registers and memory? What instructions implement the control structures?

2.11 Write the RISC-V assembly code that corresponds to the following loop. What function does this program compute?

```
int  i =0;
int  sum=0;
int  values[32];

for  (int  i=0,  i=i+3,  i<96){
   sum  +=  values[i % 32];
};
```

Explain your program. Which parts correspond to each section of the C++ program? What is the mapping of program variables into registers and memory? What instructions implement the control structures?

2.12 Write the RISC-V assembly code that corresponds to the following program including a procedure call.

```
int  needshelp  (int  n)
{
   int  j  =  0;
   for  (int  i=0,  i<64;  i++){
      if  (n % 8){  i++;}
      else  {j  +=  helper(j);};
   return  j;
};

int  helper  (int  x){
   return  x*2;
};
```

(a) How does the calling convention use jal and jr? Could you have implemented the recursion without these instructions? Could you implement general recursive programs?

(b) A common optimization for recursive programs is to pass the values of arguments and return values in registers. This saves the cost of storing values to memory and loading them back. However, this requires that the caller and callee procedure have a shared understanding of the register map. Recursion can be very deep; how does this work for all cases of recursion?

(c) Inevitably, programs exhaust the limited number of registers in an ISA. What can be done to pass arguments when this has happened?

2.13 Write the RISC-V assembly code that corresponds to the following factorial program including a procedure call.

```
int  fact  (int  n)
{
   if  (n<1){
      return  1;
```

```
      }
   else {
      return n*fact(n-1);
   };
};
```

Explain your program. Which parts correspond to each section of the C++ program? What is the mapping of program variables into registers and memory? What instructions implement the control structures? The procedure call?

2.14 Write the RISC-V assembly code that corresponds to the following Fibonacci program including a procedure call.

```
int fib (int n)
{
   if (n<2){
      return 1;
      }
   else {
      return fib(n-1) + fib(n-2);
   };
};
```

Explain your program. Which parts correspond to each section of the C program? What is the mapping of program variables into registers and memory? What instructions implement the control structures? The procedure calls?

2.15 In this problem, we will consider why there are only a few widely used instruction sets.
(a) Consider the incentives and costs for those building application software and selling it to customers. What benefits does a single instruction set give them? Are there advantages to many?
(b) Consider the incentives for those building software tools and libraries. Why should they prefer one instruction set? Or dozens of instruction sets?
(c) Finally, consider the incentives for a company that builds computers. What are its incentives to adhere to one instruction set? Does it have an incentive to make that instruction set private? (Can't be implemented by anyone else? Explain.)

2.16 Write an assembly language program that implements a simple sorting algorithm, bubble sort. Explain its parts clearly.

2.17 Write an assembly language program that implements a simple sorting algorithm, merge sort. Explain its parts clearly.

2.18 Write an assembly language program that implements a simple sorting algorithm, quicksort. This requires a procedure that calls itself recursively. Explain its parts clearly.

2.19 Here, we address fundamental elements of instruction sets.

(a) Explain why each of the four core elements of instruction sets (computation, control flow, memory access, and procedure linkage) are all required.

(b) Given these requirements, how small an instruction set is possible? Speculate why, given these modest requirements, modern instruction sets (including ARM and x86) have more than 300–400 instructions.

(c) Now look at a full instruction set reference for x86, ARM, or RISC-V. Just one is fine – they are all relatively similar at this level. How does the need for supporting various datatypes affect these numbers? What are some of the fastest growing types of instructions?

2.20 In Section 2.5 we covered the steps in instruction execution. The steps have a particular order.

(a) Explain why these steps go "in order" (and do not repeat).

(b) Could another order of steps work? Explain.

(c) Consider another variation, in which some computers allowed instructions to access memory several times (a repeat of the memory access step). What implications would this have for implementing a computer?

(d) Does it make sense for some other execution steps to repeat?

2.21 Nearly all computers have both registers and memory. It's a common question to ask "why don't we just have many more registers," 64 or 128, since we are always running out of registers. We will examine two reason why instruction sets (and computers) don't have dramatically more registers.

(a) The three operand style for many RISC-V instructions, combined with the architecture's 32 registers, requires 5 bits to specify each register for a total of 15 instruction bits. This leaves 17 bits for operations. Suppose we increased the number of registers to 128; this would consume 21 bits per three operand instruction. How many fewer instruction opcodes would be needed?

(b) Suppose we could just barely manage to switch to a 128-register architecture, reducing the number of operations as needed above. But all of the instruction encodings were used up. What is the downside of not being able to add more instructions?

(c) Hardware design engineers will tell you that adding more registers is likely to make the processor run slower, as it takes longer to read each register when we have a larger register file. Suppose each doubling of the register file slowed access by 20%. Can you formulate how many memory references would have to be avoided in order for this to make the overall processor faster? (For simplicity you can assume each memory access takes five times longer than a regular instruction; the real number is larger.)

2.22 In Section 2.6 we described two approaches to speeding to program execution: (1) speeding up each instruction in a sequence; and (2) exploiting overlapped execution of instructions in a program.

(a) To make each instruction faster, we need to increase the speed of some or all of the instruction execution steps. We will see how the shrinking of microelectronics makes this possible in Chapter 3. Another angle on this is to make instructions simpler – suggest two ways that the steps of instructions could be simpler. Explain why these changes don't restrict the computer's ability to support general programs.

(b) The second approach overlaps the execution of two instructions. In Chapter 4, we explore some aggressive techniques that have been invented. For now, explain how an assembly program depends on the **illusion** of sequential order by constructing several pairs of instructions (one follows the other), for which the program result will change if the instructions are swapped. (Hint: consider register dependences, branches, store-load, etc.)

2.23 While many computer users think of instruction sets as a fixed design, in fact any widely used instruction set is continually growing. The growth generally uses some instruction bit patterns that were not previously designed for encodings. Look at the RISC-V instruction encoding definition (https://riscv.org/wp-content/uploads/2017/05/riscv-spec-v2.2.pdf, sections 1.2 and 2.2). The RISC-V design mainly uses instructions of a fixed size 32-bit format.

(a) How many R-type instructions can the 32-bit instructions support?

(b) Approximately how many of the encodings of the 2^{32} bit patterns for instructions are unused? (Count the instructions and compare to the *funct* fields.)

(c) If we assume that instructions will need three register specifiers, how many opcode/instruction bit patterns for instructions are unused (and thus can be used for new instructions)?

2.24 While many computer users think of instruction sets as a fixed design, in fact any widely used instruction set is continually growing. While growth usually employs instruction set bit patterns not previously used, fixed size formats can cause "shortages" of available bit patterns. For background, look at the RISC-V instruction encoding definition (https://riscv.org/wp-content/uploads/2017/05/riscv-spec-v2.2.pdf, sections 1.2 and 2.2). The RISC-V design mainly uses instructions of a fixed size 32-bit format. As a result, on rare occasions, instructions will be "deprecated" and then eventually removed from an instruction set.

(a) Deprecated means that the instruction is still supported, but executes with lower performance. What are the consequences of this for software that uses the instructions?

(b) After several years of being deprecated, instructions can be removed (the bits cause some other newly defined instruction to execute). What are the consequences of this for software that uses the instructions?

(c) Imagine a situation in which a computer processor designer deprecated a set of instructions for six years, and then removed it in future products after this period. What is the consequence for machines that were sold and continue to operate in the world? What is the consequence for a software developer who is distributing program binaries (executables) as a product? The customers who bought either the processors or the software?

2.25   Computer architectures use a calling convention to pass values in a procedure call; the RISC-V uses the convention summarized in Table 2.4. The purpose of the calling convention is to allow interoperation among computer languages (e.g. a Python program calling a C or Java program), but also to reduce the amount of loads and stores to the stack for transmitting arguments and return values. Write a recursive procedure that has two arguments, and does some local computation before calling recursively.

```
recurse(int  a,  b,  c,  depth){
    int sum = a+b+c;
    if ((depth −1)<0){ return sum;}
    else {
        sum = sum + recurse(a*2,b+3,c−7,depth −1);
        return sum;
        };
}
```

(a)   How many of the arguments and return values would be stored to the stack in a call to `recurse(5,7,13,5)`? How many bytes of memory traffic is this?

(b)   How does this compare to a stack-calling approach that transmits all of the arguments and return values using the stack? How many bytes of memory traffic would be required?

(c)   Our code is contrived to focus on only procedure calling; not much other work is done. Can you describe an example of a more complex program where this kind of structure might occur? Explain the example, and how much it might save in memory traffic to the stack.

2.26   One of the most successful instruction sets is the x86 (including x86 and x86_64), which is used by processor products from both Intel and AMD. This instruction set began in the 1970s and has been updated many times since.

(a)   Look for resources on the Internet and perhaps Intel and AMD websites. How has the number of instructions (unique operations possible) grown over the years? Create a table with the number of instructions that are part of x86 in 1975, 1985, 1995, 2005, and 2015. Make a graph that shows the growth. What is the annual growth rate?

(b)   The x86 architecture has expanded the size of registers (in bits), the number of registers, and the number of instruction operation codes over time. One key aspect making this possible is the use of variable-length encoding for instructions. This means that instructions vary from very short (one byte) to about 17 bytes (in 2020), and this maximum number could even grow in the future. Explain how this enables the x86 instruction set additions over the past 45 years.

2.27   One of the most successful instruction sets is the x86 (including x86 and x86_64), which is used by processor products from both Intel and AMD. This instruction set began in the 1970s and has been updated many times since. A key design element enabling expansion has been its variable-length encoding of instructions. Instructions currently range from 1 to 17 bytes.

(a)   Explain how variable-length instruction encoding complicates the steps of instruction execution (the downside).

(b)   One additional advantage of variable-length encoding is that a clever design uses short encodings (a small number of bytes) to represent frequent operations. Look up a description of the x86 instruction set on the Internet. What are some of the shortest instructions (one byte)?

(c)   Suppose the shortest instructions accounted for 30 percent of the total instructions, 2-byte instructions accounted for 30 percent, 4-byte instructions for 30 percent, and 6-byte instructions for 10 percent. How would program size compare to a fixed 32-bit instruction format, such as used by RISC-V?

3   Processors and Scaling: Small is Fast!

In Chapter 2 we saw that a computer performs computation by processing instructions. A computer instruction set must include a variety of features to achieve flexible programmability, including varied arithmetic and logic operations, conditional computation, and application-defined data structures. As a result, the execution of each instruction requires a number of steps: instruction fetch and decode, arithmetic or logic computation, read or write memory, and determination of the next instruction. The instruction set definition is a contract between software and hardware, the fundamental software–hardware interface, that enables software to be portable. After portability, the next critical attribute is performance, so computer hardware is designed to execute instructions as fast as possible.

The speed at which a computer can complete a program is determined by the speed at which it can execute instructions. The larger the computer hardware used to perform steps, the longer each step will take. Why is this? It is because larger hardware requires information to be sent along longer critical paths that connect units of the computer, and those longer critical paths slow execution. As a result, the miniaturization of the computer logic has been a major contributor to the increasing performance of computers.

In this chapter, we discuss how and why information processing systems are amenable to scaling to smaller size. We discuss the specifics of how the size scaling has happened. Finally, we present how it has benefited computer performance and capabilities, in particular how it has reduced power and cost. This provides a perspective on how such miniaturization speeds the execution of computer programs, and has made computing remarkable. We compare these advances to those of other technologies, which serves to further highlight computing's unique impact.

3.1   Miniaturization and Information Processing

One key to computers' extraordinary capability has been the rapid advance of microelectronics that has reduced the size of electronic circuits rapidly. The earliest electronic computers were constructed from vacuum tubes (each approximately the size of a human hand, ≈ 0.25 liters). Construction of simple computers from such devices produced building-sized computers such as ENIAC at the University of Pennsylvania.

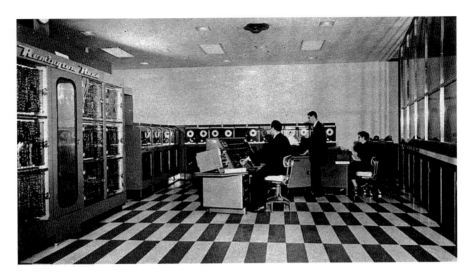

Figure 3.1 UNIVAC in 1953 was a computer as large as a house, but only achieved 5,000 operations per second.

By the end of its operational life in 1956, ENIAC contained 20,000 vacuum tubes, 7,200 crystal diodes, 1,500 relays, 70,000 resistors, 10,000 capacitors, and approximately 5,000,000 hand-soldered joints. UNIVAC, the commercial product based on ENIAC, was much simpler, with 5,000 active devices (vacuum tubes or relays), and occupied approximately 65 m^3 (spread over 1,800 square feet), about the size of a small house! Each UNIVAC weighed approximately 8 tons. Figure 3.1 shows the UNIVAC.

In contrast, today's computers are dramatically smaller. The computing power of the UNIVAC system can now be had with a tiny sliver of silicon. For example, the ARM Thumb processor is implemented on a silicon chip with an area equal to the cross-section of just a few dozen human hairs (see Figure 3.2). Designed by the world leader in small, low-power computers (ARM), the Thumb employs a minimal instruction set, enabling its implementation to require only 20,000 transistors and only micro-watts (10^{-6} watts) of power. The Cortex-M3 ARM Thumb shown in Figure 3.2 is 200 times faster than the original UNIVAC computer, and weighs only a few grams.

In the remainder of the chapter we explain how the computer miniaturization enabled by the advance of microelectronics has driven improvements in computer capability, power, and size. In doing so, we answer questions such as:

1. How is this miniaturization possible for information processing?
2. What impact does miniaturization have on processing speed?
3. What impact does miniaturization have on power requirements?
4. Why is the scale of these benefits unique to information processing? Why not in other technology areas?

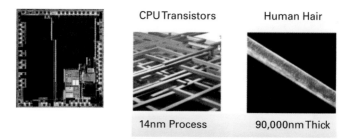

CPU Transistors   Human Hair

14nm Process   90,000nm Thick

Figure 3.2 The 0.11 mm^2 Cortex-M3 on a STM32F100C4T6B chip (300 × 300 μm) compared to the cross-section of a single transistor (14 nanometers) and human hair (90,000 nanometers). One micron is 1,000 nanometers. The area of a 24 MHz ARM microcontroller is combined with a 16 KB flash memory, and altogether is about the cross-section of 32 strands of hair.

00101010111100   11011010110011
10100101101   11100101011

Figure 3.3 A computer transforms sets of information "bits."

3.2   What Is the Natural Size of a Computer?

What is the natural size for a computer? Let us first consider what computers do. Computer programs alter one set of bits to another, reading them from storage, transforming them, and writing them back to storage. This is illustrated conceptually in Figure 3.3. These bit transformations are remarkably powerful, and are a general model for all different types of information applications, such as a database system, weather simulation, or rendering of an animated feature movie (computer graphics).

More examples include the recent wave of smartphone applications that transform photos with a Snapchat filter, or compose a feed from the activities of your social network. More precisely, in this class of applications, computers receive sets of bits from the network (from other computers), transform them, and send them out to other computers, as illustrated in Figure 3.4.

For example, a social network application presents an integrated view of your social network, a "timeline" of images, messages, ads, and news. When you open the app, the timeline (a set of elements) is downloaded and rendered on your smartphone. That rendering involves complex algorithms that convert bits to images and animation, that lay out the images, and accept inputs as you scroll, flick, pinch, and click your way through information. The cloud performs a complementary function, building an integrated database that captures your social network point-of-view. This includes accepting posts of images, animations, news, and network connection updates, continuously creating an integrated flow of activity for your app to view.

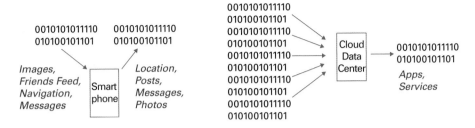

Figure 3.4 Many modern internet and smartphone applications can be thought of as transformations of bits coming from the network, cloud, phone sensors, or user inputs.

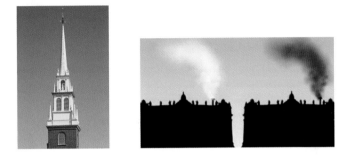

Figure 3.5 The two lanterns in the Old North Church conveyed one bit of information to Paul Revere. The color of the smoke indicates whether a pope has been chosen, or not, one bit of information.

How large must a computer be in order to transform a set of bits? How large is a bit? And, what is the physical size of a computation? Claude Shannon, widely regarded as the "Father of Information Theory," created a mathematical theory based on entropy that measures information in terms of bits (sometimes called Shannons), as the minimum quantum of information [83]. These simplest information building blocks encode information by taking on the values of 0 or 1. Interestingly, because bits are defined mathematically, their physical representation is a matter of engineering choice.

For example, a single bit of information can be encoded in physical representations as diverse as the number of lanterns lit in the Old North Church (one if by land, two if by sea), a semaphore switch at a railroad junction, or the color of smoke (black or white) at the meeting of cardinals to select a pope (Figure 3.5). The variety in both size (0.3–10 meters) and encoding of information (light, physical position, smoke color) reflect the fact that information and computations have no intrinsic size or medium; rather, computing systems can choose a technology that enables better computers. As discussed in Chapter 1, these choices have enabled faster, cheaper, and smaller computers. And, as computers evolved over seven decades, many technologies have been used in computers.

Some examples of bits are very small. For example, a "pit" (hole) in the surface of a DVD (digital video disk) is 530 nanometers (nm) on a spacing of 320 nanometer tracks, occupying an area of 0.53×0.32 μm. The pattern of pits indicates "0" or

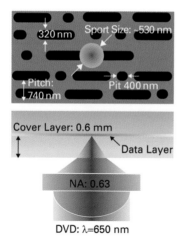
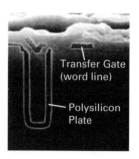

Figure 3.6 DVD "pits" on a flat disc (left) and DRAM cells (right) are examples of small single bits in a computer system.

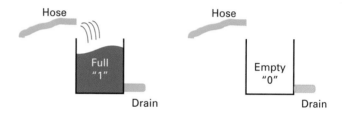

Figure 3.7 A 1-gallon bucket can be used to represent a bit, encoding a value by the level of water in the bucket. Filled by a hose and emptied by a drain, the rate of water flow and bucket size determines the rate of switching.

"1" values. A wire in a modern computer chip is even smaller, at 20×100 nm and encodes a value based on its electrical voltage. A DRAM cell (a single bit of computer memory) is approximately 0.5×0.5 nm (see Figure 3.6) and stores a bit with electrical charge on a capacitor. Assuming that the Old North Church lanterns occupy an area of approximately 1 m^2, a DRAM cell is 1/2,000,000,000 times smaller in each dimension or $1/(4 \times 10^{18})$ smaller in total area.

3.2.1   Example: Bit Size and Speed

Consider a simple example, shown in Figure 3.7, in which the value of a bit is represented in the water-fill level of a 1-gallon bucket. To switch the value from "0" to "1," we turn on the hose, which flows at 10 gallons/minute. If the bucket starts empty, it takes 6 seconds to fill it. To switch the value from "1" to "0," the drain valve is opened and also runs at 10 gallons/minute, so it takes 6 seconds to switch from "1" to "0." Thus, this bit can switch values once in 6 seconds, or at a rate of 0.1667 Hz (cycles/second or changes/second). If you prefer metric units, consider a hose with a rate of 40 liters/minute and a 4 liter bucket.

Now, suppose the buckets were smaller, say one-quarter of a gallon? Then the same hose could fill it in only 1.5 seconds, so this bit can switch values at a rate of $1/1.5 = 0.667$ Hz, four times faster. The metric analog would be a 40 liters/minute hose, and a 1-liter bucket.

Principle 3.1: Information Size Scaling

Information has no natural size, so bits and computation can be scaled down in physical size, enabling computers to become smaller and faster.

3.2.2 Shrinking Computers

If bits can be implemented in a wide range of sizes, what about computations? Computations are really transformations on sets of bits, so it turns out that computers, the engines that compute on them, can be shrunk along with the bits.

The first commercial digital electronic computer was the UNIVAC in 1951. UNIVAC was a better engineered version of ENIAC, and much smaller – about half the size (roughly 28 m^3). The electronic logic elements used in the design of computers were large, and therefore a major determinant of computer system size in the 1950s and 1960s. This continued to be true even as computers became small enough to fit onto a single chip, microprocessors, from the 1980s on through the present day.

If you look at the entirety of those old computer systems, they included additional cabinets for memory, archival storage (paper and magnetic tapes), and often large physical structures for human input/output (I/O) such as card punches, printers, and sometimes cathode-ray displays, as depicted in Figure 3.1. This situation continues to the present, as larger-capacity memory and storage such as rotating disks and now solid-state persistent storage (i.e. SSD's) or perhaps the touchscreen dominate the overall size of a computer system. However, for now, we will focus on the size of the logic part of the computer system, depicted in Figure 2.17, as this part of the system generally determines a computer's maximum instruction-processing rate.

3.3 Computer Size and Speed

What does the physical size of a computer have to do with its speed? Building on the idea that smaller size makes bits faster, the next step is to consider how a smaller computer, and the resulting shorter wires, can make a computer faster. For the different parts of an electronic circuit to agree on signal values (bits), these signals must be communicated throughout the computer. These electronic circuits use a shared clock that ticks at a constant rate. That rate is determined by the time it takes for information to spread across the computer. If the computer is physically large, it requires a longer time for information to propagate across the system, resulting in a longer clock period and therefore a slower clock rate. If the computer is small, the shorter time to propagate information allows a faster clock rate. In both cases, the clock rate limits the rate at which the computer can execute instructions. So in a very direct way, the size of a computer is related to its speed. In fact, these effects are so important that famed supercomputer designer Seymour Cray designed the Cray-1, a ground-breaking supercomputer, in a cylindrical shape to minimize the length of wires, and thereby wire delays, and finally the clock period of the machine.

3.3.1 Smaller Computers Are Faster

As you may have learned in a physics class, the fastest anything can move is limited by the speed of light. In electronic computers signals can approach the speed of light traveling on a "transmission line," tuned to match the transmitter and receiver so that the electromagnetic wave travels without loss. These transmission lines are usually drawn as in Figure 3.8 (left), and are a common tool for electrical engineers.[1] A perfect transmission line is carefully matched at both ends to avoid reflections. If a circuit has irregular connections (such as one output connected to several inputs) it is difficult to connect all points directly. However, perfect transmission lines are a useful abstraction because they represent a limit, the fastest way to communicate in an electronic computer.

In commercial computer designs, most connections in the electronic circuits are not made with transmission lines, but rather as resistor–capacitor (RC) circuits, which can be modeled as simple charge pumps. As depicted in Figure 3.8, the idea is that a transistor pumps charge (electrons) onto a wire, switching the wire from a "0" to "1" value by increasing its voltage. Intuitively, you can think of the wire as a long trough (or pipe) that is filled with water that comes from the pump. This is the same idea as our buckets in Figure 3.7. In that example, the water filled the bucket gradually

Figure 3.8 The fastest way to communicate information in a computer is a transmission line (left). These lines transmit information at the speed of light by creating an electromagnetic wave. An alternative model for wire delay in a computer is a charge pump connected to a wire capacitance (right). The rate at which charge can be pumped determines how long it takes to fill the capacitance, and thus change the value from "0" to "1."

---

[1] Strictly speaking, the speed of transmission is limited by the materials used in the transmission line; vacuum is the fastest [29].

based on the flow rate of the hose. In this case, the wire is charged gradually based on the flow of charge through the transistor onto the wire, and the increase of voltage is governed by the simple equation:

$$Q = CV,$$

where Q is the electrical charge on the wire, C is the capacitance of the wire relative to the ground plane, and V is the voltage used to reflect the digital information value of the wire. As you might expect, C, the capacitance of the wire, grows linearly with distance (or worse!). Overall, the charge-pump computer speed limit is analogous to that of the speed of light (as in Figure 3.8). An electrical engineer might use a more complete model based on an RC circuit (resistance and capacitance), capturing the transistor output resistance and wire resistance. The resistance determines how fast charge can be pumped onto the wire. However, the RC model would produce a slower speed for the communication – and corresponding longer clock period. So, the charge pump is a simpler model that illustrates the same point.

Putting it all together, we can construct a model for the clock speed of a computer based on its physical volume (V). For a cube of volume V, the length of wire required to go from one corner to the farthest corner using XYZ wires can be characterized as $3L$, where

$$L = V^{\frac{1}{3}}.$$

This relationship is depicted in Figure 3.9. We can use the transmission line or charge pump model and this maximum distance, $3L$, to determine the computer clock period, and hence the computer clock rate. Since a smaller volume enables a faster clock, this means that the smaller the computer, the faster it can be. To exploit this property, computers are miniaturized as much as possible. And computer technologists have even spent substantial energy to find materials and build structures with low dielectric constants (low k, such as air gaps) to reduce capacitance and thereby make the clock period as short as possible.

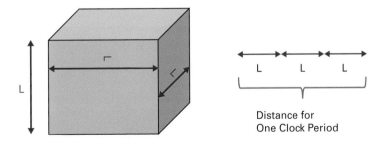

Figure 3.9 The clock speed model relates a computer's size to the maximum distance for a signal. When compared with limits in information propagation speed, it provides a minimum computer clock period.

> **Principle 3.2: Physical Size and the Clock Period Model**
>
> *To model the achievable clock period, we model a computer's size, V, as a three-dimensional cube. Within each clock period, the computer must communicate information from one corner to the farthest corner, a distance of $3L$, where $L = V^{\frac{1}{3}}$. This distance, combined with a model for the maximum speed that information can travel, produces a minimum clock period, and thus a maximum clock rate.*

3.3.2   Example: Applying the Size and Clock Period Model

Microprocessors are the most widely used computers and are employed for a wealth of computing applications. Let's apply the computer size and clock period model to a modern microprocessor, and see how it captures clock period scaling over seven decades of size scaling. We use ENIAC, a state-of-the-art computer in 1950, as one point of reference, and use our model to consider scaling. ENIAC was the size of a large room at the University of Pennsylvania, with a volume of 65 cubic meters ($V = 65$ m^3) (with approximate dimensions as illustrated in Figure 3.10). We model the size of ENIAC with a cube, which gives a value of $L_E = 4$ m and $3L_E = 12$ m. ENIAC had a clock period, T_E, of 200 microseconds (200×10^{-6}, or about five-thousandths of a second).

Next, we estimate the clock speed of the ARM Cortex-M3 depicted in Figure 3.2, using our physical size and clock period model. ARM processors are a leading type of processor in smartphones and many smaller computing devices such as web cameras, smart watches, and tablets. The Cortex-M3 has a area of 0.3 mm^2 and is a thin silicon wafer. The Cortex-M3's volume is comparable to a cube $0.2 \times 0.2 \times 0.2$ mm. This reflects a characteristic length for our model of $L_C = 0.2$ mm. The Cortex-M3 is remarkably smaller with a 20,000-times shorter characteristic length. Taking this ratio and multiplying by ENIAC's clock period gives:

Figure 3.10 The ENIAC (1950), annotated with dimensions.

$$T_C = \frac{L_C}{L_E} \times T_E$$

$$T_C = \frac{0.2 \times 10^{-3}}{4} \times 200 \times 10^{-6}$$

$$T_C = 10 \times 10^{-9} \text{ or } 10 \text{ ns.}$$

So, the *physical size and clock period* model predicts a clock period for the Cortex-M3 of 10 ns (100 Mhz). This is quite close to the actual Cortex-M3 clock period of 4 nanoseconds (10^{-9} seconds), and over 10,000-fold clock scaling, off by only 1.6 times.[2] Matching so closely is remarkable, as the ENIAC and Cortex-M3 use disparate technologies and very different processor designs. Further, the model is applied over a 70-year period of computer evolution. In short, this example shows the *physical size and computer clock period* model provides a good estimate for clock period, and hence computer performance. In the following sections we analyze how computer scaling works, and compare compute-performance scaling to that of other technologies.

3.3.3 Size Scaling Computers from Room-Sized to a Single Chip

Over seven decades the physical dimensions of computers have shrunk steadily. We have seen that the incentive to shrink is higher performance, but the key enabler was a steady reduction in size of logic and memory electronics used to build computers. In Table 3.1, we document the progression from large to small to tiny computer sizes. Starting with the ENIAC (65 m³), a house-sized computer based on vacuum tubes as electronic components (each the size of a small pickle), each generation of systems has progressed to a smaller physical size (to 11 m³ down through 5.6 m³ and the minicomputer at 3 m³). The first 35 years of computer evolution saw the reduction of computer size from an entire floor of a building (ENIAC) to the first microprocessor-based portable computers (Compaq Portable). This evolution spanned a range of logic technologies from discrete (individual) vacuum tubes and relays to transistors. Once on transistors in the 1960s, computer systems used transistors that were dime-sized, then pencil tip–sized, and then soon shrinking so small that they were difficult to see with the human eye! This progression has been steady and continues to this day.

These technology shifts enabled smaller computers, and consequently both shorter clock periods (higher clock rates) and higher performance. At a few technology transitions, the shift to a lower-cost and more scalable technology caused a temporary increase in clock period, but the benefits of miniaturization quickly reasserted

---

[2] The clock period of the Cortex-M3 is less than the model predicts due to aggressive lower-level techniques that partition the computer into multiple different clock periods, called pipelining. These techniques are discussed in Chapter 4. In some processor designs, these approaches can enable clock periods as short as 0.25 ns (4 Ghz).

Table 3.1. Computer size evolution.

System type	Technology	Memory capacity	Size	Clock period
Electronic (ENIAC/UNIVAC), 1950	Vacuum tubes	0.004 MiB	65 m^3	200 μs (10^{-6})
Mainframe (IBM360/67), 1965	TTL	0.5 MiB	11 m^3	200 ns (10^{-9})
Mainframe (IBM370), 1970	MST	8 MiB	5.6 m^3	115 ns
Minicomputer (DEC VAX750), 1985	TTL/MOS	1 MiB	3 m^3	320 ns
Portable (Compaq), 1983	CMOS	0.13 MiB	50×10^{-3} m^3	200 ns
Laptop (Compaq Presario 1610), 1995	CMOS	128 MiB	14×10^{-3} m^3	2 ns
Smartphone (Apple iPhone 11) 2018	CMOS	8 GiB	12.5×10^{-6} m^3	0.4 ns

Figure 3.11 The Apple iPhone 11 is 5.94 inches along its longest dimension (left). This size is largely due to the display and to fit a human hand. The circuit board being removed from the phone contains a CPU chip that is one-quarter the size of the smallest square on the board, 98.5 mm^2 (right).

themselves. Table 3.1 is far from comprehensive, including only a selection of computers, so the improvement in clock period are jumps of five-fold or greater.

A few entries are of particular note. The Compaq Portable, a briefcase-sized system introduced in 1983, is the first computer in Table 3.1 to use a single-chip processor, a microprocessor. It's also interesting to consider the span of size and performance from the first (ENIAC) to the most recent entry (iPhone 11). Applying our physical size and computer clock period model, we can see that the reduction in computer size from ENIAC to the Apple iPhone 11 accounts for a 500,000-fold increase in performance (Figure 3.11). So, getting small is an important part of what makes computers fast. This computing performance benefit alone would be compelling, but miniaturization has the added benefit of making computers small enough to fit easily in your pocket, so your smartphone or smartwatch can be with you all of the time!

> **Principle 3.3: Computer Size and Speed Scaling**
>
> *Smaller computers have shorter clock periods, reducing in proportion to the longest distance in the machine (see Principle 3.2). The shorter clock period shortens the time to complete each instruction, giving a proportional increase in computer performance.*

3.3.4   Size Scaling Single-Chip Computers: The Power Problem and Dennard's Solution

In the late 1950s, Jack Kilby and Robert Noyce invented the ability to integrate transistors onto a single monolithic silicon chip. In his 1964 paper, Gordon Moore posited that the number of transistors on a chip might double every two years for the foreseeable future [68]. This observation of exponential increase in available transistors per chip held true for nearly 50 years, catapulting us from chips with 32 transistors (1964) to those with 50-billion transistors (2018). Naturally, putting billions of transistors on a chip that grew only slightly larger meant that any computer logic shrank dramatically. Over this period, a fixed function of logic would be 1/1,000,000,000 times smaller than its original size. The miniaturization provided computer designers with a bounty of transistors, triggering a multitude of creative computer architecture techniques, described in Chapter 4.

Once entire processors could fit on a single chip, around 1975, "microprocessors" were born. Coupled to Moore's Law, these processors grew in performance and complexity rapidly, and despite dramatic increases in computer complexity and memory capacity, by the early 1990's a full-featured computer (central processing units, or CPUs) fit onto a single silicon chip. These single-chip computers were dramatically smaller than all prior computers, occupying a volume below 50 mm × 50 mm × 50 mm or 125 cm^3, the size of a fingernail. Since that time, while computer system size has been determined largely by external physical requirements – desktops, portable laptops, and smartphones – the computing engine (aka processor or CPU) at the heart of the system has continued to shrink. By 1990, microprocessors were the world's fastest processors. This enabled a critical phase of computer size scaling – the scaling of single-chip microprocessors. In this phase, computers benefited exponentially from the rapid progress of microelectronics miniaturization.

Moore's Law produces an exponential increase in both transistors per chip and computation density, and thus poses a significant challenge for electric power and the heat it generates in a computer. If the power for each computation remains constant, exponential shrinkage in physical size produces a corresponding increase in heat density that would destroy the circuits. In fact, the Intel CTO famously showed a graph showing that microprocessors that didn't solve this problem would soon become hotter than the surface of the sun!

In 1974, Robert Dennard proposed a new scaling rule that solves the power problem, enabling productive Moore's Law scaling. Dennard's scaling rule is so effective that it carried the computer industry from MOS (metal-oxide silicon) devices with 1,000 transistors per chip to 100 million in 2005 [23] at essentially constant power. In short, once a processor was small enough to fit onto a single silicon chip, Dennard scaling was essential to reap the benefits of microprocessor scaling ever smaller and to a fraction of a modern CPU chip. This Dennard-enabled scaling enabled computing technology to elegantly capture the benefits of "smaller is better" for information processing.

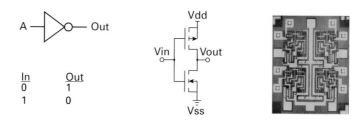

Figure 3.12 Three levels of abstraction for an inverter: logical, schematic, and physical (20 μm, circa 1980). The physical layout is a NAND gate (which can be easily used to implement an inverter). The dimensions of the physical layout determine properties such as capacitance (C).

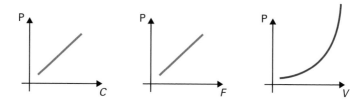

Figure 3.13 Power scaling for CMOS circuits – from inverters to full microprocessors. Power increases linearly with capacitance (C) and clock frequency (F), and increases quadratically with voltage (V).

To explain Dennard scaling, we first need some background on how digital logic functions become circuits of physical devices. As shown in Figure 3.12, each logic circuit (left) in a computer is mapped to transistors (middle), which are then mapped to a two-dimensional, planar, physical design (right). Thus, a mathematical notion, a Boolean inverter function, is manifested as an electronic circuit with a physical design that determines key properties such as capacitance (C, determined by the sizes of the wires and the gates) and frequency (F, another name for clock rate). This circuit is operated at a specific voltage (V). A microprocessor is just a much more complex logic circuit with a corresponding C, F, and V. However, these key attributes determine the power consumption of the computer circuits. Directly, the electric power (P) consumed by such a circuit can be written as:

$$P = \frac{1}{2} \times C \times V^2 \times F.$$

This equation means that power scales up linearly with increased in capacitance and frequency, but quadratically with voltage, all shown in Figure 3.13. The energy required for each transistor switching (or circuit) is $1/2\ CV^2$, required as the voltage of a capacitance is moved between a voltage of 0 and V. The rate of switching, F, in cycles/second, determines the energy required over time, the power. Dennard scaling exploits the quadratic growth of power with voltage, reducing voltage to reduce power. The voltage reduction produces a corresponding quadratic reduction in power, which is exploited for multiple scaling benefits.

Dennard's rules for scaling are:

1. scale transistors down in size by 0.7 times in each linear dimension (down to approximately 70%); and
2. simultaneously scale down the voltage used to represent logic values by 0.7 times, keeping the electric field constant.

This coordinated scaling has two important impacts:

1. It reduces the switching energy per bit value transition by one-half, making each computation require one-half the energy it previously required!
2. It enables a processor with twice as many transistors to be run 1.41 times faster without any increase in power used! (power = energy/time)

Dennard's key insight was that by holding the electric field constant (per unit distance), and thereby scaling down the voltage, the quadratic power reduction could compensate for the increased power due to a larger number of transistors. Further, it could simultaneously enable faster operation, an increased clock frequency, F. Dennard's scaling law maintains constant power per unit area (per chip!) while increasing the clock rate by 41 percent per generation. Constant power per CPU chip from generation to generation is a terrific property, enabling succeeding generations of microprocessors to be used in nearly the same surrounding design and form factor (e.g. server, desktop, laptop, or smartphone).

This idea of Dennard scaling is illustrated in Figure 3.14, where CPU_2 is the successor for CPU_1, and implemented in a more advanced, next-generation silicon progress – in this case 0.7 μm versus 1.0 μm. Because of the finer feature sizes, CPU_2 has twice the number of transistors as CPU_1 in the same chip area. We can see from the computation below CPU_2 that Dennard scaling allows all of those transistors to run 41 percent faster while consuming the same amount of power! This is because the voltage reduction compensates for the larger number of smaller transistors. Such coordinated scaling maintained power per unit area nearly constant for 25 years, from

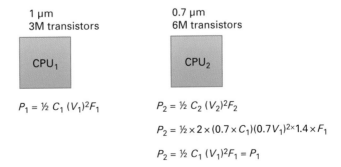

$$P_1 = \tfrac{1}{2} C_1 (V_1)^2 F_1$$

$$P_2 = \tfrac{1}{2} C_2 (V_2)^2 F_2$$

$$P_2 = \tfrac{1}{2} \times 2 \times (0.7 \times C_1)(0.7 V_1)^2 \times 1.4 \times F_1$$

$$P_2 = \tfrac{1}{2} C_1 (V_1)^2 F_1 = P_1$$

Figure 3.14 Doubling the number of transistors from a 1 to 0.5 μm process and a voltage reduction and a frequency increase in a new process generation, using Dennard scaling. Power density and chip power remain constant in the new generation, while processor performance increases dramatically!

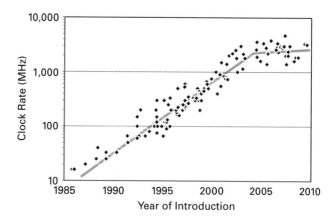

Figure 3.15 Dennard scaling produced clock rate increases of 1.4-fold per process generation without any increase in power. Over the 20-year period from 1985 to 2005, this scaling increased microprocessor clock rates from 33 Mhz to over 3 Ghz.

1980 to 2005, by reducing operating voltage from 5.0 V to 0.7 V, and shrinking transistors from 10 μm to 0.032 μm (32 nm). The dramatic, more than 10,000-fold, increase in clock rate (Figure 3.15) has been a major contributor to increased microprocessor performance.

Dennard's scaling law was employed in single-chip microprocessors from the late 1980s through 2005. It enabled the growth of logic transistors per microprocessor from 100,000 to over one billion with only modest increases in power requirements. It enabled the personal computer, smartphone, and Internet-of-Things (IoT) revolution.

3.3.5   The End of Dennard Scaling

Unfortunately, Dennard scaling came to an end around 2005. The reason for this is that transistors became so tiny (deep submicron gate lengths) and operating voltages became so low (close to gate thresholds) that reducing operating voltage to keep the electric field constant was increasingly difficult. Further, transistors with gates shorter than 1 μm (10^{-6}m) are increasingly "leaky," causing power to be consumed constantly, not only when the transistor was switched on. This makes the power scaling formulas on which Dennard scaling depends inaccurate. The end of Dennard scaling forced a radical change in the direction of computer architecture, causing the industry to turn to explicit, multicore parallelism to exploit the continued increases of transistors produced by Moore's Law. We consider multicore parallelism in Chapter 7.

3.4   Computer Size and Power Consumption

We have seen that the miniaturization of computers enables them to have higher clock rates, and therefore greater performance. More precisely, the miniaturized computers can process instructions faster than their larger predecessors. Now we will examine the benefits of miniaturization for the power required for a computer. As discussed earlier, the representation of each bit of information may be large or small. The size of bits makes computing on them either a high-power or low-power activity. ENIAC was 150 kilowatts, but computed only 5,000 instructions per second, a ratio of 33 instructions per second per kilowatt. Today's microprocessors achieve millions of instructions per second per **watt**! These units reflect a power efficiency increase of 1 million × 1 thousand = 1 billion times. For example, the Apple A13 Bionic (in the iPhone 11) operates with a maximum power of 3 watts, and delivers 7–14 billion instructions per second. This is a power efficiency of 3 billion instructions per second per watt, or nearly 3,000,000,000,000 instructions per second per kilowatt, a 10^{12} improvement over the ENIAC.

The story above captures power efficiency for an entire processor. The same question can be considered for an individual transistor or switch. Since it is complicated to compute a vacuum tube or relay's switching energy for ENIAC, let us assume the cost of 1 joule per bit (a joule is a watt-second). Applying our charge pump model of delay (Figure 3.8), scaling switching energy for bits with machine size ratios produces a switching energy for the smaller volume of modern computers, of $1/(275^3)$ $= \frac{1}{20,796,875}$ or approximately 48 nanojoules. While this seems remarkably small, 30 years of Dennard scaling has taken us even further, reducing voltage along with size. Now, computer chips can execute an entire instruction at an energy cost far below a nanojoule (10^{-9} joule).

Principle 3.4: Computer Size and Energy Scaling

Reducing computer size decreases the energy required for each compute operation. Combined with Dennard's voltage scaling, this effect has reduced the energy required for computation by one trillion times! This enables a trillion times faster computer that uses so little power (and generates so little heat) that it can be held in your hand.

Reduced energy per instruction in turn lowers the energy required for an entire computation. As the computers are scaled down in size, computations can be completed with much less energy, and the energy efficiency of computation increases dramatically. For example, if we consider the evolution of the iPhone processor (introduced in 2007), the shrinking of transistors every two years has reduced the power per computation $2^5 = 32$-fold over the 10-year period from 2007 to 2017. This means that if a particular computation had a fixed value in 2007 – for example, computing an image to display on the screen – then the 2017 iPhone is capable of generating 32 times as much value! Interestingly, the Apple designers expended much of this bounty on a 20-times increase in the number of pixels in the phone display, increasing it from 153,600 (320 × 480) to 3,338,496 (1242 × 2688). The spectacular resolutions (3.3M pixels at 458 dots-per-inch [dpi] now rival or even exceed print quality. While the new chips are a little more expensive (perhaps twice the cost), the investment is well worth it to millions of iPhone users as the modern phone is capable of a much greater total computation, computation per dollar, computation per watt, and computation per joule. The fact that smaller computers are more power efficient is a direct consequence of the malleability of information; bits can be shrunk in size and energy, so small bits – and thus computers – are energy efficient.

3.5   Size in Other Technologies

Does miniaturization produce large benefits in all technologies? Or are the benefits of size scaling in computing unique? To answer this question, we consider several leading "engine" technologies – automobiles (internal combustion engine), airplanes (jet engine), wind turbines (induction generator), and electric batteries (Li-ion cell). These technologies are successful and important, and thus have benefited from major investment and experienced significant technology advances over many decades. We will see that, among them, computing is unique in its connection between miniaturization and increased capability – faster, lower-energy, and greater memory capacity. In contrast, these other widely used technologies uniformly become less capable as they are scaled down. In some cases their capabilities decrease linearly in proportion to their size, and in a few cases the decrease is even more rapid. The primary reason for such scaling is the linkage of their capabilities to physical or chemical processes, where the amount of energy is intrinsically proportional to size (quantity of material).

We summarize the properties of these engine technologies in Table 3.2. We begin with automobile engines, where there has been significant improvement over the past several decades in horsepower per unit displacement (combustion volume). However, its a consistent trend that larger engines have greater power, growing in proportion to their size. Next we consider airplane engines – jet turbines. Again, we see that large engines are more capable than small ones. For wind turbines, renewable generators for the power grid, again power decreases with size, this time as inverse of the square of the rotor diameter; therefore larger wind turbines are much more productive. If we use area sweep of the blades as the size metric, then the comparison would be closer, with turbines maintaining nearly the same power per square meter; however, again the smaller are no more efficient than the larger. Finally, we consider an electrical technology – electric batteries – that are of great importance to portable computers, smartphones, and even electric cars. The technology that underlies all of these systems, lithium ion batteries, has made rapid progress, but again this technology exhibits reduced capacity with reduction in size, as documented in Table 3.2.

> Principle 3.5: Comparative Scaling for Non-computing Technologies
>
> *Other technologies have poor scaling with smaller size because they are linked with physical or chemical processes whose power decreases with size. Thus they do not share the extraordinary size scaling benefits of computers.*

Table 3.2. Non-computing technology scaling and capability.

Automobile engine	Displacement	Power	Figure of merit
2020 Kia Forte	2.0 L	147 hp	73 hp/L
2020 Honda Civic	2.0 L	158 hp	79 hp/L
2020 Ford Mustang	5.2 L	625 hp	120 hp/L
2020 Lamborghini Aventador S	6.5 L	730 hp	112 hp/L
Airplane Engine	**Rotor size**	**Power**	
Boeing 777 Engine (General Electric GE9X)	340 cm fan	105,000 pound-force (lbf)	308 lbf/cm
Learjet 70/75 Engine (Honeywell TFE731)	100 cm	4,750 pound-force (lbf)	47.5 lbf/cm
Wind turbine	**Diameter**	**Power output**	
Small turbine	40 m	0.5 megawatts	12.5 kW/m
Medium turbine	90 m	2 megawatts	22 kW/m
Largest turbine	164 m	9.5 megawatts	58 kW/m
Lithium-ion battery	**Weight**	**Energy capacity**	
2020 smartphone battery (Pixel 4 XL)	100 g	3,700 mAh	37 mAh/g
2020 smartphone battery (iPhone 11 Pro)	110 g	3,969 mAh	36 mAh/g
Electric car battery (2015 Nissan Leaf)	295,000 g	24 kWh	81 mAh/g
Electric car battery (2019 Tesla Model 3)	453,592 g	75 kWh	165 mAh/g

In summary, computing is unique in its ability to benefit dramatically from size scaling. Computing systems become both not only faster with decreased size, but also cheaper and more energy efficient. By aggressively exploiting this property, computers have become faster, smaller, and ever more capable over time.

3.6   Tiny Computers Enable an Explosion of Applications

In 1956, the Sperry UNIVAC system was not only large, but also heavy, estimated at 8 tons (16,000 lb). However, an equivalent computational power (instructions per second) can now fit in a much smaller space; a good example of this is the ARM Cortex-M0, which is only 0.008 mm^2, and consumes 5 microwatts, despite delivering 200 times the performance. You may be surprised how small an area 0.008 mm^2 is -0.09×0.9 mm – an area approximately the thickness of a piece of paper on each side. Comparing the areas occupied directly, 1,393 m^2 vs. 8×10^{-9} m^2, it is a staggering ratio of 174 billion. Finally, its weight is only a few grams. Not only is

Figure 3.16 Examples of everyday objects with computers inside.

the modern computer billions of times smaller, it is far more capable; these advantages have given rise to a wide range of applications, including those described in Chapter 1. The small size of computers is one of the keys to their ubiquity, and the power of software. Computers are in nearly every product we have in society, providing data processing and storage, as well as intelligence in many "tiny things" such as those portrayed in Figure 3.16. Intelligence and programmability in these "smart" devices are enabled by the shrinking of computers.

- **Automobile key fobs** are used to unlock, lock, and now to remotely control automobiles. These tiny computers fit into a pocket, and include computation for secure authentication, a radio, and in some cars record use and performance to inform maintenance or even auto-insurance rates. The computing and cryptography ensure that only you can open your car.
- **Secure credit cards** provide secure cryptographic identification of the card, record card information, and encrypt PINs. In short, the chip in a credit card authenticates the chipcard (and you!) securely. This fits in a flat credit-card format, and can even survive a trip through the washing machine (sometimes).
- **Television remote control** manages channels, television audio-visual settings, and recently a rich set of controls of "Smart TV" applications such as Netflix, or DisneyPlus, or YouTube TV. The controls include a flexible computer, allowing software-defined behavior of buttons.
- **Network-connected video cameras**, commonly called web cameras, include computers that capture video. The camera not only performs adaptive illumination and video capture, but advanced cameras can perform machine-learning for video analytics. These can analyze video for motion, human faces, and even detect particular faces. The computers are often used to filter and save only the most interesting video clips.
- **Electronic door locks** are often used in hotels or electronically secured buildings. They contain computers that are network-connected to a centralized computer

system, allowing convenient control of access granted to individual key cards and individual locks in a building – or even a university campus. The intelligent hotel door locks allow convenient generation of new keys that expire with your stay, solving several hotel safety problems.

- **Flying drone for video**, where onboard computing is essential to their navigation and level flight; many employ video cameras, capturing video intelligently as with surveillance cameras. The speed at which drones fly makes the small size and low weight of computing critical.

While we have described a half-dozen uses for miniaturized computers, there are literally hundreds more. In fact, many homes have 20 or more computerized devices per resident, ranging from laptops and smartphones to smart speakers, thermostats, and intelligent dishwashers. And the number continues to grow! Some current innovations include computerized eyeglasses and even toothbrushes (though no one knows how popular they will turn out to be).

The shrinking of computers by factors of billions not only makes computers fast, but also small and energy efficient. Both properties are essential for many of these new applications. There are now hundreds of computers for every human on Earth, and the number is increasing rapidly; perhaps someday there will be millions of computers for each person on Earth.

Principle 3.6: Overall Computer Scaling

Altogether, size and voltage scaling of computers has reduced their size by one-million times and the energy for computation by more than one billion times. The smaller size, increased clock speed, and reduced energy enable a performance increase of 500,000 times, and the computer is smaller than the cross-section of a few dozen human hairs. This scaling benefit is unmatched by any other technology.

3.7 Summary

Computers can be miniaturized because their function is not tied to physical scale. This follows directly from the principle that information and computation have no natural physical size. We represent information by embedding it in some physical phenomena, such as electric charge on a transistor gate; consequently, both information storage (memory) and information transformation (computers) can be shrunk dramatically. We have accomplished one-billion-fold progress in computer miniaturization over the past 75 years, delivering a dramatic reduction in size and energy that produces the astounding increase in computing capability and number of applications.

- **Small is fast.** Computer clock rates are limited by the time to propagate information across a computer. In electronic computers, this is limited by the speed of light. Therefore, the physical dimensions of a computer pose a limit on its clock rate, and thus its computation rate. The radical reduction in computer size relaxes this limit, providing a performance increase of a cube root of the computer's volume. This has yielded performance increase of more than 100,000-fold over the past 75 years.

- **Small is energy efficient.** Individual bits are typically stored as electrical charges, and as these charges are scaled in size, the energy to "switch" a bit between 0 and 1 decreases in proportion to their volume. Consequently, miniaturization has reduced energy required per bit switch (an essential part of computation) in proportion to the cube of the linear dimension of the volume, resulting in one-billion-fold energy-efficiency improvements over the past 75 years.
- **Small is small.** As computers have shrunk, they have become useful in an increasing number of application niches, enabled by their miniscule size and reduced cost. Small microprocessors are now embedded into automobiles, car keys, hotel doorknobs, credit cards, and virtually every small manufactured device produced in the economy. This makes computing and software a critical part of all of these devices.
- **Memory is a problem.** Despite miniaturization, the increasing complexity of computer applications and software creates growing demands for memory capacity. Even billion-fold increases in memory density are overwhelmed by even larger increases in application needs. This poses a significant challenge to improving computing performance in the face of ever-larger memory systems. We address the challenges and limitations of solutions to these problems in Chapter 5.

The basis of computing's unique role in society and economy is not only its extraordinary versatility, but also its exceptional performance and energy efficiency, derived largely from miniaturization. It is often said that "small is beautiful," but in computing small is fast and energy efficient, as smaller size makes computers faster, more capable, and more parsimonious with energy. This scaling with miniaturization is unique among the technologies that underpin our economy and energize computing's powerful transformative role.

3.8   Digging Deeper

The foundation of digital information systems is information theory, which establishes the notion of a bit and the notion that information has no intrinsic size. An introduction to information theory [83], and a very nice portrait of Claude Shannon and how this discovery happened, can be found in several books [34, 90].

J. Presper Eckert and John Mauchly led the design of the ENIAC system, which later led to the UNIVAC system – the first commercial computer. The story of ENIAC and its role in predicting the 1952 US presidential election is well documented [26, 104].

In a 1964 paper, Dr. Gordon Moore posited that the number of transistors on a chip might double every two years for the foreseeable future [68]. The history of Moore's

Law and its impact on the path of computing technology and the larger computing revolution in society is documented in several books [10, 94].

Robert Dennard was a dynamic-random access memory (DRAM) designer at IBM when he formulated constant electric-field scalings, now known as "Dennard scaling." This scaling provides the formula for how to scale from thousands to one billion transistors on a single chip [23]. Mark Bohr's 30-year retrospective on Dennard scaling chronicles its history and impact [7].

The design of the Cray-1 computer is a storied tale that happened on Seymour Cray's farm in Wisconsin. It was the latest of a long series of the world's leading supercomputers that he designed, but the first one that bore his name [80]. The company named after him is a leader in supercomputing to this day.

A Wire-Delay Optimized Computer: The Cray-1 (1976)

The design of the Cray-1 supercomputer illustrates the importance of short wires in achieving high performance. The Cray-1 supercomputer was launched in 1976 with the fastest clock rate of its era, and delivered the best computer performance in the world for nearly 10 years after its introduction.[3] Given the rapid pace of computer progress, such longevity in performance leadership is unprecedented and, as we'll see in Chapter 6, not likely to happen again. Seymour Cray, a renowned computer designer later known as the "Father of Supercomputing," designed the Cray-1 with the circuit boards arranged in a cylindrical shape, as shown in Figure 3.17. This shape allowed each circuit board to have an edge close to all others (the inside of the cylinder), minimizing wire delay and thus clock period. The processor logic circuits were then placed on the boards, but the connections to other boards were arranged to arrive at the edge close to the cylinder. This arrangement minimized the wire lengths, and hence wire delays, enabling the Cray-1 to achieve a clock rate of 80 Mhz (clock period of

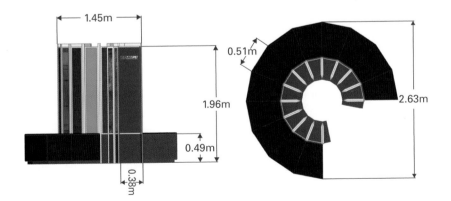

Figure 3.17 In the Cray-1 supercomputer, short wire lengths were critical to performance, engendering a cylindrical structure (gray sections) in which each circuit board had one edge close to all others.

---

[3] Highest performance based on measurements on scientific computing applications.

12.5 nanoseconds), despite a machine diameter of nearly 5 feet (1.45 m). This Cray-1 clock rate is close to the speed-of-light limit from Figure 3.8, based on the computer's physical size. By comparison, an IBM mainframe of the same vintage had a clock rate of 8 Mhz (10 times slower).

The Cray-1 example illustrates how the *physical size and clock period* model captures the limits of a fast supercomputer.

3.9   Problems

3.1   Consider a few examples of hoses and buckets that might be considered to improve a computer switching technology. Starting from our baseline of a hose/drain capable of 40 liters per minute, and a bucket size of 4 liters, consider several different scenarios for an "improved" technology, and their impact on the speed that bits can be switched on and off.
(a)   Consider smaller, 1-liter buckets. How fast can bits be switched?
(b)   Consider smaller hoses, 10 liters/minute. How fast can bits be switched?
(c)   Consider 1-liter buckets and 10 liters/minute hoses. How fast can bits be switched?
(d)   Consider 1-liter buckets and 80 liters/minute hoses. How fast can bits be switched?

3.2   Given the analysis from Problem 3.1, what is the best combination for speeding the switching of bits? Explain why.

3.3   Let's take our example of a hose and buckets to an extreme. Suppose we take the metric example of a hose/drain (40 liters/minute), and shrink the bucket.
(a)   How fast can we switch between "1" and "0" (called toggle) a bucket of 1 liter? 100 milliliters? 10 milliliters?
(b)   How about if we increased the hose's pumping rate; how fast can we toggle a 4-liter bucket if the hose is 80 liters/minute? 160 liters/minute?

3.4   Consider using the 4-liter volume of water that was used in a bucket to communicate a bit across a schoolyard. We want to transmit the signal as a rise in the water level across a distance of 50 meters.
(a)   How much water is available per meter to communicate the information?
(b)   If we use a trough that is 1 cm wide, how tall would it be? (This is the water level rise that would be read as a "1" at the other end.)
(c)   Now, using the hose/drain rate of 40 liters/minute, how fast can this trough be used to communicate a toggle "1 to 0 to 1" across the schoolyard?

3.5   Using your answer from Problem 3.3, and your common sense, how much faster can this switching be done by increasing the pumping power of the hose? What is going to limit the performance?

3.6 Relays are mechanical switches that change the physical position of an "armature" to change the electrical connections between the terminals of the relay. An armature has a mass. Here we will use a simplification of classical physics to explore the benefits of size scaling. Assume the armature has a mass of m grams, and to switch from open to closed, it must move d millimeters. We will assume there is no friction, and the armature is accelerated at a constant rate, a, until it is halfway across and then decelerated at that same constant rate, stopping just at it reaches the other contact.

(a) If $m = 1$ g, $a = 1$ cm/s^2, and $d = 5$ mm, how long does it take the relay to switch from open to closed?

(b) How much faster would the relay be if d were reduced to 2.5 mm?

(c) How much work is done accelerating the armature until it is halfway across the gap? (Work = force × distance)

(d) How much would this work be reduced if m, the mass of the armature, were reduced to 0.1 g?

(e) Reducing the gap and armature mass are two examples of benefits one might get from scaling. Suppose that we reduce the size of our original relay to one-tenth the size. How much might you expect m and d to reduce?

(f) How much might those size reduction benefits improve the switching speed of the relay? And how much might they reduce the work required to switch?

3.7 The model of a hose and bucket is a pretty good analogy for how dynamic random-access memory (DRAM) works. As we will see in Chapter 5, DRAM has been the main type of computer memory used since 1975 (approaching 50 years). However, real DRAM has several complications – it leaks and the filling and reading of buckets is noisy. Consider a DRAM cell with a capacitance of 1 picofarad (10^{-12}), and a charge pump that can pump 100 microcoulombs/second (0.1 milli-amp), allowing the cell to be charged in 10 nanoseconds (10×10^{-9}) to 1 volt.

(a) The DRAM cells are called "dynamic" because they leak charge, so a "1" will eventually lose enough charge to be considered a "0." If the cells leak at a rate of 0.01 microcoulombs/second, how long will it take a full cell to leak all of its charge?

(b) In practice, DRAM values have to be refreshed (rewritten to ensure they are not lost) frequently. They must be rewritten long before their values have decayed to 0. Suppose we can allow the cells to lose 25 percent of their charge; how long can a DRAM cell hold the value before it needs to be refreshed?

(c) As DRAM cells are scaled to smaller size (producing higher bit density per chip), balancing these properties is a challenge. If cells are reduced in size by 50 percent and their capacitance decreases by the same factor, but leak charge at the same rate, what is the problem that arises?

(d) Given the problem you've just outlined, what new capabilities do DRAM technologists need to enable DRAM scaling to higher density? Describe the requirements for the higher-density technology.

3.8 As we saw in Section 3.5, size scaling does not create major benefits for the other engines. Consider the internal combustion engine, and analyze it in some detail. Are there fundamental physical challenges to scaling small? If the productivity problem could be solved, is there a way to address the heat density?

3.9   Complete Problem 8 for the case of wind turbines.

3.10   Complete Problem 8 for lithium ion batteries used in electric cars.

3.11   Complete Problem 8 for a technology of your choice. Be sure that it has a long history (at least 30 years), and that you have clear performance metrics.

3.12   Think about scaling. Some technologies might increase in capability as they are scaled smaller, but their dominant use remains about the same size. This can have to do with human (or industry) uses of the technology.
(a)   For example, laptop computers have remained about the same physical size for the past 15 years, but the available memory and recently SSD storage have continued to grow in capacity. Why haven't laptop computers shrunk in size?
(b)   Many people are surprised that smartphones have generally not decreased in physical size over the past 15 years, and in fact over the past 5 years have perhaps grown larger. Give one or two reasons for these trends, despite improving technology for computing, radios, storage, and even displays. Explain.
(c)   What is another technology whose miniaturization would allow smaller and smaller devices? Give a specific example of a technology, and several examples of products that use it. What is the trend in size of those products? Explain.

3.13   In Section 3.3.4, we explored Dennard scaling that gave rise to both computer speed and energy efficiency.
(a)   Read the Dennard paper [23], and provide a detailed description and analysis of how the scaling worked.
(b)   What are the assumptions on which it depends, and how can it be applied to the design of the logic for processor chips, not dynamic RAM.
(c)   Dennard scaling ended because the reduction in supply voltage became more difficult due to increasing transistor leakage. Assuming this happened around 2005, how many voltage-reduction steps (a Dennard scaling step) were achieved?

3.14   The end of Dennard scaling is widely dated to around 2005. Since that time, we have had to settle for limited versions of the scaling, with smaller increases in speed and reductions in power. Despite that, there have been significant increases in performance (and increases in performance per power). Pick a line of processors such as the Qualcomm Snapdragon, Intel Core, or the Apple Ax (A9, A10, A11, A12, A13, A14). Find the processor data sheets or internet information that describes the performance these processors from 2010 to 2020.
(a)   How have performance and power of these processors scaled over time?
(b)   Estimate how performance and power would have changed if Dennard scaling had continued, and compare. How much have we lost with the end of Dennard scaling?

(c) How much will we lose in the next decade if these trends continue at the same rate?

3.15 We asserted that information has no natural size, enabling the extremely productive scaling of computer systems. Using your background in chemistry or physics, analyze and discuss what fundamental physical limits might exist for the minimum size of information "bits."

3.16 In Section 3.3.1, we showed that our size–speed scaling model can be used to estimate the clock rate of a Cortex-M3 across 75 years of computer evolution. Calculate the error in our model based on those results in predicting the speed scaling factor. (Hint: it's a very small number.)

3.17 The size–speed scaling principle (Figure 3.9) uses a three-dimensional cube to estimate how the volume of a computer affects the length of the maximum distance that a signal must travel in a single clock period. However, in Section 3.8, we saw that a highly optimized design, the Cray-1 computer, packed its circuits into a cylinder, and furthermore tuned the circuit designs on each board so that the critical connections were at the edge of the circuit boards (and thus along the cylinder surface). In this problem, we will explore how much faster such a design could be compared to our basic scaling model.

(a) Let's assume the circuits for the computer have total volume V, and are packed into a cube for our size–speed model. Compute l, the characteristic length.

(b) For the cylindrical design, assume the volume of the circuits must fit into a cylinder that has a height, h, and an inner diameter $h - 0.3$ meters, and outer diameter $h + 0.3$ meters. Write the value of h as a function of V.

(c) The design of the Cray-1 has the complex claim that they optimized the circuit paths to arrive at the inner edge of the cylinder. We'll give them partial credit for that, and assume the longest path must go from the top to the bottom of the cylinder, and across the an intermediate diameter of h (which is the distance between two circuit boards opposite each other). Again, compute l, the characteristic length.

(d) Finally, we can compare the speeds of these computers. Assuming the computers have the same total circuit volume, V, how much faster clock rate is possible with the Cray-1 design? Does the advantage of the cylindrical design increase with computer size? (Look at the real sizes in Figure 3.17.)

3.18 Just for fun (and to emphasize how exceptional the improvement of computers has been), consider what would have happened if the same level of size scaling and resulting benefit worked for internal combustion engines. Consider the 1959 Chevy Corvette (Figure 3.18), which had a 290-horsepower engine with a displacement of 283 cubic inches (4.64 liters) and achieved a 0–60 mph time of 6.9 seconds.

(a) Suppose we decide to build a smaller engine (1/1,000 in volume or 10 times smaller in each dimension) suitable for a bicycle or small scooter, what power could it produce? How fast could it accelerate the scooter from 0 to 60 mph? (Assume the power of the engine scales down with displacement.)

Figure 3.18 1959 Chevy Corvette, the sportscar of its day.

(b)   Estimate the fuel efficiency of the resulting scaled Corvette. Assume the amount of fuel burned decreases with the displacement, and the fuel efficiency of the 1959 Corvette is 15 miles/gallon. How does it compare to today's internal combustion engine cars?

3.19   Consider what would have happened if the same level of size scaling and resulting benefit worked for lithium ion batteries. Suppose we decide to build a smaller battery (1/1,000 in volume or 10 times smaller in each dimension), taking as an example a Tesla Model 3 battery down from 1 m^3 size to make it small enough for a bicycle or small scooter. What battery capacity would it have? How long do you think it would run the original car (in miles), and how long do you think it would power a smaller vehicle such as a scooter?

3.20   Macrobiology studies animals that vary in scale dramatically from tiny insects to the largest mammals – elephants and blue whales. Take two characteristics similar to those we studied that relate speed and scale, and fill a few intermediate animal sizes in.

(a)   How does the heart rate of animals scale with size? What is the reason for this? What implications does it have for the creatures?

(b)   How does the speed of movement of animals scale with size? Note that speed of movement might not correlate directly with "speed of travel." What is the reason for this? What implications does it have for the creatures?

(c)   How does the life span of animals scale with size? Life span is certainly one form of performance metric. What is the reason for this? What implications does it have for the creatures?

(d)   Identify another attribute of animals and answer the same questions.

(e)   Compare and contrast computer scaling with these animal scaling properties. Be specific.

3.21   Make up your own scaling analogy (pick a high-value, important function in society), develop a scaling study, and show what capabilities a smaller system 1/1,000th of its original size could produce.

Credits

4 Sequential Abstraction, But Parallel Implementation

A computer instruction set defines the correct execution of a program as the instructions processed one after another – that is, sequentially (see Chapter 2). This sequential abstraction enables composition of arithmetic operations (add, xor), operations on memory (state), and also grants extraordinary power to branch instructions that compose blocks of instructions conditionally. In this chapter, we explore the central importance of the sequential abstraction for managing the complexity of large-scale software and hardware systems. Subsequently, we consider creative techniques that both preserve the illusion of sequence and allow the processor implementation to increase the speed of program progress. These techniques are known as **instruction-level parallelism (ILP)**, and accelerate program execution by executing instructions in a program in pipelined (overlapped), out-of-order, and even speculative fashion. Understanding ILP provides a perspective on how commercial processors really execute programs – far different from the step-by-step recipe of the sequential abstraction.

4.1 Sequential Computation Abstraction

One of the most fundamental concepts in programming is the notion of sequence, the idea that in a computer, conceptually only one instruction happens at a time. This instruction set architecture (ISA) defines the state of the program precisely before and after each instruction. Thus, the overall memory and variables in a program collectively pass through a sequence of steps. The sequential abstraction provides the basis for reasoning about the state of the program and its evolution over time and is used for software design and debugging.

4.1.1 Sequential Programs

Consider the bubble sort algorithm, taught in many introductory programming courses (illustrated in Figure 4.1). It involves a sequence of passes through an array, each comparing and swapping adjacent array elements. Specifically, each iteration of inner loop is a sequence of comparisons and conditional swaps, and the loop sweeps over the array.

```
for  (i=0; i<N; i++){
    for  (j=0; j<N-i; j++){
        if  (A[j] > A[j+1]) {
            tmp = A[j];
            A[j] = A[j+1];
            A[j+1] = tmp;};
    };
};
```

Figure 4.1 A bubble sort program consists of two nested loops that gradually create the sorted array.

	Initial	After i=0	After i=1	After i=3	After i=4
A[4]	0	15	15	15	15
A[3]	3	0	10	10	10
A[2]	15	3	0	7	7
A[1]	7	10	3	0	3
A[0]	10	7	7	3	0

Figure 4.2 Progression of sorted sections at the top, after each iteration of the i loop (for a five-element array).

The bubble sort algorithm uses a two-level structured sequence of steps to "bubble" the largest element to the top of the array, then the second largest, and so on, such that the outer loop on i, creates a larger sorted section at the top of the array after each iteration.

This process is illustrated for a five-element array ($N = 5$) in Figure 4.2. After the first iteration of the i loop, the largest value is guaranteed to be in A[$N - 1$], and the size of the sorted section increases with each successive iteration of the i loop. The notion of a sequence of larger and larger sorted sections can be used to reason about the correctness of the bubble sort program. For example, in an inductive proof you can use this sequence to prove that bubble sort does in fact produce a sorted array – that it is a correct sorting program.

The notion of state sequence is fundamental to reasoning about correct execution for software. It is the foundation for explaining algorithms, debugging programs, and even reasoning about correctness. For example, Dijkstra's framework of reasoning about program correctness based on weakest postconditions [24] can be applied to the sorting algorithm to prove it sorts the array correctly. The postconditions for each iteration of the inner and outer loops for the bubble sort program are illustrated in Figure 4.3. Nearly every programmer has used a debugger to examine program state as it proceeds from statement to statement, or perhaps instruction to instruction, during execution. This state sequence is important conceptually to help a programmer understand how to make a program work. It also defines the fundamental semantics (definition of correct behavior) of the computer program. Likewise, computer

```
for  (i=0;i<N;i++){
   for  (j=0;j<N-i ;j++){
      if  (A[j] > A[j+1]) {
         tmp = A[j];
         A[j] = A[j+1];
         A[j+1] = tmp;};    // {Post #1:} A[j]<A[j+1]
      };  // {Post #2:} A[N-i-1]::A[N-1] is sorted.
   };
```

Figure 4.3 Postconditions define properties of the machine state after each iteration of the loop. A sequence of postconditions is used to ensure program correctness.

architects use this notion of the semantics of sequence of states to define the correct behavior for a computer (machine).

Sequential state reasoning can be applied hierarchically. From the perspective of the outer loop, each execution of the inner loop is a collection of state changes with a net result. Some of these state changes are transient; others are visible after the inner loop completes. For example, as a high-value element "bubbles" to the top, as in the $i = 0$ iteration, its assignment to intermediate locations in the array is only transient. Likewise, this happens to the value 10 in the $i = 1$ iteration in our five-element bubble sort example. More generally, from the perspective of the outer loop (or any "outer program"), each activation of the inner loop (a set of $N - i$ iterations) produces changes to the array A, depicted as a step in Figure 4.2.

The sequential state evolution model applies at multiple levels, including in C programs, assembly code, and even machine instruction execution. As we covered in instruction execution (Chapter 2), each instruction changes the machine state as shown in Figure 4.4. This is analogous to each statement in our bubble sort program. Just as we did with the C program, from the outer, surrounding program we can view the set of machine state changes as a composite or summary set of changes. Directly, this enables sequential and hierarchical composition of state changes.

The composition view provides an opening to increase processor performance while maintaining the sequential abstraction. Computer architects developed the idea of executing a group of instructions in parallel, in order to reduce the execution time of a loop iteration (sometimes called a basic block). The approach employs hidden parallelism in the execution of instructions and is called **instruction-level parallelism**, and was previously highlighted as a major approach to speed up computers in Chapter 2. In the next section, we explore the ideas for how computers can identify instructions that are safe for parallel execution.

Principle 4.1: Sequential Abstraction

The sequential abstraction is a powerful tool for composition, modularity, and reasoning about execution and correctness in computing. Therefore, it is important and valuable to preserve sequential abstraction for software.

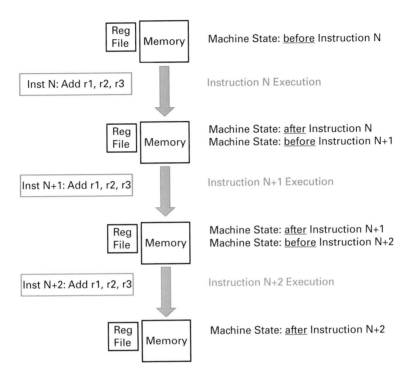

Figure 4.4 Each instruction modifies the machine state in sequence.

4.1.2 Instruction-Level Parallelism: Pipelining and More

To define sequential execution for a computer program's instructions, consider the simple program in Figure 4.4. The machine state – registers and memory – is well defined before and after each instruction. Very little of the state is changed by each instruction. For the instruction sets discussed in Chapter 2, each instruction modifies only a single register or memory value. The rest of the machine state remains the same.

As Moore's Law provided a growing bounty of transistors, the number available on a single chip first matched, then exceeded, that required for a full 32-bit computer. By the late 1980s the available transistors exceeded that needed for a 64-bit computer, first by 10-fold and later by 1,000-fold. Naturally, computer architects sought to apply the bounty of low-cost transistors to speed up the execution of traditional sequential programs. They created a set of techniques that identify (or create!) parallelism across instruction execution, thereby translating the growing number of transistors into improved performance for sequential programs. As a result, the number of transistors used in a core (sequential computing engine) grew from 200,000 in 1989 to 100 million in 2006 (a 500-fold increase). The instruction-level parallelism techniques that use many transistors to increase performance are as follows Figure 4.5):

- **Pipelining:** The overlap of six steps of instruction execution for successive instructions (e.g. instruction fetch, decode, read registers, execute, access memory, and write results).

Figure 4.5 Three types of instruction-level parallelism: pipelining, multiple issue, and out-of-order. Time progresses from left to right, so each instruction starts at the left and finishes at the right. The three approaches create different structures of parallelism (overlap). The fourth, speculative execution, is depicted in Figure 4.16.

- **Multiple issue:** Executing sets of successive instructions simultaneously, following the determination that doing so does not change program results. Typically this means they do not share any registers or memory locations, and thus do not need to be ordered.
- **Out-of-order execution:** Dynamically tracking the values being created and used, then forwarding them appropriately to ensure that each instruction gets the values that correspond to the sequential program order. This is the most relaxed framing of instruction execution, and generalizes the parallelism exploited by pipelining and multiple issue.
- **Speculative execution:** Speculating on the path that program execution will take beyond each conditional branch and executing the instructions on that path based on that speculative choice. These instructions are not needed if the speculation is wrong, in which case the machine must erase the effects of the speculative execution.

All four techniques increase the performance of sequential programs, and are used in essentially all computers from small to large. Collectively, these four techniques are known as "instruction-level parallelism." These techniques increase the computer's throughput for a given program by finding a way to execute the instructions with more parallelism than the strict sequence specified by the program. In this chapter we explore how these ideas in instruction-level parallelism safely accomplish overlapped execution of instructions while preserving the illusion of sequence. These ILP techniques account for a large, 100-fold performance increase, trading vast numbers of transistors for higher performance.

> Principle 4.2: Instruction-level Parallelism (ILP) Cheats the Sequential Abstraction
>
> *At the instruction level, sequential abstraction is a key property of the ISA. Despite that, nearly all programs can have instructions executed in parallel, invisible to the programmer. Exploiting this ILP is an essential factor in making processors fast.*

4.1.3   Data Dependence and the Illusion of Sequence

If we think of a program as a collection of changes to the state of memory, then a program's computation is the sequence of instructions that performs those changes on

```
for  ( i = 0; i < N;  i ++ ){
    sum  += A[ i ]  * B[ i ];
};
```

Figure 4.6 Dot product source program.

```
Loop:    . . .
         addi  x2,  x3,  #8
         lw  x3,  Aaddress[x2]
         lw  x4,  Baddress[x2]
         mulw  x5,  x4,  x3
         addw  x6,  x6,  x5
         . . .
         bne  x1,  Loop:
```

Figure 4.7 Dot product loop body assembly program.

the memory. The length of this sequence, the number of instructions, is the program **work**. And if they are executed one at a time, sequentially, then this count would be directly related to time required to execute the program. However, we know that many pairs of instructions do not need to be ordered this strictly to maintain the sequential abstraction because they compute (use values, produce values) for unrelated parts of the machine state. That is, they read and write disjoint sets of registers or memory locations. For example, consider the dot product program in Figure 4.6. For each i groups of instructions (read from $A[i]$, $B[i]$ arrays and multiply them) the sequential order can be relaxed and still produce the correct result. Instruction-level parallelism takes advantage of these "partial orders," enforcing only those necessary to ensure the correct sequential results.

When we translate a C program to assembly code, each C line or expression typically turns into multiple instructions, as shown in Figure 4.7. Among these instructions, **dependences** arise from the creation and use of values in the program. We will focus on the dependences called **flow dependences**, **data dependences**, or **true dependences**. These dependences, simply put, are the ordering required to maintain the illusion of sequence, the correct execution of the source program (sequential programming language) and the machine program (sequential instruction execution).

Consider the dot product program from Figure 4.7, redrawn in Figure 4.8 where the instructions are shown as blocks and the dependences are indicated as arrows between them. This partial ordering shows that several load, addi, and mul instructions can be executed in parallel while maintaining the sequential illusion. Further, due to using multiple instructions per C expression, we see that the assembly program in fact has multiple instructions that can be executed in parallel, even within one iteration, and even more across iterations. Specifically, index increments, memory operations, and multiplies all contribute to the potential ILP. In short, at the assembly code level, there are more units of work, allowing for an amount of instruction parallelism higher than might appear possible at the source level program.

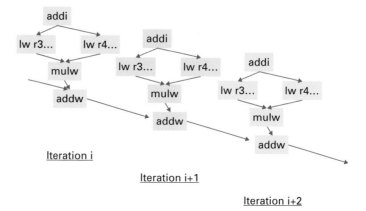

Figure 4.8 The assembly code for the dot product has parallelism both within each iteration and across iterations. Arrows represent dependences.

```
A[][]; B[][]; Result[][];
for (i=0;i<N;i++){
   for (j=0;j<N;j++){
      sum = 0;
      for (k=0;k<N;k++){                    // dot product begins here
         sum = sum + A[j][k] * B[k][j];
         };                                 // dot product ends here
      Result[i][j] = sum;
      };
};
```

Figure 4.9 A matrix–matrix product program, consisting of N^2 overlapped dot product computations, gives an even higher level of parallelism.

In general, when analyzing the dependences as in Figure 4.8, the longest chain of dependences determines the **critical path** for program execution, and the resulting breadth of the graph is the effective instruction parallelism of the program. The wider the graph, the more parallelism is available, and the essential idea of instruction-level parallelism is to exploit this breadth (parallelism) to increase the rate of instruction execution, that is, computer performance. Today's computers extract a great deal of ILP from nearly every software program.

How much ILP is there? There can be a large amount. For example, consider a matrix–matrix multiply computation. One program for matrix–matrix multiply is simply a loop wrapped around our dot product example (Figure 4.9). This multiply nested loop structure contains a high degree of ILP. As illustrated for an 8×8 matrix–matrix multiply in Figure 4.10, this parallelism peaks at over 35 instructions. As the outer loop executes, an out-of-order processor will unroll and expose parallelism across the dot products. Within each of the eight dot products, the processor also exposes ILP. In a real implementation, parallelism that can be exploited varies based

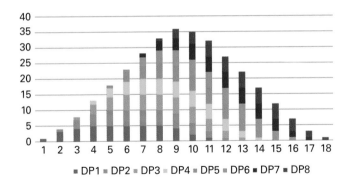

Figure 4.10 The overlapped execution of matrix–matrix product (8 × 8 matrix) gives ample opportunities for parallelism.

on the speed that the "spine" of the critical path can be unrolled. Note that the results from the multiplications can be reorganized in software as a reduction tree, providing an additional source of ILP. There is potential for a lot of ILP in programs.

However, exploiting ILP in a processor has multiple challenges. First, the computer must detect opportunities to execute instructions in parallel at runtime based on dependences between creation and use of values. These dependences evolve dynamically as the program is executed based on control flow (branches and procedure calls) as well as memory addresses. Second, the program execution must correctly enforce and preserve the illusion of sequential execution, particularly for debuggers or for operations to memory. And third, in order to maximize the parallelism that can be exploited for higher performance, the machine must "guess" which conditional paths will be executed, and recover when these guesses are incorrect. We will discuss how all these challenges are solved in modern computer processors.

4.2 The Illusion of Sequence: Renaming and Out-of-Order Execution

Out-of-order execution generalizes both pipelining and multiple-issue execution. To provide a simple picture, we consider ILP in a high-level abstract form, exploring when the execution order of instructions can vary from source order to enable higher performance.[1] How can we maintain the sequential abstraction correctly? While programs conceptually pass through a sequence of states, many of these states are not important to the correct functioning of a program. Consider the previous example of a dot product program, but now for the specific vector size of eight elements.

We show an unrolled dot product code for a vector of length eight in Figure 4.11, and then another version optimized for parallelism. The rewritten code computes the same function, but reorders the memory loads and multiplies. As a result, the first eight

---

[1] In commercial processors, implementation of ILP is remarkably complex. Since our goal is not training of computer engineers, but rather sophisticated computer users, we do not delve into those complexities. But if you are interested, see *Digging Deeper* at the end of the chapter.

```
sum += A[0] * B[0];
sum += A[1] * B[1];
sum += A[2] * B[2];
sum += A[3] * B[3];
sum += A[4] * B[4];
sum += A[5] * B[5];
sum += A[6] * B[6];
sum += A[7] * B[7];
result = sum;
```

(a) Simple version, unrolled.

```
sum0 = A[0] * B[0];    // multiply the elements
sum1 = A[1] * B[1];
sum2 = A[2] * B[2];
sum3 = A[3] * B[3];
sum4 = A[4] * B[4];
sum5 = A[5] * B[5];
sum6 = A[6] * B[6];
sum7 = A[7] * B[7];
sum0 = sum0 + sum1;    // 1st level partial sums
sum2 = sum2 + sum3;    //      others reorganized
sum4 = sum4 + sum5;    //      for parallelism
sum6 = sum6 + sum7;
sum2 = sum0 + sum2;    // 2nd level sums
sum4 = sum4 + sum6;
result = sum2 + sum4;
```

(b) Optimized for parallelism and faster execution.

Figure 4.11 Two versions of the dot product program for vectors of length eight.

statements can all be executed in parallel (comprising 24 instructions). This rewrite highlights the idea that the computation does not require the sequential execution of iterations, and is what an out-of-order processor achieves dynamically with ILP. At the end of the program, a parallel reduction using partial sums produces the correct final machine state (the result). This version of the program could be substituted, producing higher performance, yet maintaining the correct behavior of the dot product computation and its sequential composition with the surrounding program.

The data dependences for the code in Figure 4.11b are shown in Figure 4.12. The figure shows that the 16 load instructions require no specific order, and likewise all 8 multiplies require no specific order. These unordered operations can be executed in parallel while maintaining the sequential abstraction for the program. The reduction across product terms can be reorganized into a reduction tree, allowing a smaller amount of parallelism to be exploited.[2] These levels of parallelism are for vectors of length eight; longer vectors would produce commensurately higher ILP. In fact, for a

---

[2] This type of reorganization is common on high-quality optimizing compilers and popular parallel programming interfaces such as OpenMP [111].

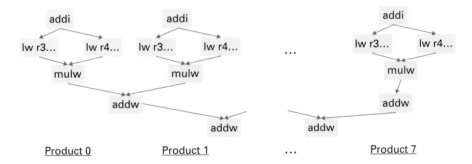

Figure 4.12 Graph of data dependences for each of the multiplies and the reduction for dot product (A[0:7],B[0:7]).

dot product of size N, the instruction parallelism could reach $2N$. For a matrix–matrix product of two $N \times N$ matrices, as shown in Figure 4.9 and 4.10, it could reach N^2.

4.2.1 Variable and Register Renaming

The dot product example showed how an application program can be rewritten with new variable names, then reorganized to increase parallelism. The original program reused program variables, and that reuse could be eliminated by introducing new variables names. Doing so increased the freedom of execution order – that is, the parallelism. Directly, **variable renaming maintained the original program's sequential semantics** while increasing the program parallelism. This variable renaming can be generalized and is similar to what happens at every procedure call in which each call gets its own set of variable names. Renaming combined with reprogramming can significantly increase the amount of program parallelism available. However, such reprogramming is an additional effort, and can be error-prone.

To avoid this programmer effort, yet still reap the benefits of ILP, computer architects have developed computer hardware techniques that can **discover parallelism while the program is running**. For example, a modern processor can automatically identify the freedom to execute multiple load, multiply, and reduce instructions from the dot product program in parallel. Once identified, the parallelism could be exploited by pipelining, multiple-issue, and out-of-order execution microarchitecture techniques.

But how to rename variables systematically to increase program parallelism? There is a simple way to understand this conceptually. The key is to shift to thinking about the evolution of the variables' values in a two-dimensional space–time structure. In space–time, illustrated in Figure 4.13, a sequential program execution happens left to right. Each variable is a row, and each column is an instant in time, capturing the program state. Each step to the right is a program statement. For correct sequential program behavior, to execute each statement, we look to the left (to the most recent update) to read the value for each variable. The example in Figure 4.13 illustrates this for the beginning of a matrix–matrix multiply program. Each operation computes its

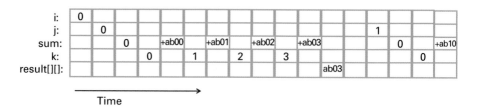

Figure 4.13 Space–time structure for selected variables in the beginning of the matrix–matrix multiply from Figure 4.9.

result and updates (writes or defines) a variable at its time of execution. We denote this by adding an entry for that variable in the current column. That value may be used by future operations (to the right). At any point in the execution space–time, each variable has a well-defined value. In Figure 4.13, we can see that i, j, sum, and k are initialized to 0, and then as the products are accumulated, the value of sum is updated repeatedly. Eventually, the dot product value is written into the result array, and the program goes on to the next dot product.

To maximize the opportunity for parallelism, **variable renaming** creates a unique name for each segment of the row for each variable. In our space–time figure, it is easy to see that each segment between definitions (updates) of a variable corresponds to a distinct value for it. That is, in Figure 4.13, each update (new value) and all of the blank spaces in the row to its right until the next update defines a segment. Assigning a unique name to each new value for the variable (each update or segment) ensures that variable value will not be confused with any others.[3] Next, renaming re-expresses the program relative to this larger set of variable names. This is done by replacing each use of the original variable with thew name of the variable's segment that is currently active (new variable name) when the operation happens (column). These two steps remove many unnecessary ordering constraints in the program such as those involving variable reuse, and thereby increase ILP. Below we define renaming for registers precisely, and prove the transformation is correct (preserves program function).

Considering renaming at the assembly (or machine) instruction level, we can apply the same technique used for variables to register names. Renaming registers in a program is an algorithmic approach that ensures execution that faithfully implements the sequential state abstraction of the instruction set. Modern computers implement **register renaming** to dynamically generate the dependence graph shown in Figure 4.12 from the machine code program in Figure 4.11. The register renaming algorithm eliminates dependences from the reuse of an ISA register for different program values. Each reuse of an ISA register constrains ILP in the machine program – we cannot put a new value there until all of the readers of that value have completed their reads. So, modern processors all use register renaming to map the ISA registers used in a program to a succession of physical registers in the microarchitecture. This is the same

---

[3] If you have used MacOS's Time Machine feature, the idea is similar; each version of the file gets a unique icon in the stack.

space–time idea illustrated in Figure 4.13. To implement renaming the processor needs two new capabilities: (1) the ability to create new register names; and (2) the ability to point pending register reads at one of these new register names. These two functions are used in Algorithm 4.1.

Algorithm 4.1 Register Renaming Algorithm

```
//
// Each instruction of form INST( operation , outreg , inreg1 , inreg2 )
//
rename  ( INST ){
      tmp1 = R[ last_name ( INST . inreg1 )]
      tmp2 = R[ last_name ( INST . inreg2 )]
      new_target = new_name ( Rdest )
      R[ new_target ] = execute ( operation , tmp1 , tmp2 )

Where
      new_name ( x ) generates a new **register** name **for** x , records in map
      last_name ( y ) returns the last new_name generated **for** y
```

Conceptually renaming assigns the results of instructions unique names from "space–time" of the computation, carefully ensuring that the correct names are used by subsequent instructions to find the right value. This correspondence ensures the correct implementation of the program's sequential abstraction. As shown in Figure 4.13, we can use the tuple of space (source register name), time (instruction cycle count) to uniquely define the program value. Thus, using this pair of space–time factors to identify the right value is sufficient to ensure the illusion of sequential execution.

Consider a program example. The register renaming algorithm transforms an assembly program as it is executed, as shown in Figure 4.14, assigning a new name for the result of each instruction. Next, as it continues scanning the program sequentially, it substitutes the new names for the corresponding uses of these computation values. Recall that each value has a unique name and corresponds directly to the set of data

```
// Base code ( ISA Regs )          // Renamed code , rename registers are Tn
ld    x2 , A[ x3 ]                 ld    T1 , A[X3]
ld    x3 , B[ x4 ]                 ld    T2 , B[X4]
add  x2 , x2 , x3                  add   T3 , T1 , T2
addi x3 , x3 , 100                 addi  T4 , T2 , 100
add  x2 , x3 , x3                  add   T5 , T4 , T3
ld    x7 , C[ x5 ]                 ld    T6 , C[X5]        // start parallel
ld    x4 , D[ x6 ]                 ld    T7 , D[X6]
add  x3 , x7 , x4                  add   T8 , T6 , T7
add  x2 , x2 , x3                  add   T9 , T5 , T8
slli x2 , x2 , −8                  slli  T10 , T9 , −8
```

Figure 4.14 Register renaming algorithm applied to a simple code sequence (no particular program).

dependences that are required for that value in the program. In the original program, only a few instructions can be executed in parallel. But after register renaming, the program is separated into two large groups of instructions (from load through the third add, and from the third load to the second to last add). Renaming increases ILP by allowing the two groups of instructions to be executed in parallel (and each also has internal parallelism).

THEOREM 4.1 (Correctness Proof for Register Renaming)   *The register renamed program computes the same results as the original program.*

Proof by contradiction.

We label each instruction execution with the program cycle it executes, uniquely identifying it in the original sequential execution, and compare its results to the corresponding instruction execution in the renamed program.

   Define operation OpB = <instruction, program cycle> that computes a result X in the original program. OpB' is the corresponding operation in the renamed program.

   If the renamed program does not compute the same results as the original program:

1. *There must be at least one OpB' that computes X' != X. Because the computer executes instructions correctly, OpB' must receive different input values than OpB.*
2. *Consider Input1(OpB), Input2(OpB), Input1(OpB'), and Input2(OpB'). Our renaming algorithm picked the names for Input1(OptB') and Input2(OptB') to match the current values of the corresponding registers in the original sequential program (by picking the name of the value last written to that register, last-name(Input(OptB))).*
3. *So, we must have Input1(OptB') == Input1(OptB) and Input2(OptB') == Input2(OptB).*

   This is a contradiction. Therefore, the register renamed program computes the same results as the original program.

Principle 4.3: Renaming Safely Encodes Sequential Structure, Enabling ILP

Renaming enforces the sequential abstraction of a program and creates parallelism by giving values "space–time" names. Renaming can be applied by a compiler or by processor hardware, enabling instructions to execute in parallel to increase performance.

4.2.2   Implementing Register Renaming: The Reorder Buffer

Register renaming is implemented in all modern processors. To make this possible and to maximize benefits, its implementation must be fast. Fortunately, it turns out this is possible! In renaming, each value is given a unique name and place to store a value, then subsequent uses of the value are redirected to this unique name. The key hardware innovation that makes this possible is the reorder buffer (ROB) (Figure 4.15).

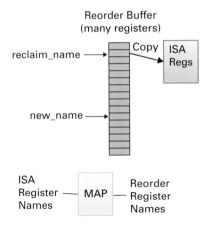

Figure 4.15 Register renaming uses a MAP and a set of physical registers called a reorder buffer (ROB). The state for instructions in flight is held by the ROB to preserve the sequential abstraction. Values that persist are eventually copied from the ROB to the ISA registers.

The ROB supports these two functions: (1) allocating new unique register names; and (2) keeping a map of the current "renaming" for each of the ISA registers.

The ROB provides new names from a large set of **physical** registers that are not visible to software as they are not part of the ISA. The key is the function new_name(), which is used in the renaming algorithm to create unique names for values in the program execution. The ROB allocates new names by incrementing the new_name pointer, as shown in Figure 4.15, supplying an unused register (and its name). The renaming is then added to the MAP to keep track of the information needed for the last_name() functions. While the physical registers can be reused by making the new_name pointer wrap around, the number of physical registers limits the maximum number of unique names that can be active simultaneously. Thus, to increase the effectiveness of register renaming, modern processors provide a large set of physical registers in the microarchitecture – as many as 256, over 16 times the number of registers available to software in ISA! This is possible thanks to the plentiful transistors provided by Moore's Law.

The out-of-order execution enabled by register renaming provides a 1.5–2.5 times increase in the instruction throughput for a processor. And the idea of a ROB is key for even more aggressive ILP, so we will revisit it when discussing speculative execution in Section 4.3.

4.2.3 Limits of Out-of-Order Execution

Register renaming and out-of-order execution can increase the quantity of ILP significantly. However, they have two key limitations. First, conditional branches create boundaries that can limit the instructions subject to parallel execution. Beyond the conditional branch we do not know what code will be executed, blocking further instructions from consideration for parallel execution. In effect, a conditional branch becomes a dependence for all instructions that follow in the sequential execution, commonly called a "control dependence." The examples we studied included many instructions between conditional branch instructions, but typical programs average 10 machine instructions between conditional branches. Thus, if the critical path between branches is two or three instructions, then out-of-order parallelism is limited to 10/2.5 or approximately four. Second, load and store instructions access memory, causing a difficult problem. Without executing the address computation of the memory access instruction, it is difficult to tell if there is a connection between a memory load and a store. But to examine the address computation, the processor needs the values used by these instructions, and thus would delay renaming. We will discuss the general topic of memory references in Chapter 5.

4.3   Illusion of Causality: Speculative Execution

The idea of speculation is to create parallelism from instruction execution – before it is known if those instructions are needed. Speculative execution exposes this parallelism by allowing instructions beyond a conditional branch to be considered for parallel execution. Because this allows some instructions to be executed *before* the branch instructions that cause them to be part of correct program execution, we call this maintaining the **illusion of causality**. And despite the complexity of speculation, essentially all modern computers implement it.

Branch prediction is the key to enabling speculative execution; each prediction "guesses" the next block of instructions that will be executed by predicting whether the conditional branch is taken or not. An example of the two different blocks that are considered based on the prediction is shown in Figure 4.16. By allowing more instructions to be considered, more instruction parallelism is exposed to potentially increase processing performance.

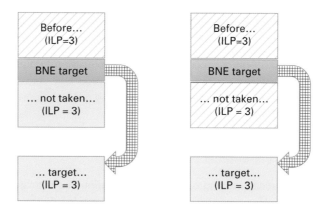

Figure 4.16 By speculating across a conditional branch, more instructions are available for ILP. In the base case (left), only one block is available. With speculation (right), two blocks (orange hash) are available for ILP.

In the current state-of-the-art, one direction for the branch is pursued. It turns out that one path works better than two because high-accuracy **branch prediction** is possible. With such prediction, executing only one path reduces the wasted instruction executions and increases the progress along the program's real execution path. First, let us consider the challenge of accurate branch prediction. After that, we will discuss how to handle incorrect guesses, which are only detected when a branch is resolved – the condition is computed.

4.3.1 Branch Prediction

As shown in Figure 4.16, branch prediction allows ILP to exploit instructions from a window that goes past a conditional branch. At each branch, the processor guesses and speculatively executes the instructions on that path. If the guess is correct, there are two benefits. First, speculation significantly increases the number of instructions that can be executed concurrently, improving the instruction execution rate. Second, if the branch prediction is correct, we are accelerating progress along the true program execution path, effectively executing the branch instruction and instructions beyond it.

Most processors actually go further, and make multiple branch predictions, chaining them together and allowing speculation across multiple guesses. This produces even greater potential benefits in ILP. For example, if three consecutive branches are predicted correctly, then the degree of concurrency may be as high as 12 (four basic blocks times three-fold instruction parallelism per block). But if these branch predictions turn out to be wrong, we will have wasted a lot of work, and further will need to clean up the speculated execution. Speculation across multiple basic blocks is depicted in Figure 4.17, where the chain of five basic blocks reflects the predicted patch from which instructions can be scheduled for parallel execution.

So, the key enabler for productive speculative execution is high-accuracy branch prediction. Branch predictors have been the subject of much research, and the results

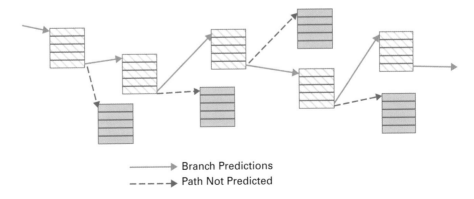

$\longrightarrow$ Branch Predictions
$----\rightarrow$ Path Not Predicted

Figure 4.17 Speculation allows instructions to be executed in parallel from any of the blocks along the predicted executed path (gold). This path can span multiple predictions, and thereby increase available ILP significantly.

Table 4.1. Branch counts, correct prediction counts, and the resulting accuracy for the matrix–matrix multiply program in Figure 4.18.

Matrix size	Inner loop branches	Inner loop pred. correct	Middle branches	Middle pred. correct	Outer branches	Outer pred. correct	Branch pred. accuracy (%)
8×8	576	512	72	64	9	8	88.9
32×32	33,792	32,768	1,056	1,028	33	32	97.0
64×64	266,240	262,144	4,160	4,096	65	64	98.5

```
A[][]; B[][]; Result[][];
for (i=0;i<N;i++){                  // loop N times, exit once
   for (j=0;j<N;j++){               // loop N*N times, exits N times
      sum = 0;
      for (k=0;k<N;k++){            // loop N*N*N times, exit N*N times
         sum = sum + A[j][k] * B[k][j];
      };
      Result[i][j] = sum;
   };
};
```

Figure 4.18 Matrix multiplication has nested loops with highly skewed trip counts. For each branch, there are N not-taken decisions for every taken decision.

show that accurate branch predictors are possible. This is due to the structured nature of program behavior. In general, programs contain many loops and if–then–else structures with highly unbalanced trip counts (counts of the decisions taken or not taken at each branch). For loops, the major reason for this is that most loops execute more than one iteration, skewing their branch distributions. For if–then–else structures, the reasons are manifold. Such structures often arise from termination conditions for recursion, error test, or even categories over skewed data (e.g. right-handed versus left-handed), producing a skewed branch distribution. As we will see, these skewed distributions can be easy to predict accurately.

A branch predictor guesses whether a branch is taken or not taken. To capture skew and temporal correlation, these predictors often use behavior history to hone their predictions. Let's look at a specific example. Consider the matrix–matrix multiplication program (Figure 4.18). In this example, each of the branches is skewed by a factor of N. That is, the decisions to continue the loop outnumber loop exits by $N : 1$, so for the exit test, this translates into a branch not taken to branch taken ratio of $N : 1$. Such skewed branches can be predicted accurately with a simple "always not taken" predictor! The accuracy of this predictor increases with the value of N, and is 96.9 percent for $N = 32$. The accuracy of the always not taken predictor is shown in Table 4.1 for several matrix sizes. With prediction accuracies from 88 to over 98 percent, the data in Table 4.1 shows how looping structures can be predicted accurately with only simple branch predictors.

More sophisticated branch predictors can handle more complex control structures that occur in programs, achieving prediction accuracies in excess of 95 percent. When combined with speculative execution, such branch prediction accuracies increase the number of instructions available for ILP and the instruction execution rate. In fact, modern computing processors (cores) routinely execute 30–40 instructions concurrently and at peak can reach 100–150 concurrent instructions. This aggressive speculation is not unique to any one company, but rather deployed in all modern server processors available from Intel and AMD x86, ARM, and IBM POWER processors. These rates depend on both successful branch prediction and speculative execution. But we have not completed the speculation story, as so far there has been no description of what the processor does when a branch prediction is incorrect.

4.3.2   Speculative Execution

Having outlined the motivation for speculative execution and discussed its benefits, we now complete the story by presenting the speculative execution algorithm (Figure 4.19). This algorithm not only enables speculation, but also ensures the correct program results are computed even when the branch prediction is incorrect. How is this possible? Each time a processor speculates on the direction taken by a conditional branch, it keeps track of the guess and creates a log of the speculative computation results – the register and memory changes. As the branch prediction continues guessing, the speculation continues through multiple branches and basic blocks, and the log of pending speculated changes continues to grow. The speculative execution algorithm captures this in Figure 4.19.

The speculative execution algorithm consists of two parts. The first part speculates and executes the code blocks along the speculative path. The `execute()` operations

```
// Speculating actor, executes ahead based on predictions
//
execute(BlockA);
flagA = predict(endA_cond_branch);
if (flagA == true) execute(target(endA_cond_branch))
    else execute(fall_through(endA_cond_branch)
...
// Resolving actor, completes branches, cleans up if necessary
//
result = actual_result(endA_cond_branch);
if (result != flagA){  // oops prediction ERROR!
    if (flagA == true) cancel_updates(target(endA_cond_branch));
        else cancel_updates(fall_through(endA_cond_branch));
    cancel_all_further_speculative_updates();
    }
    else go_on_to_next_speculation();
...
```

Figure 4.19 Speculative execution algorithm.

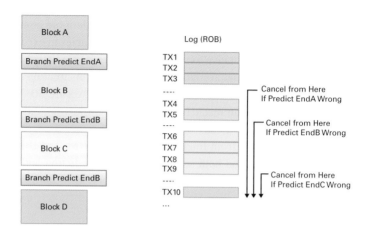

Figure 4.20 In a speculated path of basic blocks A;B;C;D, each block produces a set of updates in a growing log of changes, associated with the renamed register values. If the speculation is correct, these values can be copied into the ISA registers; if not, the entire log is cancelled from the incorrectly predicted branch instruction.

compute the results of a basic block and commit them to a log. This log is represented in the ROB as a set of renamed register names, and thus reflects the path of speculation. Entries are written at the bottom of the log, shown in Figure 4.20. At the end of basic BlockA, there is an endA_cond_branch, `flagA` records the prediction and path taken for that branch. This `execute()` creates ILP across blocks, increasing the instruction processing rate.

The resolving actor follows behind, and when the endA_cond_branch is completed, it checks if the result matches the prediction. If yes, then all of the speculation for the target(endA_cond_branch) is good, and we continue forward having benefited in performance from the speculation. If the branch result does not match the prediction (incorrect), then the speculation for target(endA_cond_branch) is invalid and must be flushed. This means we must cancel the updates for the target(endA_cond_branch) basic block and for all further speculated basic blocks on the path. As shown in Figure 4.20, this could be three, four, or even more colored ROB sections! While this sounds like a lot of work, with a log structure all of these changes can be discarded by simply moving the write pointer in the ROB back to the position where BlockA finished. So, this elegant ROB mechanism gets us back to the correct processor state easily, but there is still the cost of losing all of that speculated work!

Proof that the speculative execution preserves sequential execution semantics, despite mispredicted branches and recovery, is shown in Theorem 4.2.

THEOREM 4.2 *The program executed with speculation always computes the same results as the program executed without speculation.*

Proof by contradiction.
Consider the execution of two basic blocks A followed by B in our program. As before, we will use its place in the order of the regular program execution to identify it, Blocknum. So this basic block A = < BlockA, Blocknum> and B = <BlockB,Blocknum+1>.

Note that a basic block in a loop will show up many times with different Blocknum values as it is executed many times.

Let pre-MS(X) denote the machine state before executing block X, and post-MS(X) denote the machine state after execution.

If a speculative execution does not compute the same results as the original program, then:

1. *There must be at least block B, such as that post-MS(B) != post-MS(B′), while pre-MS(A) == pre-MS(A′), and post-MS(A) == post-MS(A′).*
2. *This means that both B and B′ see the correct machine when they begin; however, post-MS(B) != post-MS(B′). There are two possibilities.*
3. *First, B′ != B, that is our speculative algorithm executed this block incorrectly. This could happen if the speculated branch decision to execute B′ didn't match the actual branch decision. However, if this happened, the speculation algorithm would have "cancelled all of the updates," so this is a contradiction.*
4. *Second, B′ == B, but then given the post-MS(A) == post-MS(A′) == pre-MS(B) == pre-MS(B′), then after executing the block, we must have post-MS(B) == post-MS(B′). This is also a contradiction.*

Both paths produce a contradiction. Therefore, the program executed with speculation always computes the same results as the program executed without speculation.

Let's review the effect of speculative execution again in Figure 4.20. As branch predictions are made (speculative choices), the path of execution is determined; this path creates a log (series) of potential changes which are recorded (committed) only when the corresponding branch predictions are confirmed as accurate (correct).[4] As the log grows, the computation after each guess simply uses the values produced by the speculation chain, captured in the TXn labels from the register renaming algorithm. When branches are resolved and the predictions are correct, then changes are committed, becoming part of the program execution. Typically, this commitment can trail the speculation by 3–7 branches and is reflected in a large log of changes in Figure 4.20. At the top of the figure, updates from the renamed registers are eventually copied into the ISA registers. The hardware design of the machine microarchitecture limits the amount by which commitment can trail speculation; however, many machines today have about 256 registers in their ROB [109]. It is worth noting that if for some reason the machine runs out of ROB space, the speculating thread can simply wait for more branches to be resolved and hence for space to be released.

The importance of speculative execution for processor performance means that the cost of incorrect branch predictions (and corresponding mis-speculation) is extremely high. If the speculation is incorrect, branch misprediction, all of the speculated work is wasted. Further, the potential changes to registers and memory must be cleaned up (erased). Finally, the processor must restart its speculating actor, which takes a

---

[4] If there is an interrupt (external event) or trap (an exception, usually an error), the step-by-step sequential machine state semantics must be precisely maintained. This presents an important challenge for exploitation of ILP.

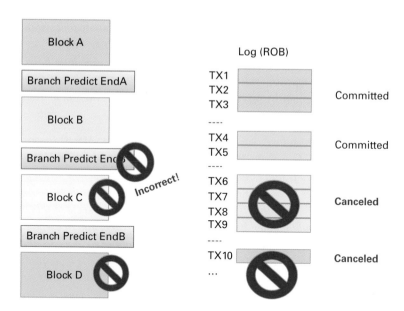

Figure 4.21 Speculation: if the branch prediction for endB is incorrect, then the updates for both C and D are canceled, as is any ongoing execution of blocks C and D. This causes significant loss of work.

number of cycles to expose enough ILP to refill the microarchitecture's parallelism. Thus, it is a number of cycles before performance recovers to full speed. In short, each incorrect prediction and speculation incurs a significant hiccup and performance loss. The importance of making good choices for speculative execution led to a bounty of research in branch prediction.

Let's continue the example in Figure 4.20. If any branch prediction turns out to be incorrect, then the corresponding changes and all subsequent predictions and associated changes are discarded. The ROB structure makes this easy, but discarding changes wastes all the speculated work.[5] Both successful and unsuccessful speculation resolution are illustrated in Figure 4.21. This logical structure maps the log directly on the ROB implementation of ILP shown in Figure 4.15, but here the ROB is being used to support speculation and rollback after incorrect branch prediction.

> **Principle 4.4: Speculative Execution Uses Prediction to Increase Execution Speed**
>
> *Speculative execution combines register renaming, branch prediction, and the ability to recover from incorrect predictions. Speculative execution exposes ILP from as many as 3–7 basic blocks, enabling higher processor performance.*

---

[5] In Section 4.3.4 we consider what happens when these effects are erased imperfectly, causing a major security problem in the Spectre/Meltdown [53] situation.

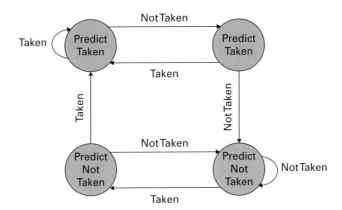

Figure 4.22 A simple 2-bit branch predictor.

4.3.3   Accurate Branch Predictors

As we saw in Section 4.3.1, branch prediction is surprisingly easy at first. For some program structures a simple predictor of "not taken" can achieve branch prediction accuracies of over 98 percent. In general, branch prediction accuracies of over 90 percent are easy to achieve.

State-of-the-art branch predictors used by today's microprocessors employ branch history to refine the basic branch prediction approach. These improved predictors use several bits of storage to record the history of decisions at a branch (one bit per decision!) as context. This context allows the branch predictor to model some common control structures with a finite-state machine (FSM), enabling them to increase prediction accuracy.

For example, the 2-bit branch predictor shown in Figure 4.22 uses a 2-bit FSM for each branch instruction in the program. The FSM encodes the recent sequence of branch decisions made at a branch, enabling capture of typical loop behavior – a run of taken or not taken, followed by a prediction error. This 2-bit FSM predictor takes two mispredicts to change its prediction, thus eliminating one mispredict on each entry to the loop. The two-bit predictor minimizes misses – only one for each execution of a for–while–do loop structure – achieving an accuracy of greater than 95 percent on a broad variety of programs [115].

> **Principle 4.5: Effective Speculative Execution Relies on Excellent Branch Prediction**
>
> *Because of the cost of misprediction, speculative execution depends critically on high-accuracy branch prediction to improve performance.*

Loops are the most common conditional branching structures, but the quest for even higher accuracy has led to aggressive techniques that target the less frequent conditional branches. For example, empirical studies show that in if-else or even

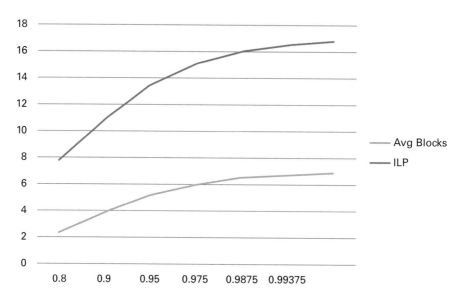

Figure 4.23 Average ILP available from increasing branch prediction accuracy.

switch() structures, branch decisions can be correlated with recent behavior of other branches nearby. A more sophisticated type of branch predictor exploits this correlation by hashing branch program counter addresses into shared predictor tables. With an appropriate hash function, the nearby branches can inform a prediction for a given conditional branch. With these techniques, branch predictors can achieve over 97–99 percent for an even broader range of programs – again at the cost of additional hardware, provided courtesy of Moore's Law.

How much branch prediction accuracy is enough for speculation? Each misprediction incurs a significant loss of ILP. And, as accuracy gets very high, prediction can enable speculation over as many as seven basic blocks. Figure 4.23 shows the benefits of increased prediction accuracy, assuming a base of ILP of three, and an increase of two for each basic block that is enabled for ILP by successful branch prediction. Here we ignore the overheads of speculative execution and rollback, and examine only the benefits.

As branch prediction accuracy exceeds 90 percent, the number of basic blocks that can be exploited for ILP increases beyond four blocks, and enables high levels of ILP. When accuracy exceeds 95 percent the benefits are even larger. Conversely, if branch prediction accuracy falls, performance drops precipitously. For example, if a branch prediction accuracy were only 50 percent, performance might drop 10-fold or more compared to typical performance. Such a performance drop reflects misprediction penalties such as refilling the instruction fetch pipeline and flushing incorrectly speculated instructions. At such poor branch prediction accuracy, performance is worse than if there were no speculation at all.

> Principle 4.6: Excellent Branch Prediction Is Easy
>
> *Branch prediction can reach accuracies as high as 95–99 percent. These branch predictors exploit structured programs and typical software behavior, and are essential to the three to four-fold ILP performance benefits of speculative execution.*

4.3.4 Security Risks of Speculation: Spectre and Meltdown

Most computer architecture research and design focuses on higher performance and functional correctness (performs the computation correctly). Additional goals are computers that are smaller and more power efficient. But as computing applications have grown to include every aspect of society, computing naturally takes on a much wider range of concerns, such as a growing concern about making computers *secure* from malicious attack or compromise. With computers widely used in critical functions of society (e.g. finance, law, factories, etc), as well as nearly every aspect of personal behavior (e.g. communication, health, sleep, records, etc.), securing the information in a computer is a definite requirement. The entire computing community was surprised in 2017 when researchers showed that performance features such as speculative execution could be used to create unauthorized access to data in a computer – a violation of hardware protection used by the operating system. We discuss two examples of how these foundational security mechanisms were circumvented in a modern processor.

In late 2017, security researchers demonstrated exploits, called Spectre and then a related variant called Meltdown, that showed how to use speculative execution to provide unauthorized access to privileged information on servers [54, 60]. This novel attack approach using speculative execution reflects a general security problem for Intel server processors (Xeon) that underlie most of the servers used in the worldwide cloud. This attack uses the performance variability produced by speculative execution to leak protected information. In 2018, Intel disclosed a broader class of speculation-related side channel attacks, as well as software patches and later hardware patches to plug the holes. An overall summary is available [65].

Spectre was the first exploit that demonstrated how a thread without privilege could create an execution-time based side-channel that revealed the contents of privileged data in the operating system kernel. This exploit used speculative execution to access privileged data. Because the access is done under speculated execution, not the confirmed execution path, it does not cause an access violation because the failed speculation must be invisible to the application. However, the exploit cleverly detects the speculation's decisions based on the data in changes in the memory system (caches; see Chapter 5). In this way, Spectre and Meltdown break down the isolation either between an application and the operating system or between two applications. In today's cloud computing environment, applications from different companies,

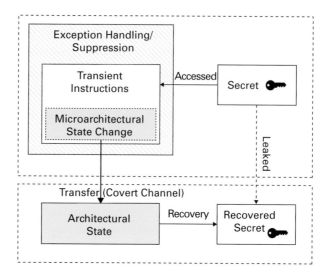

Figure 4.24 Spectre and Meltdown create a side channel that leaks information from the operating system or between processes by manipulating speculative execution. Meltdown [60] uses exception handling or suppression (e.g. TSX) to run a series of transient instructions. These transient instructions obtain a (persistent) secret value and change the microarchitectural state of the processor based on this secret value (top). The receiving side (bottom) can detect the microarchitectural state.

individuals, and even governments run side-by-side on the same cloud servers. Thus, such a security exploit presents a critical problem.

Spectre and Meltdown represent a key challenge to the definition and design of computer architecture because they exploit speculative execution, a microarchitecture performance feature that is intended to be functionally invisible to application programs. Both of these exploits expose information by manipulating the performance visibility of speculative execution to create information side channels (Figure 4.24). This disrupts the basic definition of the ISA specification, which only defines state change in defined architectural state, not performance. If performance must be specified in the definition of an ISA, such as x86, it would disrupt the traditional basis of portability that began with the IBM 360 in the 1960s. The functional definition of the ISA alone would not be a sufficient description of architecture portability for security purposes. Directly, making assurances of application security on a computing system would require detailed performance information normally associated with a specific chip implementation (e.g. Intel Coffee Lake chip, 2017), not the ISA (e.g. x86). The accretion of performance specifications to functional specifications, the traditional definition of the computer architecture interface (or extension of the interface) complicates things significantly. Spectre and Meltdown are just the first of a much larger set of security challenges that exploit computer architecture features!

> Principle 4.7: To Increase Performance, Computers Execute Instructions in Parallel, but Preserve the Sequential Abstraction to Ease Programming and Use
>
> *Techniques such as renaming, branch prediction, and speculation reshape program execution, maintaining the sequential abstraction but producing a hardware execution order that increases performance dramatically. Altogether, these ILP techniques (pipelining, multiple-issue, out-of-order, branch prediction, and speculative execution) increase processor performance reliably by 30 times and as much as 100 times in bursts. This net contribution by processor architects is a key pillar of computer performance.*

4.4   Summary

Computers (and most programming languages) implement strict sequential abstraction in order to make reasoning about complex sequences of state easier. These abstractions are powerful tools for managing the complexity required by sophisticated algorithms and data structures, as well as large-scale software. As such, they are non-negotiable and represent a key element of the software–hardware interface, the ISA.

With a bounty of transistors, architects have developed a set of techniques for hidden parallelism – pipelining, multiple-issue, renaming, branch prediction, and speculation – that allow instructions to be executed out-of-order, while maintaining strict sequential semantics. The results of these techniques are two-fold:

- The hardware execution order of a program's instructions is often radically different – unordered, overlapping, and even a different order – than simple instruction sequence. The unique renaming of values (from registers or memory variables) is the key, and ensures the correct sequential semantics. This complex approach is how commercial processors really execute programs – far different from the step-by-step recipe of the sequential abstraction.

- These **instruction-level parallelism (ILP)** techniques deliver a 30 times increase in performance, based on successful branch prediction and speculative execution! However, these techniques are implemented at a tremendous cost in power and transistors. For example, a modern processor core is often over 200 million transistors – a sharp 400-fold inflation from the 500,000 transistors required for the simplest early 64-bit microprocessors.

The dramatic increase in processor complexity was enabled by plentiful, inexpensive transistors delivered by Moore's Law, and is a trend in all modern high-performance compute engines (cores) such as Intel and AMD x86, ARM, and IBM POWER processors. We provide a deep dive into a commercial processor design in Section 6.1.

However, growing the complexity of processors to increase their performance is not without downsides. First, the use of hundreds of millions of transistors for out-of-order increases processor power consumption significantly. And the number of transistors being used per processor in all commercial designs continues to grow. Second, if branch prediction accuracy falters, then processor performance can drop precipitously. And finally, with new security attacks, such as Spectre, that exploit implementation properties (microarchitecture), there is no shortage of future challenges for computer architects to continue the growth of computer performance.

4.5   Digging Deeper

Many computer-architecture textbooks describe *instruction pipelining*, the division of instruction execution multiple stages, and the partial overlap of instructions. Kogge's classic text gives a clean analysis of fundamental pipelining performance properties [55]. Modern chips include multiple-issue (aka superscalar), that allow more than one instruction to be initiated in a single clock period. The idea of superscalar, embodied in the MIPS R4000, Intel Pentium Pro, and IBM POWER [66], issues multiple instructions per cycle (parallel execution). Out-of-order execution and register renaming were pioneered by Tomasulo in the IBM 360 Stretch project [96], allowing overlapped execution and even instruction passing, and have evolved into the modern ROB.

Several architectures considered ISAs that employed compiler-based renaming instead of hardware renaming, but the software challenges proved insurmountable [28, 82]. Speculative execution began in the academic research community with the multiscalar architecture [89] and is now available from all of the commercial processor vendors. The flexibility engendered by renaming and speculative execution allowed the CISC processor to overtake and outperform RISC processors starting around 2008 [5, 49].

Branch prediction has a long history, going back to the 1980s [88], but reached the levels of accuracy needed to make speculative execution flourish in the late 1990s and has continued to progress [115].

We have covered two drivers for increased computer performance: size/technology scaling and ILP. Size/technology scaling accounted for improvement by a factor of 100,000, and ILP by a factor of perhaps 100. In a 2011 paper, Borkar and Chien separated the effects of technology and ILP over a 20-year period [8], and suggested that the performance improvement balance would be quite different in the future. Another excellent study collected a wide variety of microprocessor performance data in an open database, and analyzed technology and microarchitecture effects [21].

4.6   Problems

4.1   Statement sequence is important in program blocks. It is used by programmers to compute more complex functions. Consider this code example:

```
{
    int i, j, k;
    i = j = k = 0;
    i = 24*7*365;      // hours   in  a  year
    j = i * 60;        // minutes in  a  year
    k = j * 60;        // seconds in  a  year
}
```

(a) Explain how the sequence between the initial assignment to i, j, k is important to the correct behavior of this program block.

(b) Explain how the final values of the program variables would differ if the second assignments to i and j were executed in the opposite order to their order in the program listing? What would be their final values?

(c) Would the reordering considered in the prior problem part affect the final value of k?

(d) What operations in the program could be reordered (executed without the same sequence as program order), and still produce the same results for i, j, k?

(e) Draw a graph of the dataflow dependences between statements that is sufficient to ensure correct program execution (as in Figure 4.12).

4.2 Statement sequence is important in program blocks. It is used by programmers to compute more complex functions. Consider the code example:

```
{
    int jane, fred, elise;
    jane = fred = elise = 100;    // all   start  with  \$100
    jane = jane + 1000;           // paycheck
    fred = fred * 2;              // gambles and wins
    elise = elise + 0.2*(jane + fred);   // elise taxes them
    jane = jane - 0.2*jane;
    fred = fred - 0.2*fred;
}
```

(a) Explain how the sequence between the initial assignment to *jane, fred,* and *elise* is important to the correct behavior of this program block.

(b) Explain how the final values of the program variables would differ if the last three statements (elise taxes) were performed out of sequence, before the prior two statements (paycheck, gambles and wins).

(c) What operations in the program could be reordered (executed without the same sequence as program order), and still produce the same results for *jane, fred,* and *elise?*

(d) Draw a graph of the dataflow dependences between statements that is sufficient to ensure correct program execution (as in Figure 4.12).

4.3 The sequential state abstraction is a central element of how we reason about algorithms and about the correctness of programs. Here we will consider several different ways in which this model is useful.

(a) Procedures are a key element of structuring programs. Explain how we reason about the state of a program at the location of a procedure call. What do we assume before, and what do we assume after? How do we reason about changes in the state made by the procedure?

(b) Sequential abstraction is used by programmers to reason about state change and program correctness. The simplest model is to think of each textual program statement happening in order (no change). What would you have to know to change the order of the statements? Optimizing compilers can do this; what do they need to prove in order to transpose two statements? For example, consider the following C program statements that assign values to *mixed_fruit* and *mashed_fruit*:

```
int apple , pear;
int mixed_fruit , mashed_fruit;
mixed_fruit = apple + pear;
mashed_fruit = apple ^ pear;
```

(c) Most programs use complex data structures that reside in the stack or the heap. To reorder statements using such structures to enable their parallel execution, what property would a programmer or compiler have to prove?

4.4 From the earliest days of software, debuggers have been used to show programmers the state of registers and memory (the architectural state) as the program executes one statement at a time.

(a) Explain why debuggers show progress only one statement at a time. Why would this make sense to a programmer?

(b) Consider the instruction-level parallel execution discussed in this chapter. What does the machine do when a debugger breakpoint stops the program? Does it have to do work to recreate the sequential abstraction?

(c) Now consider a magic debugger (not like the ones we have!) that stops the machine executing with the 30–100 instructions "in-flight" due to ILP. Is it possible to define the machine state precisely? What might a programmer think of this?

4.5 The sequential state abstraction for computers also applies to the memory. This means that data structures on the stack or even in the heap (both a part of the computer memory) obey the sequential state abstraction. This means keeping the entire memory, which can be gigabytes or even terabytes, consistent with a sequential abstraction. For example, consider the following C program that updates data structures in memory:

```
struct cabinet {
    long item;
    long IDnumber;};
cabinet office[64];
// initialize
for (int i=0; i++; i<64){
```

```
    office [i]. item  =  (i +17)  /  8;
    office [i]. IDnumber  =  i ;
    };

  int  val  =  37;
  int  q  =  49;
  int  rho  =  17;
  office [val/rho]  =  office [q];   // assmt 1
  office [office [2]. item]  =  office [(val/rho)];   // assmt 2
  office [rho+rho]  =  office [val/rho];  // assmt 3
  office [val/rho]  =  office [q+10];      // assmt 4
```

(a)   How do the assignments 1, 2, 3, and 4 depend on sequential abstraction? Give an example of how the values in memory would be different after executing this program if two of the assignments changed their order.

(b)   Assignment 2 includes a memory reference to find the index for the target of the assignment; how does that memory reference and the subsequent assignment depend on the correct sequence for execution?

(c)   Assignment 1 and 4 both update the same element of the array office. Why do they need to be ordered? (Hint: it depends on sequential abstraction.)

(d)   All of the assignments involve the memory, and could be operating on structures in any part of the computer address space. What requirement does this impose on the computer hardware, as more and more memory is added to computers?

4.6   Sequential abstraction applies across the iterations of a loop. Consider the program below, which iterates using the variable i as a counter variable. Because loops are presumed to execute iterations – in order – the iteration for each value of i is presumed to execute in sequence.

```
  long  elements [4096];
  for  (int  i =0;  i++;  i <4096){
    elements [i]  =  (i <<10)  −  i ;
    if  (i >1)  elements [i −1]  =  elements [i];
  };
```

The program example creates a set values and writes them into the array, oddly overwriting the values it wrote in the previous iteration.

(a)   What is the resulting content of the array for correct execution?

(b)   Each iteration overwrites the elements[i] entry written by the prior iteration, so correct execution requires execution of the iterations in order. If the program iterations were executed in another order, say descending iterations (backward), what would the results of the array elements[ ] contain?

(c)   Write a simple variant of the program that computes the same results as our original sequential program, but doesn't depend on the sequential execution of iterations to produce that result. Explain why it does so, and was it easy? Explain how you decided what code to write.

4.7 Apply the variable renaming algorithm to variables a, b, c for the following program:

```
int a=1, b=2, c=3;
for (int i=0; i++; i<4){
    a = b + c;
    b = c;
    c = i;
};
return a;
```

(a) By applying renaming, how many names did you end up using for the three program variables, a, b, and c?

(b) The original program would have required all three loop statements in sequence, effectively no parallelism. How many statements in the renamed program can be executed in parallel for each iteration?

(c) If the compiler substituted constant values for i (0, 1, 2, 3) for the three loop iterations, how many statements from the iteration body could be executed in parallel for this entire four-iteration program?

4.8 The idea of renaming is to relax the sequential state abstraction restraints on program execution. Consider the following program:

```
long values[128];
for (int i=0; i++; i<128){
    long sq = i * i;
    long sum = i + i
    long two_each = 0;
    two_each = two_each + sq + sq;
    two_each = two_each + sum + sum;
    values[i] = two_each;
};
for (int i=0; i++; i<128){
    long sum;
    sum = sum + value[i];
};
```

(a) Consider the first loop; ignoring the dependence for i, consider the dependences with an iteration. Draw a picture of the data dependences within an iteration (one copy of the loop body) at the level of statements. Which statements depend on each other? What is the longest patch of dependences (critical path)?

(b) Rename one of the program variables to eliminate a dependence, and thereby shorten the critical path. How much can it be shortened?

(c) The i (loop index) variables are technically a dependence from one iteration to the next, but because the values involve only a simple increment, a compiler can figure out how to enable iterations to execute with dependences on each other by substituting a constant i value for each iteration. For example, the first iteration would get $i = 0$, the second would get $i = 1$, and so on. However, the dependence in the second loop on the value *sum* is not so easily broken. Think about this, and explain why the compiler cannot substitute a value for *sum* in each iteration?

4.9 Let's consider the renaming algorithm and build some deeper understanding of why it is correct. Consider the following declaration:

```
long i, j, k, l, m, n; //assume all are registers a2–a7 (x12–x17)
```

(a) Write a program that computes the sum of six integers (longwords) i, j, k, l, m, and n using only one register, a2, to store any intermediate values and the final result.

(b) If the program was run on a processor without renaming, how many instructions could execute at a time? (How much ILP?)

(c) Apply the renaming algorithm; how many instructions can execute at a time?

(d) Rewrite the program to use two registers, a2 and a3, to store intermediate values. Under renaming, how many instructions can execute at a time?

(e) Prove that the renamed execution of your new program computes the correct answer by showing that each of the renamed values is the correct result.

(f) Even with renaming, your program can't achieve the full potential parallelism of this computation. Explain why. And explain what additional program transformation is needed to make it possible.

4.10 In modern compilers, an extensive analysis allows the program to be transformed significantly for higher performance. We have come to depend on these transformations that often produce a program execution structure quite different from the source program. In short, they can make it difficult to reconstruct the sequential abstraction view of the program execution. As a result, many debuggers do not work on optimized programs.

(a) Consider a program with a loop (write an example), and then perform loop unrolling on the program to increase its ILP.

(b) Now consider a breakpoint in the unrolled program. Why would reconstructing the sequential abstraction for the original program be difficult? Give some specific examples.

4.11 Program correctness and precondition/postconditions are a framework for reasoning about programs, developed by Edsger Dijkstra. It was formulated in the context of sequential abstraction.

(a) How is it affected by the presence of ILP?

(b) How would it be affected by parallel execution (multiple threads), as we will explore in Chapter 7?

4.12 Consider the following program, which has two conditional branches:

```
long values[128];
for (int i=0; i++; i<128){ // branch 1
    long sq = i * i;
```

```
if ((i*7)%5 >= 2){        // branch 2
    do ... something1
} else { do ... something2 };
cleanup;
};
```

(a) Consider branch 1 in the program example. Estimate the prediction accuracy for it. Explain your estimate.

(b) Consider branch 2 in the program example. Estimate the prediction accuracy for it. Explain your estimate.

(c) Given what you've learned about speculative execution, how much work is going to be wasted on speculation executing "cleanup"?

(d) Given what you've learned about speculative execution, how much work is going to be wasted on speculation executing "do...something1" and "do...something2"? Compared to each other? Compared to "cleanup"?

4.13 Consider the following program with one conditional branch:

```
int aprocedure (int a, b){
    if (complex ... condition){ // branch 1
        do ... something1
    } else { do ... something2 };
    ...
    return 1;
};
```

You run this program, and use performance instrumentation to determine the number of times the conditional branch is executed (five million times), and its prediction accuracy.

(a) You find much to your surprise that it is correctly predicted 95 percent of the time. How is this possible? Explain.

(b) In another program you find a similar structure of code, but when you measure it you find that it is mispredicted 75 percent of the time. Give several explanations for how this could be possible.

4.14 Branch prediction and matrix multiply. Run the matrix multiply program example from Figure 4.18. Run it for matrix sizes of $16 \times 16, 64 \times 64, 256 \times 256$, and $1,024 \times 1,024$. Use performance instrumentation to collect the number of branches taken and the branch prediction accuracy.

(a) What is the number of branches for each size?

(b) What is the branch prediction accuracy? As you increase the matrix size, how high can you get the branch prediction accuracy?

4.15 Run the bubble sort program example from Figure 4.1. Run it for array sizes of 4K, 64K, 256K, and 1M elements. Use performance instrumentation to collect the number of branches taken and the branch prediction accuracy.

(a) What is the number of branches for each size?

(b) What is the branch prediction accuracy? As you increase the bubble sort size, how does the branch prediction accuracy change?

(c) How does this change with size compare to the matrix multiply example in Problem 14?

4.16 Run an open-source benchmark program suite, and report the number of branches executed and the number of correct predictions. What is the branch prediction accuracy? How does it vary over the programs in the benchmark suite? How does it vary with input/data set size for each benchmark?

4.17 Write a program designed to get a low branch prediction accuracy. Explain your program design and the reason it should have a low prediction accuracy.

(a) Measure the achieved branch prediction accuracy using performance counter tools. Was it as low in accuracy as you expected? Why or why not?

(b) For the lowest branch prediction accuracy, report the number of instructions executed and the number of cycles used. What is the effective ILP?

4.18 Speculation is based on accurate prediction. In this question, we will explore how accurate a prediction must be to enable speculation to achieve specific levels of performance improvement.

(a) Suppose that each basic block has 12 instructions and an average ILP of three. If we can perform a prediction in a single cycle, how long does it take us to get to predictions running four basic blocks ahead of the oldest executing block?

(b) At that point, what is the average ILP for the machine across the five basic blocks?

(c) Now, suppose the branch prediction accuracy is X and consider your answer for the first part of this question. What is the effective average ILP for this machine if X is 90, 95, or 99 percent?

4.19 Speculation depends critically on accurate branch prediction, which as we have seen is typically feasible due to structured programming and to high skew at branches.

(a) How low can branch prediction accuracy be for a given branch? 75, 50, 25 percent? Lower?

(b) Write a small C program that results in low branch prediction accuracy. Using the PERF tool, measure the branch prediction accuracy. How low can you make it? Analyze and explain this number.

(c) If you knew the branch prediction scheme for a machine, explain how you would design the lowest possible prediction accuracy program.

4.20 Consider the program below, and several different scenarios in which speculation can cause extra instructions and other work to occur. Suppose this program section is executed one million times in a program.

```
if ((a+3)/(residue >> 4)){
    retval = a->left + b.right->deepvalue;
} else {
    retval = doLotofWork(a,b,a->left+512);
```

```
    };
    return  retval;
```

(a)   Suppose the if conditional fails 90 percent of the time, but the branch prediction does an exact 50/50 split. That is, half the time it predicts taken, the other half not taken. And consider that these decisions are not correlated with the actual branch decisions. How many memory references will be speculated in the true arm for each time its mispredicted? Overall in the program?

(b)   Memory references are tricky for speculative execution. If a and b.right only pointed to user program data, there's probably little harm in fetching them (except perhaps some loss of performance due to cache pollution – see Chapter 5). But what would happen if they accessed outside the segment, creating a "segmentation fault"?

(c)   The scenario sketched above isn't that far-fetched. Suppose we used a marker at tree leaf nodes (or linked lists), where the last value was −1 (think while (val! = −1)a = a–>next; ...) What address would speculation access? Look up the Linux memory map; is that address likely to be safe?

(d)   Now lets consider the wasted work in the else clause. Out of the one million executions of this code section, how many will incorrectly speculate on the else branch? What are the elements of work that might be wasted to compute the arguments? And perform the procedure call? Suppose 10 instructions were executed, how far might we get before canceling?

4.21   As discussed in Section 4.3.4, speculative execution can be used to provide unauthorized access to privileged information on servers. Spectre and Meltdown create execution timing–based side channels that reveal the contents of privileged data in the operating system kernel [54, 60]. The basic idea is to use speculation in the "not taken" side of the conditional to bring data into the cache, and then to observe the runtime of an privileged routine. For example, consider the following program:

```
if  (nevertakethis){
    access –>privileged_data1;
    access –>privileged_data2;
    access –>privileged_data3
    access –>privileged_data4
} else {
    thispathalwaystaken;
};
```

If the conditional is speculated to be taken, it will speculatively execute the loads in that arm, and bring the privileged data into the cache. This will affect the running time for the privileged routines that use that data, making the speculation visible, and if the code in the privileged routines is known, it is possible to determine the values in the privileged data. Traditional ISAs do not describe performance behavior or speculation.

(a)   What would a performance specification for a branch instruction look like if it were to prevent exposing information in this way?

(b)   What does this vulnerability tied to speculation mean for future ISAs? Is it possible to hide any microarchitecture features, which exist to increase performance but were not supposed to be functionally visible?

(c)   What kind of constraints might this specification have for future computer implementations?

4.22   In the early days of microprocessors, the reduced instruction set computers (RISC) were able to achieve higher performance through both higher clock rates and the ability to integrate larger caches.

(a)   A classic paper on why early RISC computers were faster used extensive measurements and a few simple formulas to explain the performance difference between a DEC VAX and MIPS computer [6]. Read the paper and explain in a few bullet points why RISC chips were faster.

(b)   A later paper compared CISC chips whose performance had caught up with RISC designs, explaining how they were different and what RISC implementation approaches were adopted to close the gap [5]. Read the paper and explain in a few bullet points how the CISC microprocessors caught up to the RISC microprocessors.

(c)   In the early 2010s evidence began to grow that RISC instruction sets had important disadvantages, and CISC chips demonstrated some significant performance advantages [49]. Read the paper and explain in a few bullet points why the CISC microprocessors now outperform the RISC microprocessors.

4.23   Take a large open-source program (for example, the PARSEC benchmark suite: https://parsec.cs.princeton.edu/) and run it on a modern microprocessor using a performance tool that gives you access to the performance counters. An example of such a performance tool would be PERF. Most of the performance information necessary for this exercise can be acquired by running "perf stat [program]". Further documentation can be found at the perf wiki: https://perf.wiki.kernel.org/index.php/

   For each of the programs:

(a)   How many instructions are executed by the program?

(b)   How many clock cycles does the program take to execute?

(c)   How much ILP does the program achieve on average? Does this correspond to what you expected? Or does it not? Explain.

4.24   We have seen that "small is fast" accounts for nearly 100,000-fold benefit over the past 75 years, and that ILP allows for another 100-fold improvement in performance.

(a)   Are you surprised at this ratio? Specifically, are you surprised that a much larger performance increase has come from miniaturization and technology compared to the impact of architectural design changes? Why? Why not?

(b)   In their 2011 paper, Borkar and Chien tried to separate the effects of technology and architecture innovation (mostly ILP) over a 20-year period [8]. Read their paper. What did they find as the ratio of technology improvement to architecture improvement on performance?

(c) In Chapter 3 we learned that Dennard scaling is over, and Moore's Law scaling is nearing its end. What do you think might be the balance of contribution between technology and architecture innovation to performance improvement in the future? Explain and justify your answer.

Credits

Figure 4.24 M. Lipp, M. Schwarz, D. Gruss, T. Prescher, W. Haas et al., Meltdown: Reading Kernel Memory from User Space, *Communications of the ACM* 63(6):46–56, 2020.

5 Memories: Exploiting Dynamic Locality

Memory is a critical part of computing systems. In the organization of computers and the programming model, memory was first separated logically from the computing (CPU) part, and then later physically. This separation of CPU and memory in a structure known as the von Neumann architecture[1] was covered in Chapter 2 and is illustrated in Figure 5.1.

The separation of CPU and memory is reflected in the logical structure of computers. The software interface (instruction set architecture, or ISA) structure that limits memory access to only **load** and **store** instructions, commonly called **load–store**, is typical in modern computers. At the physical or hardware level, separation of compute and memory specifically allows specialization of the hardware technologies used, producing fast computing elements (CPUs) and low-cost, high-capacity, but much slower memories. Within the hardware, memory is physically separated from the processor, allowing memory capacity to be increased independently from compute capability.

In this chapter, we discuss memory scaling, which reflects the different technologies used for memory and the voracious demands of applications for memory capacity that result in large, relatively slow memories. The separation of CPU and memory also creates a bottleneck (called the von Neuman bottleneck), limiting the rate of memory accesses, and further increasing memory latency. With this perspective, we explore the program behavior of dynamic locality, and computer architecture techniques that exploit it. Successful exploitation of dynamic locality with caches can ameliorate the memory bottleneck and memory latency. With these insights, we discuss an application program modeling technique, reuse distance, that enables programmers to understand and tune program performance on multiple levels of caches (a memory hierarchy).

5.1 Memory Technologies, Miniaturization, and Growing Capacity

As we saw in Chapter 3, the rapid progress of microelectronics enabled a radical size reduction in computing logic and memory bits that has made fast, cheap computing possible. We explained how electronics miniaturization enables the parts of a computer to be placed close together. This smaller size reduced the clock period

---

[1] This term predominated from the 1950s through the early 2000s, but is now recognized as a misnomer, and this computer organization is largely attributed to J. Presper Eckert and John Mauchly [104].

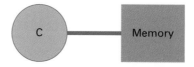

Figure 5.1 The von Neumann architecture separates processor from memory in a computer, shaping the instruction sets used by software, and creating a hardware bottleneck for memory access.

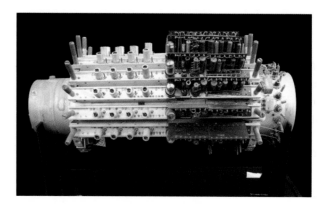

Figure 5.2 Size of a bit: the mercury delay-line memories stored 11-digit registers; each of the 16 registers is a horizontal column. The entire set of UNIVAC registers was approximately 1 meter long and half a meter in diameter.

of the computer from 200 microseconds to below 1 nanosecond, a 200,000 times improvement in computing speed.

The miniaturization of memory also yielded powerful benefits, reducing size and cost, increasing speed, and most notably increasing capacity. First, the smaller size per bit of memory made the physical size of the memory system small, allowing a larger memory to be packed into the same physical size. This made computers with larger memories possible. Second, the cost of a bit of memory shrinks with the amount of material needed, which shrinks as the cube of the linear dimension. As we have seen, size is related to speed. Making each bit smaller enabled memory of a fixed capacity to become faster. And finally, lower cost per bit allows memory capacity to be increased.

But as memory has been miniaturized, it has progressed through several technologies. To establish a perspective, we first consider how memory has progressed through three major memory technologies: mercury delay lines, magnetic cores, and semiconductor static and dynamic RAM.

Mercury Delay Lines   The earliest electronic computers, such as ENIAC and UNIVAC, used heated mercury delay lines. These large units, as shown in Figure 5.2, encoded information as acoustic waves in the mercury, and included heaters to keep the mercury at 104 °F for more stable wave propagation speed. Talk about a challenge for energy efficiency!

In a mercury delay line, bits were encoded in acoustic pulses that traveled through the lines. Each line contained 1,000 bits that traveled down the line in a fraction of a second, using vacuum tubes to control each register. The delay lines were used to implement the registers, the fastest-changing memories in the computer.

The entire tank was approximately 268 in^3; allowing for surrounding circuitry (including heaters!) the volume per bit was approximately 2 in^3/bit or 33 cm^3. The UNIVAC included several one- and two-word registers, each of which encoded an 11-digit decimal number (the equivalent of 32 bits), and computation was done serially, one decimal digit at a time.

Magnetic Cores   In the early 1960s a new memory technology based on ferromagnetic cores emerged. Core memories are depicted in Figure 5.3. These cores were magnetized either clockwise or counterclockwise by running current through wires strung through the cores (Figure 5.3a). A two-dimensional array of wires with cores at the crossings was used to address the bits individually, allowing the memory to be random-access. As shown in Figure 5.3b, a small section of core memory (a few inches square) includes a large number of wires and cores at each crossing. These cores were wired by hand! Over time, these cores became smaller and denser within each plane, then were stacked into three-dimensional structures. These mats were held in a rigid frame to allow a standard size unit (8 KB), to be racked together into a

(b) Close-up of wires and ferrite cores.

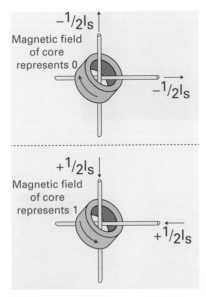

(a) Cores store bits in magnetic fields.

(c) An 8 KB board from IBM 360 (1966).

Figure 5.3 Magnetic core memories.

larger memory system (Figure 5.3c); IBM 360 computers in the 1960s typically had only a few hundred kilobytes of memory, and 1 MB would have been a memory-rich computer indeed! The term "in core" reflects data being in the computer memory to system programmers to this day!

Semiconductor Memory: Static and Dynamic RAM   The next major memory technology to emerge was based on semiconductors – the same electronics technology that drives logic circuits and CPU clock speeds. In 1969, Intel produced the first semiconductor static random-access memory (SRAM) based on MOS electronics technology, the 3101, a 64-bit memory chip (Figure 5.4). That's right, the entire chip could store only 64 bits of information. This dual-in-line package (DIP), approximately $1 \times 2 \times 2$ cm, connected by inserting its pins through holes in the printed circuit board. Once inserted, the chip was wave-soldered onto the boards, yielding a density of $64/4 = 16$ cm^3. At this density, a 1×1 m square (1 cm high) could store only 160 kilobits, and an area of 50 m^2 (twice the area of a large house) would be needed to store a single megabyte. From this humble beginning, semiconductor memories (dynamic random-access memory, or DRAM) grew rapidly in density and speed, as shown in Figure 5.5 – the three example memory elements from 1970, 1989, and 2019, illustrating an increase in bits per chip from 1 kilobit to 1 megabit to over 8 gigabits. This exponential increase benefited from both Moore's Law increases in density and Dennard scaling that together reduced power consumption and increased speed.

Figure 5.4 Introduced in 1969, the Intel 3101 was the first MOS semiconductor memory. It stored only 64 bits.

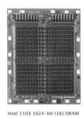  

Intel 1103 1024–bit (1K) DRAM

Figure 5.5 The evolution of the MOS DRAM from Intel 1 kb DRAM (1 cent per bit), to 1 MiB DRAM in 1989, and 8 GiB DRAM chips packed on a 128 GiB DIMM in 2019.

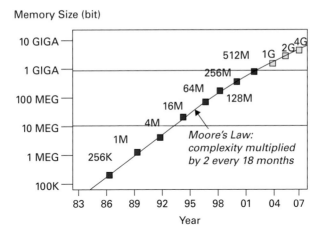

Figure 5.6 Shrinking the bits increases density and the number of DRAM bits on a single chip. NAND flash memories have seen similar trends.

Through this period, the cost per chip remained about the same, producing an exponential reduction in cost per bit capacity. As a result, semiconductor memories eventually replaced core memories due to their density, low cost, and reliability. The rapid scaling of memory density on semiconductor chips produced the rapid increase in capacity per chip depicted in Figure 5.6, rising from 256 kilobits per chip in 1986 to 4 gigabits in 2007. The cumulative increase from 1986 to 2007 is (4,000,000,000)/(256,000) represents a 16,384-fold increase. From Intel's 64-bit SRAM in 1969 to DRAM in 2007, the increase is even larger, (4,000,000,000)/64 = 60 million-fold. As a result of this dramatic increase in semiconductor memory density, combined with an equally large reduction of cost-per-bit capacity, from 1980 to 2020, semiconductor memories, both SRAM and DRAM, have been the dominant memory for all computing systems.

Since 2010, DRAM density scaling has slowed as the number of electrons on each DRAM capacitor reached a few hundred, increasing the challenge of keeping leakage to acceptable levels (Figure 5.6). As a result, the state-of-the-art DRAM chips in 2019 were 8 gigabits – only twice the per-chip capacity of those available in 2007.

The slowing increase in DRAM density has created a growing interest in alternative memory technologies. Of these, the most promising is the phase-change technology, part of a larger class of so-called resistive RAMs (ReRAM). The idea in these technologies is to encode a bit in the phase change of a material, called an Ovonic material, inducing this change with heat or electrical current and detecting the phase change (i.e. reading the bit) as a change in resistance. These resistive RAM technologies have the potential to scale far denser than DRAM, and are simple enough to be fabricated in deep three-dimensional stacks. A leading example is Intel and Micron's 3D Xpoint technology (see Figure 5.7). Despite higher densities and good read performance, these technologies have been slow to catch on because of poor write performance and wear-out. Compared to DRAM, these phase-change memories have higher write

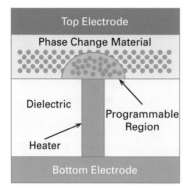
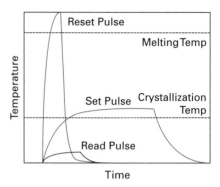
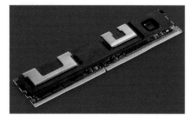

Figure 5.7 A new memory technology uses the phase changes of Ovonic materials to encode a bit. Heat or current creates a crystalline or amorphous structure. These memories are persistent – that is, they keep their bit values when powered off.

latencies and energies, and lower write bandwidths. Further, they have a limited number of write cycles before failing (wear-out).

Principle 5.1: Memory Technologies Change and Progress

Computer memories have progressed through several technologies, including mercury delay lines, magnetic cores, and charge-based semiconductor memories. Semiconductor DRAM has been the mainstream technology for 40 years, from 1980 to the present. With slowing improvement of DRAM, new technologies continue to emerge, but daunting requirements of density, performance, and cost make it difficult for a new technology to compete successfully.

5.2   Software and Applications Demand Memory Capacity

Semiconductor memories benefited from the same exponential miniaturization (microelectronics scaling) that produced the processor-shrinking that we characterized in Chapter 3. The digital logic in processors became smaller by four trillion-fold over 75 years, and thereby more than 100,000 times faster. Memories have seen similar size improvements, and as result, ENIAC's memories (8–16 kilobytes) are as fast as these modern processors. In fact, the ARM Cortex-M3 processor on a die shown in Figure 3.2 includes 4 kilobytes of SRAM. In the photo, the ARM processor is approximately the same area as 4 kilobytes of SRAM, and just as fast.

But modern applications and software use far more memory than the programs run on ENIAC. In fact, the growth of computer memory demands by software has been rapid and vast since the beginning of computing. There are three reasons for this:

1. larger, more complex application programs;
2. larger data sets; and
3. higher-level programmming languages, abstractions, and interfaces.

First, recognition of computing's broad utility and applicability led to new applications, and a rapid expansion of software complexity to, first, thousands and now as much as hundreds of millions of lines of code. This remarkable increase in software application complexity requires much larger memories to represent the software and its data structures for applications that are literally of global scale or model scientific studies at molecular scale. Second, computing applications operate on ever larger data sets – derived from sensors such as still and video cameras in the millions, and by the unceasing computations of billions of computers. Terabyte and petabyte data sets are already common. Finally, the adoption of higher-level programming languages such as C++, Python, R, Rust, Swift, and JavaScript, as well as powerful higher-level frameworks such as Unity, Unreal Engine, and even Android and iOS enable small teams of developers to build applications of extraordinary scale and complexity. The higher productivity of these high-level tools are critical enablers for the explosion of computing applications for mobile devices, the Internet of Things (IoT) and the cloud. As a result of these three powerful drivers, the memory needs of applications and therefore the capacity in computing systems has grown rapidly.

To illustrate the growth of memory capacities, several typical computing systems are shown in Figure 5.8. We see the steady exponential increase of computer memory

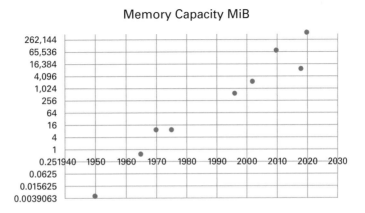

Figure 5.8 The growing appetite of software applications for memory drives greater computer memory capacities (1950–2020).

Table 5.1. Evolution of computer memory capacity.

System type	Technology	Memory capacity	Size	Clock period
Electronic (ENIAC/UNIVAC), 1950	Vacuum Tubes	0.004 MiB	65 m^3	200 µs (10^{-6})
Mainframe (IBM360/67), 1965	TTL	0.5 MiB	400 ft^3	200 ns (10^{-9})
Mainframe (IBM370), 1970	Various	8 MiB	200 ft^3	115 ns
Supercomputer (Cray-1), 1975	ECL	8.4 MiB	113 ft^3	2.5 ns
Laptop (Compaq Presario 1610), 1995	CMOS	128 MiB	0.5 ft^3	2 ns
Desktop (HP Kayak XU), 1996	CMOS	512 MiB	15 ft^3	3 ns
x86 server (Google Node), 2002	CMOS	2 GiB	7 ft^3	0.5 ns
x86 server (Cloud Node), 2010	CMOS	64 GiB	7 ft^3	0.33 ns
Smartphone (Apple iPhone 11) 2018	CMOS	8 GiB	12.5×10^{-6} m^3	0.4 ns
x86 server (Cloud Node), 2020	CMOS	512 GiB	7 ft^3	0.33 ns
x86/ARM server (Cloud Node), 2022	CMOS	4 TiB	7 ft^3	0.33 ns

capacity from 4 KiB to 512 GiB (note the semi-log plot). In Table 5.1, we present data for the same set of systems, elaborating on computer size and clock period. The contrast between shrinking clock periods and growing memory capacity highlights the challenge for computers to meet application software needs at the ever-higher speeds computing users expect.

So, if memory capacity had remained constant, the progress of microelectronics would allow ENIAC's memory (4–8 KiB) to be as small as a processor; however, the rapid increase in the memory capacity of computers soon made this impossible. As computers became faster and more widely useful, computer memory systems grew from 4 kilobytes to gigabytes to even terabytes, as shown in Figure 5.8. In short, memory capacity has increased by $512 \times 10^9/4 \times 10^3 = 128$ million times in 75 years. This large growth in capacity means that memory systems are physically larger than processors – despite very small bits! And this larger size also means that computer memory systems are inevitably slower than processors.

How much slower must memory systems be? Let us revisit the physical size and clock period model from Chapter 3, and adapt it for memory. We will assume that the size of a memory bit is finite (and scales down with Moore's Law, just like the logic). However, the dramatic increase in memory capacity means that the memory

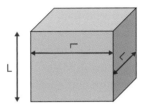

Figure 5.9 Manhattan distance and memory access latency.

system's physical size grows. We assume the memory capacity is packed into a three-dimensional space, and as before use the Manhattan distance model in Figure 5.9 to compute how the memory latency scales with size.

Principle 5.2: Memory Physical Size and Latency Model

To model the memory access latency, we assume the memory is packed densely into a three-dimensional cube. The finite size of each bit of memory and total memory capacity defines the smallest possible cube. To access an arbitrary word of the memory, the access must reach the farthest corner, and then return with the value. Thus, latency is proportional to the Manhattan distance between the farthest corners of the cube.

Applying the memory physical size and latency model, given that processors and memory have scaled down equally, the larger required memory capacity requires memory of physical size 128 million times larger than the processor. Further, the memory latency – the time to retrieve information from a given part of the memory – should have grown $(128,000,000)^{\frac{1}{3}} = 473$ times, relative to the speed of the processor. For simplicity, let us use the approximate value of 500. For a modern 3 GHz processor, the model suggests a memory system access time of 167 ns. This is very close to a typical memory access latency of 150 ns.

So, how to span this 500-times gap in memory latency and to do so in the face of continued rapid application demand for more memory capacity? Computer architects are extremely resourceful and have invented effective solutions that are the subject of the remainder of this chapter. These inventions are effective for a wide range of applications and computing systems.

Principle 5.3: Software Demands for Memory Capacity Create the Effect of Slow Memory

The voracious appetite of software applications for memory capacity demands rapid growth. Today's computers have 100 million times greater memory capacity compared to ENIAC. Despite extraordinary microelectronics miniaturization, this greater capacity makes memory systems much larger than processors, and produces latencies 500 times longer that a processor clock period.

5.3   Memory System Challenges: The Memory Wall

The basic computer structure known as the von Neumann architecture separates the processor and memory (as in Figure 5.1), and requires all memory accesses to pass through the **von Neumann bottleneck**. This architecture allows processors and memory to be scaled independently (memory and compute capacity) as well as to exploit different technologies. While providing many benefits, the von Neumann architecture creates challenges in both memory access rate and memory latency.

The separation of computing and memory operations is codified in instruction set architectures (see Chapter 2) with explicit generation of memory addresses to access a linear address space. It is a basic characteristic of all modern computer architectures, including the x86, ARM, and RISC-V families [40]. Some architectures accentuate this distinction further by allowing only a few special instructions (load and store) to access the memory. Because all memory operations must pass through the connection between the processor and the memory, computer architects have developed techniques to overcome the limits of access rate and latency.

Separation of processor and memory constrains the ability of computers to bring data from the memory for processing. To keep a processor busy requires a prodigious number of accesses to memory. First, every instruction execution requires the instruction itself to be fetched from memory, typically requiring one word (4 or 8 bytes). Second, 10–15 percent of the instructions in a computer program are load or store operations, and thus on average another 0.15 words per instruction needs to pass between processor and memory. Finally, instruction-level parallelism (ILP), described in Chapter 4, increases the instruction execution rate by 30 times, increasing memory demand to 35 memory words per processor cycle. When combined with the fast clock rates of modern computers (1–3 Ghz), these memory access rates are 100s of gigabytes/second, far greater than a sequential memory system can achieve. This growing mismatch is often called the "memory wall" [64, 114], as in "marathon runners hitting the wall" that makes it much more difficult to increase performance. The growing gap is illustrated in Figure 5.10, where the number of computing operations per memory access (operations/access) and per memory bandwidth (operations/byte) continue to grow at an exponential rate with time. The memory wall has been the focus of computer architecture research for decades.

5.4   Memory Latency

With processors that have the ability to execute instructions at tens of billions per second, (as in Chapter 4), how can we build a memory system that can complete memory operations (instruction fetch, load, and store) with latency of a nanosecond or less? This short latency is needed because each computer instruction needs results from memory in one or at most a few clock cycles. However, typical DRAM memory access latencies are 150 ns. So, a vast gulf of nearly 500-fold exists between a typical processor clock and DRAM access time. As we saw in Section 5.2, this gap arises

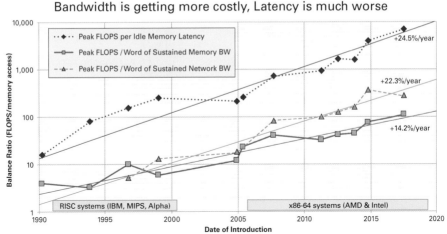

Figure 5.10 The memory wall: the growing ratio of computation/instruction processing rate compared to memory bandwidth (courtesy of [62]).

fundamentally from the physical size of the memory required to meet software applications' voracious demand for memory capacity. Thus, in short, the challenge is how to reduce latency to the high-capacity memories.

In this section, we discuss how computers "warp" space, reducing memory access latency and thereby enabling high-speed program execution. We will see that computers can not only make some memory addresses close, but also cleverly choose addresses to warp to ensure the most important memory values are close to the CPU. This technique is the key for modern computers to maintain high processor clock rates while providing memories large enough to meet application needs.

5.4.1   Warping Space–Time (Caches)

How can we make accesses to some addresses fast? How can we "warp space"? The memory physical size and speed model in Section 5.2 was based on dense packing into a three-dimensional cube, and the physical limits in communication speed such as the speed of light to reach the furthest corner of the cube. In effect, the model assumes a uniform access latency that is determined by the memory bits that are the farthest away.

Computer architects solved this problem with two key insights. First, not all memory operations need to complete with the same latency. Second, computers can "warp" space selectively, choosing the memory addresses. These two observations are exploited by **all** modern computers to provide the illusion of a fast, large-capacity memory.

To exploit these observations, computers filter all memory operations, detecting those on a small part of the address space to be served by memory close to the processor. This enables part of the address space to have a short access latency. Compared

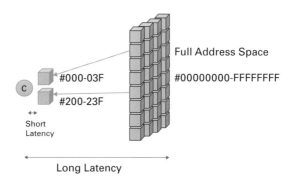

Figure 5.11 Warping space allows an arbitrary part of the memory to be closer, resulting in lower access latency. For example, addresses in ranges 0x000–0x03F and 0x200–0x23F are popular and kept in the small, fast memory. The address range chosen can be changed dynamically. The slow memory supports the full range of application addresses.

to the three-dimensional cube model with uniform access, the filter creates an effect akin to warping space, pulling a section of the three-dimensional cube of memory much closer to the CPU. We will see how computers both "warp" space and choose frequently used addresses to be close to the processor. These techniques are used in combination to implement what is commonly called **caches** or **cache memory**.

We illustrate the notion of warping space in Figure 5.11. For example, consider the situation in which the addresses 0x001F0 and 0x00200 are the most popular 8-byte (64-bit) words from a much larger address space, 0x00000000 to 0xFFFFFFFF. If the addresses of the nearer memory locations correspond to these popular addresses, then access latency for requests to those addresses could be reduced dramatically.

A bit more rigorously, let's consider how this idea is related to the memory physical size and speed model. We start with the idea that the addresses of the entire memory are uniformly spread out through the three-dimensional cube surrounding the CPU. The model assumes a uniform access time determined by the most distant memory, as in Figure 5.12. The large cube is the entire memory of the system and therefore is physically large, with high access latency. If you recall calculus and integration of three-dimensional volumes, it turns out that most of the memory is farther away, so this is a good approximation. In response, the computer architect decided to have varied memory access latencies, and then use a trick of "warping" a small address range (corresponding to the low-latency, low-capacity cube) to be closer. The address range warped closer to the CPU is accessible at both a low latency and higher access rate, because the distance has been reduced. It's important to reinforce that the closer memory, as in Figure 5.12, must have much smaller capacity.

However, even computer architects cannot overcome the laws of physics! Because there is much less space close to the processor (compared to the overall physical size of the memory), the short latency memories must have small capacity. So, choosing which address range to warp is an important challenge. The warped latency–capacity

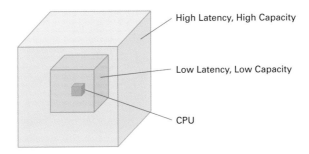

Figure 5.12 Partitioning the three-dimensional cube into nested concentric hollow cubes allows a small quantity of memory to be close to the processor and thereby accessed with much lower latency. The idea can be applied recursively.

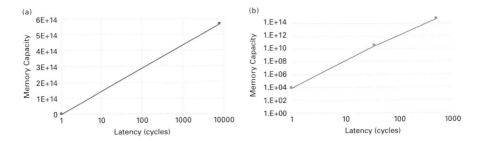

Figure 5.13 (a) Warping creates varied memory access latencies. However, the capacity available at low latencies is small (16 kilobytes). (b) Additional levels of warping create intermediate latencies and capacities.

space is illustrated in Figure 5.13 for a typical modern processor (Intel Skylake). The graphs suggest that for each 10-fold decrease in capacity, latency can be reduced 5-fold. The address range that can be warped closest to the processor is miniscule, as only about 16–32 kilobytes can provide access latency low enough to match the speed of the processor. An intermediate size of 256 kilobytes achieves a latency of 12 cycles. Finally, the full memory capacity of 6×10^{11} bytes (512 gigabytes) requires a latency of 500 processor clock cycles.

Thus far, we have not solved the performance problems of large-capacity memories – only presented some initial seeds. After all, how could a program use just a few kilobytes of memory capacity? Most modern application programs such as web browsers, games, and social network applications need at least megabytes, if not gigabytes, to execute. Further, application software has little interest in dealing with varied memories of different sizes and speeds. So, beyond warping efficiently, computer hardware must quickly decide which addresses should be closer to the processor. Because of limited capacity, it can only be a few addresses. Further, because of the high speed of computer instruction execution, these decisions must be made very quickly!

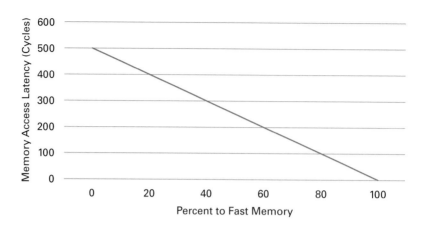

Figure 5.14 Warping has a "hit rate" – some accesses are filtered by the fast memory. If that hit rate is high, it reduces average memory access latency.

> Principle 5.4: A Small Amount of Memory Can be Close, Creating a Space–Time Warping Opportunity to Reduce Memory Latency
>
> *If varied memory latency is allowed, address range filters close to the processor can provide low latency for a small subset of addresses. Dynamic management of the address ranges provides the opportunity to have both low-latency access and large memory capacity.*

How much can the ability to warp space (address filter or cache) improve average memory latency? That is, if we compute the average across varied memory access latencies and use that as a measure of average memory latency performance, how much can we improve it? Let's consider a simple case.

Keep in mind that an address filter fast enough to match the processor clock rate could only capture 0.002 percent of memory addresses of a program using 1 GiB of data, so this is a tremendous concentration of memory address use. If 90 percent of a program's memory accesses used addresses in the address filter (cache), the average memory access latency could be reduced dramatically from 500 to a little more than 50 cycles by associating those addresses with the small, fast memory. The potential impact for a range of "hit" rates (a common term for filtering success rate) is shown in Figure 5.14. Clearly, hit rates need to be very high to bring average memory access times anywhere close to even 10 processor cycles. But such high hit rates if achieved can dramatically reduce memory access latency, and thus increase processor performance.

5.4.2   Dynamic Locality in Programs

Which addresses should be warped close to the processor?   Arranging software's memory accesses to a small, fixed address range is inconvenient at best, and a major complication to programming at worst. If computers had the ability to warp space for a fixed range of memory addresses, then to maximize benefit, software would need to place the most frequently accessed data into that "fast" region of memory.

To avoid this difficult, low-level software effort and attendant inflexibility, computers are designed with the ability to dynamically select address ranges for filtering. Modern processors provide hardware mechanisms that filter address ranges, associating memory addresses with the fast, close-by memory. This is space warping. And because processors operate with clock periods shorter than 1 ns, they must make these decisions quickly. This hardware capability is powerful, enabling the exploitation of **dynamic locality** – temporary, concentrated use of a memory address range. Such temporary concentrations are a common feature of most software due to structures such as stacks, loops, arrays, structures, and common algorithmic idioms. We call this dynamic locality, as it emerges from the dynamic evolution of the program and its data structures as it executes.

With the ability to dynamically select address ranges to filter in fast memory, the question arises – how to choose which addresses to filter? In short, answering the question: *What addresses should be close to the processor?* The best choices are those address ranges that will yield the greatest benefit in reducing memory latency for future accesses. A few simple rules are sufficient to capture a large portion of the dynamic locality in computer programs. These rules select address ranges as follows:

- memory addresses recently used; and
- memory addresses close [Address – k:Address + k] to those recently used.

These first of the rules captures the reuse of the same address or data as often arises in loops, stack frames, and procedure local variables. By keeping recently used memory addresses in the filter (cache), after the first use every subsequent memory access to this address will be captured by the filter. This means that the subsequent access will have low latency. The second rule captures the tendency of data structures, and their use, to be nearby in the address space. By using an address range of $2k$ bytes (a typical value for k is 32 in modern processors), the filter captures not only the entire memory word (4 or 8 bytes), but can also capture nearby parts of an object, struct, or array. These simple rules are depicted in Figure 5.15 and can effectively identify memory addresses that are frequently referenced; these properties have been conclusively demonstrated as empirical properties of most computer programs.[2]

Algorithm 5.1 is a more formal algorithmic description that implements these ideas.

While these rules may seem simplistic, they are the foundation of all cache memory systems in billions of modern computers. All modern computer systems use these basic rules to determine which addresses to warp close to the processor, and which ranges should be removed. But clever computer designers have added a wealth of minor variations and additional rules around them for smaller improvements. But essentially these few simple rules suffice to make decisions about what addresses should be warped close to the processor – to remarkable effect!

---

[2] See *Digging Deeper* for more references on this topic.

Figure 5.15 Rules for capturing dynamic locality. Recently used addresses capture references that are temporally close to each other – temporal locality. Nearby addresses capture references that access data structures laid out close to each other in memory – spatial locality. The filter rules capture the memory references indicated in blue.

Algorithm 5.1 Selecting Address Ranges for Warping

---

load(address){
    if not-member(fast-set, address){
        add-address(fast-set, address)
        add-address(fast-set, address+k) ;; add surrounding addresses
        add-address(fast-set, address-k) ;; add surrounding addresses
        };
    if out-of-space(fast-set){
        remove-oldest(fast-set)
        };
    };
};

How to Warp Space Dynamically   The key to understanding how a computer can warp space to make some addresses appear closer to the processor is the idea that the memory implements a mathematical **map** that is a function from memory addresses to values:

$$memory() : address \mapsto value.$$

A load operation reads the value of the map at a given address, and a store operation changes the value of the map at a given address. In a normal memory, the map is implemented in a regular, static layout in the three-dimensional cube. That is, each address has its value stored in a fixed location in the cube shown in Figure 5.9. To warp space and enable low-latency access to the most popular addresses, the challenge is to change the locations of an address and the map dynamically.

5.4.3   Address Filters (Caches)

To warp a region of address space close to the processor, computer architects invented the idea of an address range filter (also called a "cache" memory). These filters can

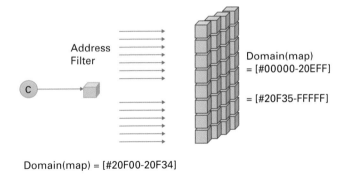

Domain(map) = [#20F00-20F34]

Figure 5.16 A cache filters the memory accesses, servicing the ones for its programmed addresses, and passing the remainder on to the full memory (and full memory latency). In effect, the map is partitioned, with the filter handling a small part of its domain – with low latency – and the slower memory handling the remainder of the map's domain.

be set to hold an address range from any part of the address space, implementing load and store operations for that range. The filter receives all memory operations and quickly decides whether it is programmed to filter each memory address, as shown in Figure 5.16.

The key to address range filters is to think of memory as a "map" or function from addresses to values. Load operations read values in the map, and store operations modify values. Algorithm 5.2 captures formally how this works for a load. With the idea of a map in mind, an address range filter must simply determine whether its range contains the memory address being accessed. To do this, each filter (cache) compares the memory address to its stored value of the addresses (address range or part of the "map") for which it is responsible. These are called **tags**. There are two possibilities. First, if the access falls within the address range, then the filter will complete the memory operation using the memory data corresponding to the address. This is called a "match" or a "hit." Second, if the access does not fall within the address range, then the filter cannot complete the memory operation, and the memory operation is passed on to the large and slow memory. Note that this means that using the filter increases the work required when a "miss" occurs. Not only is an access to regular (slow) memory required, but we have added an access to fast memory (address map). For a "hit," two accesses to fast memory are required (the address map, and then access for the actual data).

Algorithm 5.2 Access Filtered Memory Algorithm

```
load(address){
  if member(tags, address){
   return(load(data[address]); }
  else {
   return(RegMemory[address];} };
```

How does filtering reduce memory access latency? Because the filter holds only a few address ranges, it is much faster than the full memory. In fact, the time to access both filter tags and data can be as much as 300–500 times faster than an access to the full, slow memory. And the combination of a much faster address range filter (cache) and effective identification of dynamic locality can produce remarkable performance improvements.

Adding address range filters complicates the memory implementation. A natural question to ask is: Does this combination of a filter (fast memory) and regular memory give the correct results? More precisely, does it produce the same response to every load operation as the regular memory alone? We prove its correctness in Theorem 5.1.

THEOREM 5.1 (Operations on the [Filter+RegMemory] give the same results as on the [RegMemory])   *Specifically, given a sequence of memory operations $\{R_{i-1}, W_i, R_{i+1}, W_{i+2}, \ldots\}$ and corresponding load results for a regular memory (RegMemory), the sequence of memory operations returns the same load results on a filter and regular memory (filtered).*

Proof by contradiction.
First, assume a read R_j receives a different result in the regular memory and filtered systems.

Denote the immediately preceding write to the address in R_j as W_i. In the base system, the value returned by R_j is determined by the value written by W_i (definition of memory).

In the filtered system, there are several possibilities:

1. *R_j was serviced by the filter (cache). The preceding write, W_i, was processed by the cache, so the cache would return the value of W_i for R_j. This is a contradiction.*
2. *R_j was serviced by the filter (cache). But the preceding write, W_i, was processed by the RegMemory. In this case, for R_j to be processed by the filter there must have been an intervening action (say, R_k) to load the address's value from the memory into the filter (filter behavior). The value of that memory address was defined by W_i, so the filter value is the address's value. This is a contradiction.*
3. *R_j was processed by the RegMemory, then the value must have been loaded from the memory written by W_i to set up the filter entry (filter behavior). This is also a contradiction.*

Because all three possibilities are contradicted, the initial assumption of different results is contradicted. The theorem is proven. □

It is worth noting that cache (filter) design is an important activity in the computer industry today, and various optimizations are used to reduce the cost of filtering many address ranges (e.g. fast hardware hashing). We will consider a tangible modern cache hierarchy design and its full complexity in Section 6.2.

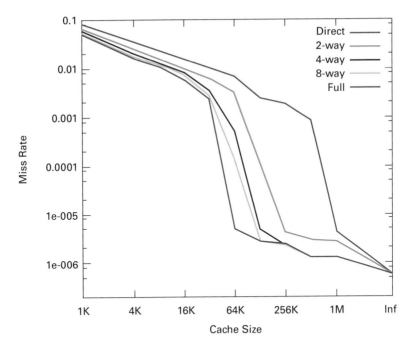

Figure 5.17 Filter effectiveness for data memory accesses on a industry-standard benchmark SPEC [58]. The instruction memory access miss rates are even lower.

5.4.4 The Effectiveness of Filters (Caches)

How effective can a small filter be? Per scaling of electronics, a filter that is comparable to the processor in physical size might have 16 KiB capacity. This size of filter (cache) can be effective even with simple rules for selecting address ranges for filtering. As shown in Figure 5.17, in measurements of the SPEC benchmarks behavior (a widely used suite of programs designed to evaluate processor performance), the application of a 16 KiB filter can produce match rates of over 97 percent or, equivalently, miss rates of under 3 percent. This remarkable effectiveness is a direct reflection of the amount of dynamic locality that exists in programs and reduces the access latency for 97 percent of a program's memory references.

> Principle 5.5: Dynamic Locality Is Plentiful in Computer Programs
>
> *Small address range filters are remarkably effective due to dynamic locality in the address reference patterns of most computer programs.*

The design space for address range filters is large, and the two most important dimensions of design are capacity and organization. Capacity is the total address range (say, in bytes) that can be held in a filter. Organization is the flexibility of the combination of address ranges that can be in the filter at the same time. In Figure 5.17, the impact of capacity and organization on miss rate is illustrated. The x-axis reflects filter (cache) sizes from 1 KiB to 1 MiB in powers of 4. Even for small filters of 1 and 4 KiB, the miss rate for the SPEC benchmarks is below 10 percent (note log–log scales). As the cache size increases further, the miss rate drops even further, approaching the ideal for a cache of infinite capacity (no limit to the data that can be stored[3]). In Figure 5.17, the different-colored lines show the impact of organization (from direct-map, 2-way, 4-way, 8-way, and fully associative) increasing the flexibility in filtered addresses that can co-exist in the filter (cache). These filters do a better job of matching, but are more complex to implement at the high speeds at which computers operate. We illuminate these features in a realistic cache design in Section 6.2.

5.4.5   Implementing Caches (Warping and Filtering)

Computer architects have been designing sophisticated caches for nearly 50 years. These systems implement the key concepts of space warping and address range selection to capture dynamic locality in application memory use. The resulting implementations are based on decades of empirical study of the access patterns from a broad variety of application domains and computer programs. The behavior of these programs is affected by programming languages, algorithms, and even programming style (e.g. recursive versus iterative).

In these caches, space warping is implemented via an optimized tagging scheme that minimizes the number of tag bits to identify each block of addresses uniquely. Caches further add status bits to reflect data modification (dirty), coherence with other processors (shared, private), and a few other features. To enable fast access, the caches are organized using a simple hardware hashing function, allowing the check for an address range to be done with a hash, and the time of a single fast memory operation – though several fast memories may be accessed. Other dimensions of design include:

1. replacement (which address range to remove);
2. prediction (which address ranges to bring in – anticipation of use);
3. flexible range filters (bring in part of a range);
4. multiple outstanding "misses" processed concurrently; and
5. many more topics!

There is a rich literature on filter (cache) design, and the interested reader is encouraged to look at the Digging Deeper section to learn more.

Principle 5.6: Space–Time Warping Exploits Dynamic Locality to Give the Illusion of Low-Latency Memory

Address range filters close to the processor can provide low latency for some memory operations. If enough memory operations are captured, this "warping" of space can improve average memory access latency significantly.

---

[3] Note that this is an "ideal" case that cannot actually be built.

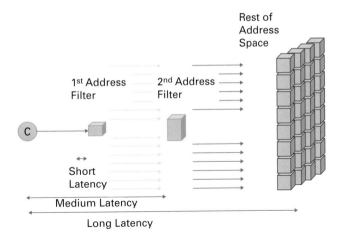

Rest of
Address
Space

1st Address   2nd Address
Filter   Filter

C

Short
Latency

Medium Latency

Long Latency

Figure 5.18 Recursive filtering: multiple levels of filters. They divide the domain of the map function across the levels, and collectively implement the full map of memory values.

5.4.6 Recursive Filtering (Multi-level Caches)

The concept of filtering memory operations with a small, fast memory can be applied recursively, creating a **memory hierarchy** of caches. The stream of memory operations that comes out of the first filter can be fed into a second filter, as shown in Figure 5.18, applying the filtering idea recursively. In fact, many current computer systems have three levels of filters (caches) above the regular memory (DRAM). The familiar address filtering and address selection ideas we have described apply to each level of the caches.

The simplest approach to managing a hierarchy of caches is to ensure **inclusion** – that is, all of the data in the first-level caches are also contained in the second level. All of the data in the second-level cache are contained in the third level. Because the filters operate on blocks of size $2k$ $(-k, +k)$ aligned with uniform boundaries of $2k$ byte blocks in the address space (e.g. 64 bytes aligned so that the lowest 6 bits are all zero), inclusion is maintained on the blocks. If a block is evicted from the first-level cache, it can remain in the second-level cache. However, if the block is evicted from the second-level cache, that corresponding data cannot remain in the first-level cache. Similar rules are also enforced for the second and third levels.

However, the recursive application works less well at each level of filter. This is because the filters close to the processor capture dynamic locality, leaving less opportunity in the filtered memory operation stream. Thus, in order to be effective, each successive filter is at least four times larger in capacity. This greater capacity implies that each successive level of caches has significantly higher latency. If multiple levels of filters (caches) are applied, then each is successively larger and slower.

To illustrate how these complex trade-offs are resolved, a more complex model is required. We will walk through the key elements of a real commercial memory hierarchy from multiple levels of caches and memory.

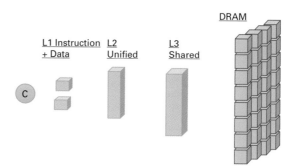

Figure 5.19 The Intel Skylake has a three-level cache hierarchy backed by DRAM. Each core (processor) has separate instruction and data caches at level 1, backed by a unified 1 MiB cache at level 2. All of the up to 32 processors shares a single, large cache.

A Real, Commercial Cache Design: Intel Skylake   Consider the memory hierarchy of a state-of-the-art server processor, the Intel Xeon Skylake-SP. This server chip has a mature three-level memory hierarchy as depicted in Figure 5.19. Closest to the processor there are separate instruction and data caches (filters), each of 32 KiB with 64 sets of 64-byte blocks. This means that addresses contained in the filter are divided into sets, meaning the hash function maps the current memory address to one of the 64 sets. Thus, each address can be kept in only one of these sets. Each set can filter 512 bytes of address space, and this is further divided into eight independent, contiguous address ranges of 64 bytes each. Access latency for these first-level or level-one Skylake caches is usually four cycles.

At the next level, there is a single level two (L2) cache with 1 MiB capacity of both address range and corresponding data. This capacity is divided into 1,024 sets, and the hash function selects one of these sets for each address. Each of the sets has 1,024 bytes of capacity, which is two times larger than in the level one caches. This means each of these fast sets can contain 16 address ranges, and as before each range is 64 addresses/64 bytes. Typical access latency for these level two Skylake caches is 14 cycles. For the fastest levels of the memory hierarchy, the number of sets is carefully chosen to be a power of two, allowing the hash function for set selection to simply drop some of the address bits (fast!). The eviction or replacement policy for cache blocks is simple for the L1 and L2 caches.

The third level (L3) of caches is much larger, with a capacity as much as 38 MiB shared across multiple cores on the chip (see Chapter 7), with a per-core amount of 1.375 MiB. However, a single program can use the entire L3 cache. The entire L3 cache has $28 \times 2,048 = 57,344$ sets, each with 11 entries. As with the L1 and L2 caches, each entry in these fast sets is 64 bytes of address range and 64 bytes of data. The L3 cache for Skylake typically has an average of 60 cycles latency, but because of its large physical size it is implemented with a range of latencies. For the L3 cache, with an average access time of 60 cycles, a more complex hash function can be used

Table 5.2. Key parameters of the Intel Skylake multi-level cache hierarchy.

Hierarchy Parameters	Capacity	Latency
Level 1 caches	32 KiB instruction cache	4 cycles (1 ns)
	32 KiB data cache	4 cycles (1 ns)
Level 2 cache	1 MiB unified cache	14 cycles (3.5 ns)
Level 3 cache	38 MiB unified cache	60 cycles (15 ns)
	Shared across 32 cores	

to flexibly exploit the tens of thousands of sets. The replacement policy for the L3 cache can be complex and even involve pattern-matching across multiple memory accesses for the L3 caches. These key parameters for the Skylake memory hierarchy are summarized in Table 5.2.

The final level of the memory hierarchy is what is commonly called the memory of a computer system. This memory is implemented with DRAM as described in Section 5.1. The memory capacity is typically expandable, and might be 2–8 GiB on a smartphone, 8–16 GiB in a laptop, and 128–1,024 GiB in a server. A high-performance server DRAM system is 6 channels × 2666 Mhz, with an aggregate bandwidth of 128 GB/s and estimated latency of 500 cycles (150 ns) for a processor at 3.5 Ghz.

Principle 5.7: Simple Address Filters Combined into Hierarchies Efficiently Capture Dynamic Locality

With simple rules for control, caches (filters) can effectively capture empirically observed dynamic locality in memory accesses. A set of simple rules determines the address ranges assigned to filters and is approximated in commercial caches with fast hardware implementations. The result is fast hierarchies of filters that efficiently exploit dynamic locality to reduce memory access latency.

5.4.7 Modeling Average Memory Hierarchy Performance

In Section 5.4.1 we introduced the idea of warping space to reduce the access latency of some memory accesses. The warping means that the access time for memory is varied – some accesses would be fast, and others slow. It was easy to reason about access latency when we had only one type of memory, but a more complex model is required when there is varied memory access latency arising from multiple levels of caches, a **memory hierarchy**. A basic approach used to estimate average performance is to combine the "hit" rates and latencies at each level into an average. Recall that a "hit" is defined as when the desired address for a memory operation is found in a filter (cache). With this statistic, an average memory access latency can be calculated using

Table 5.3. Notation for modeling memory hierarchy performance.

Term	Definition
$fl[x]$	Latency of filter x
$hit[x]$	Hit rate of filter x
$mr[x]$	Fraction of memory operations after filter x; $mr[x] = (1 - hit[x - 1]) \times mr[x - 1]; mr[0] = 1$
max	Number of filters + 1
$fl[max]$	Regular memory latency $= 500 \times fl[1]$
$hit[max]$	1 (regular memory serves all requests)
AMAT	Average memory access time (latency)

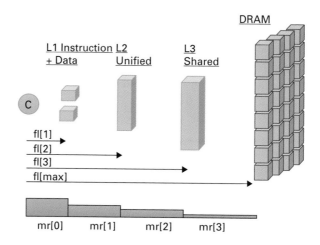

Figure 5.20 Illustrating the multi-level memory hierarchy notation – filter latency ($fl[x]$), and the remaining traffic at each level $mr[x]$. The traffic decreases by $(1-hit[x])$ at each level.

the notation defined in Table 5.3. Thus, the average memory access time (AMAT) is the composition of accrued latency at each level as follows:

$$\text{AMAT} = \sum_{x=1}^{max} fl[x] \times hit[x] \times mr[x - 1], \tag{5.1}$$

where each term in the sum ($fl[x] \times hit[x] \times mr[x-1]$) captures the latency contribution of the memory operations that are serviced by the xth filter. The regular memory is a special case because it serves all requests it receives, and it has a latency of 500 times the computer clock period. The concepts of AMAT and their relation to the cache hierarchy are illustrated in Figure 5.20.

The AMAT formula captures the behavior of the hardware for a specific memory hierarchy (set of caches and memory), and a variant of this formula is used by computer architects to design memory hierarchies using large computer applications and large simulations of their behavior [40]. This approach captures average application behavior – an appropriate goal for a hardware designer or perhaps a buyer of computing equipment.

However, for a software architect or application developer, AMAT is not the most useful. There are two basic problems with it. First, the terms $hit[x]$ (effectiveness of filter x) and $fl[x]$ (latency of filter x) used to compute AMAT are averages across large suites of programs, and in any particular application these statistics will vary depending on application behavior. Second, as we saw in Chapter 4, sophisticated instruction execution engines can execute instructions in parallel, out-of-order, and even speculatively. For this reason, how a varied collection of memory operation latencies (e.g. a load instruction) contributes to overall program execution time is unclear. These two shortcomings mean that AMAT often does not accurately predict memory hierarchy performance for a specific application. Further, we know that an application designer can choose algorithms and data structures that increase dynamic locality, improving filter effectiveness. Beyond that, compilers can rearrange program structure to increase locality. As a consequence, application developers need a different perspective, one we will visit in Section 5.6.

5.5   Why Caches Work so Well and Programming for Locality

Computers can exploit dynamic locality extremely well. For example, a recent research publication studying datacenter applications documented instruction cache hit rates of 99.7 percent (first level or L1). In fact, the authors were concerned that the cost of fetching instructions became a serious performance problem when the same hit rates fell to 98.9 percent [1]. These stratospheric hit rates illustrate that filters (caches) are so good at exploiting dynamic locality that the typical instruction memory access time is practically equivalent to the small, fast cache access time. For data accesses, in general miss rates are also low, but slightly higher than with instruction accesses. As shown in Figure 5.21, typical data cache L1 miss rates are below 3 percent for compute-intensive benchmarks (SPEC). For some applications the L2 and L3 miss rates are significantly higher (10–20 percent), showing the lesser effectiveness of the additional levels of memory hierarchy. This is despite their much larger size. These low miss rates are a key pillar of computer performance, reducing the effective memory access latency by over a factor of 100.

Why do these simple filters (caches) capture so much dynamic locality? The major reason is the bounty of dynamic locality in nearly all programs. So, it is interesting to understand the sources of program behavior (memory reference patterns) that give rise to dynamic locality. Let's discuss examples of program structures and patterns of thinking that naturally lead to instruction and data locality.

Instruction Memory Access Locality   First, let us consider program behavior. Programs written in languages such as Python, C++, JavaScript, and Java use control structures – loops, conditionals, procedure calls, and even straight-line execution

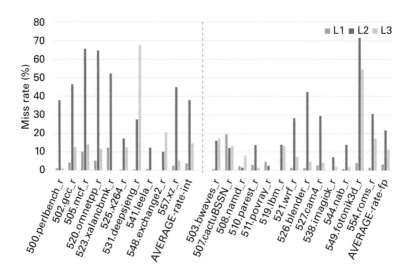

Figure 5.21 Cache miss rates (L1: 32 KB, L2: 256 KB, L3: 30 MB) for SPEC17 **rate** benchmarks [58], a compute-intensive benchmark. Note that overall hit rates are 97 percent (L1), 78 percent (L2), and 88 percent (L3).

```
for  ( i =0; i <N; i ++){
    for  ( j =0; j <N–i ; j ++){
        if  (A[ j ] > A[ j +1])  {
            tmp  = A[ j ];
            A[ j ]  = A[ j +1];
            A[ j +1]  = tmp ; };
        };
    };
```

Figure 5.22 The bubble sort illustrates common program constructs and instruction reference patterns, and creates significant instruction memory access locality.

that naturally lead to dynamic locality. Consider the bubble sort program in Figure 5.22. This simple program illustrates four major programming constructs, so we can examine how their behavior naturally produces dynamic locality in instruction fetch.

First, the straight line code in the inner loop and the if statement (conditional) produce sequential memory access for instruction fetch. That is, the references reflect a linear sequence of addresses (n, n + 4, n + 8, …) and thus are likely to be captured by [–k, +k] within each range of addresses in a filter. This structure is often called called **spatial locality** (locality in the address space of the program) by computer architects. In fact, this property is so pronounced that many instruction caches use large blocks of addresses, thereby increasing the hit rate for sequential instruction fetch. Next, the two nested loops over i and j, create a instruction reuse, fetching the instructions in the body of the j loop N^2 times, including the loop exit test.

```
// A utility function to swap two elements
void swap(int* a, int* b){
    int t = *a;
    *a = *b;
    *b = t;
}

/* Partition function takes last element as pivot, places
the pivot element at its correct position in sorted
array, and places all smaller (smaller than pivot)
to left of pivot and all greater elements to right
of pivot */
int partition (int arr[], int low, int high){
    int pivot = arr[high]; // pivot
    int i = (low - 1); // Index of smaller element

    for (int j = low; j <= high - 1; j++)
    {   // If current element is smaller than the pivot
        if (arr[j] < pivot){
            i++; // increment index of smaller element
            swap(&arr[i], &arr[j]);
        }
    }
    swap(&arr[i + 1], &arr[high]);
    return (i + 1);
}

/* low --> Starting index, high --> Ending index */
quickSort(arr[], low, high){
    if (low < high){
        /* pi is partitioning index, arr[pi] is now
            at right place */
        pi = partition(arr, low, high);

        quickSort(arr, low, pi - 1);  // Before pi
        quickSort(arr, pi + 1, high); // After pi
    }
}
```

Figure 5.23 Quicksort also creates extensive data memory access locality.

The instructions in the i loop (but not j) are also executed repeatedly, N times. This is what computer architects call **temporal locality** (locality in time) in the instruction memory accesses.

Data Memory Access Locality Program structures naturally lead to dynamic locality in data memory accesses. For example, consider the Quicksort program shown in Figure 5.23. This is a widely taught, efficient sorting program. Careful analysis of its data memory references reveals a wealth of dynamic locality.

In quickSort, the heaviest work is done by the partition() function that takes a pass through its section of the array, swapping data elements within the address range for the array (spatial locality). Each recursive call to quickSort() in turn calls partition() over a subset of the array, which creates data reuse (temporal locality). In a C program, the procedure calls are executed in a "left-first" order, so each successive set of recursive calls works over a shrinking subset of the array. These recursive calls touch each element of the array multiple times. Further, the recursive calls to quickSort() create a stack that grows and shrinks for the calls and returns, creating data reuse in procedure implementation. Not only does the program in Figure 5.23 have significant dynamic locality in data memory accesses, it also exhibits tremendous dynamic locality in instruction fetch by executing the small quantity of code in these three functions many times.

Let's look at the locality impacts of common structures such as a program stack, data structures, and arrays more generally. Each of these typically created sequences of repeated access to individual memory locations as well as frequent memory accesses to nearby addresses. These two forms – temporal and spatial locality – create an abundance of dynamic locality in memory accesses to be exploited by computers.

For example, consider the program in Figure 5.24. The program stack used for recursive procedure calls creates multiple accesses to local stack variables and repeated accesses that arise from procedure arguments (x, temp, xminusone, and other temporaries) and return values. In many cases, procedure arguments cannot fit in registers and must be spilled to the stack to observe calling conventions. Compounding this locality visible at the program level, the implementation of the program stack creates further dynamic locality, producing repeated accesses to the same addresses as the stack grows and shrinks. These may appear as logically different variables to the programmer, but to the computer hardware reuse of these addresses creates exploitable dynamic locality. Finally, other program data structures such as structs lead to spatial locality in the access to different members. Arrays also lead to locality as they are indexed with regular or repeated patterns under algorithmic control. So, remarkably, the collection of programming structures and practices designed mostly for programmer convenience turn out to create significant dynamic locality, enabling optimization of computer implementation with caches.

```
int factorNOT(int x,y){
    int temp, xminusone;
    temp = x+y;
    xminusone = x - 1;
    if (x<=1) return 1;
    return (temp * factorNOT(xminusone,y));
}
```

Figure 5.24 Procedure calls and local variables create data memory access locality.

Principle 5.8: Traditional Programming Languages and Data Structures Produce Ample Dynamic Locality, Rendering Filters Highly Effective in Reducing Memory Latency

High-level programming languages, code structures, and algorithms shape program behavior to produce ample dynamic locality. As a result, filters (caches) are highly effective in exploiting dynamic locality to reduce average access latency.

Computer Performance without Dynamic Locality? Dynamic locality is one of the miracles of modern computing. Without it, computers would suffer in performance (hundreds of times slower), consume more power, and cost much more. However, the presence of dynamic locality depends directly on the program behavior. So if programs do not have ample dynamic locality, what happens to computer performance?

To highlight this point, in Figure 5.25, we compare two program examples: (1) a program that makes sequential and repeated accesses to an array (high dynamic locality, Program #1); and (2) a program that makes memory references to random memory locations (little dynamic locality, Program #2).

In Program #1, typical execution would have all local variables in registers (i, j, sum), and the A[] array references are nearly all cache hits in the repeating reference program. Every array reference A[] will be a cache hit. In the Intel Skylake memory hierarchy, this cache hit takes approximately four cycles. The rest of the program operations take only a handful of cycles per iteration. However, in the irregular program, Program #2, while the local variables will be in registers, all of the B[] array

```
// Program #1
// Sequential, Repeated References

int A[2^28];   // a 4 GiB array
for (i=0;i<1000;i++){
    for (j=0;j<1000;j++){
        sum = sum + A[i*j];
        };
    };

// Program #2
// Random-like Irregular References

int B[2^28];   // a 4 GiB array
for (i=0;i<10000000;i++){
    sum = sum + B[(1000000000*i)/887;
    };
```

Figure 5.25 Two programs: random references, and sequential, repeated access; 887 is a prime number.

references will be cache misses. In a modern computer, Program #2 will run 50 times (or more!) slower than Program #1 because Program #2 has little dynamic locality. Because of this difference, the sequential, repeated access program (Program #1) gets tremendous benefits from caches, running at a speed as if it needed only a 16 KiB memory. In contrast, the random-like, irregular reference program (Program #2) gets little benefit from caches because the random-like references confound our filter management rules. We expect that every reference to the array B [] will produce a cache miss, potentially at multiple levels, all the way to the regular memory. Each cache miss incurs a penalty of approximately 500 cycles, dominating the rest of the execution cost for the loop, and producing the dramatically lower performance (>50 times). This forces the irregular reference program to suffer the high memory access latency of the 4 GiB memory. Thus, Program #2 represents the poor scaling of memory latency as application memory requirements grow to gigabytes and beyond. So, the extremes of dynamic locality can make as much as 50 times difference in performance.

Should programmers worry about this? Not for routine programming, and as it is difficult to write a program with such little data locality. Programs written in any of the widely used programming languages will generate substantial data access locality.

5.6   Measuring Application Dynamic Locality and Modeling Performance

Multi-level cache hierarchies pass memory accesses through a sequence of address range filters. Depending on which filter matches the request (or none at all), an application program will experience a different memory access latency that can vary by as much as 100-fold. Given that programmers do not often reason about individual memory references in their programs, it would be useful to have a way to measure and characterize a program's dynamic locality.

Traditional computer architecture texts discuss dynamic locality in terms of hit rates against a specific cache design [40] – in short, from a computer designer's perspective. A good example of this is using AMAT to evaluate computer memory hierarchy designs, as we saw in Section 5.4.7. Unfortunately, these measures are of little help for an application programmer who wants to understand the dynamic locality of their application program, how to estimate its performance with respect to a steep hierarchy of latency across multiple levels of cache, and finally how to improve the application program's performance by increasing dynamic locality. To this end, we describe an application-focused perspective that uses the concept of **reuse distance** and our physical latency model for memory hierarchies to provide a basis for reasoning about and optimizing dynamic locality and performance.

5.6.1   Measuring Dynamic Locality: Reuse Distance

The reuse distance graph for a program captures the amount of dynamic locality in its execution, summarizing it in a histogram of **reuse distances** for each memory reference. *The reuse distance is defined as the number of memory references since the previous time the address in the current memory operation was accessed.* For example, if there were 100 memory references between the first and second loads from 0x001F0000000, then the reuse distance for the second reference would be 100. The reuse distance can be computed for each memory operation in a program execution, and is a portable characterization of the dynamic locality of that program execution across different cache hierarchies and computers.

Consider our bubble sort program in Figure 5.22 and its accesses to the A[] array. Because the bubble sort program sweeps the largest elements from the beginning to the end of the array, its reference pattern for an array of size 8 looks like this:

$$A[0], A[1], A[2], A[3], A[4], A[5], A[6], A[7],$$

$$A[0], A[1], A[2], A[3], A[4], A[5], A[6],$$

$$A[0], A[1], A[2], A[3], A[4], A[5],$$

$$A[0], A[1], A[2], A[3], A[4],$$

$$A[0], A[1], A[2], A[3],$$

$$A[0], A[1], A[2],$$

$$A[0], A[1]$$

We are simplifying slightly by ignoring the loads and stores, and assuming that each innermost loop iteration only accesses the next element. This is possible if the compiler is clever. Looking at the structure of references, it's clear that A[0], sees a sequence of reuse distances 8, 7, 6, ..., 3. A[1] sees a similar structure of reuse distances 8, 7, 6, ..., 3. A[2] sees a similar sequence, but is slightly shorter at 8, 7, 6, ..., 4. And likewise shortening for A[3]: 8, 7, 6, 5. Summing these together produces the reuse distance plot for A[] shown in Figure 5.26. Another way to understand this is that for a second pass through the array (second row), all of the reuse distances are 7. For the third row, all are 6, and so on. The references for the first iteration are not shown, as they can be thought of as having "infinite" reuse distance – first uses of data. An example reuse distance graph for a more complex program is shown later, in Figure 5.28.

5.6.2   Reuse Distance and Dynamic Locality

The intuition for reuse distance is that the lower the number, the easier it is to capture the dynamic locality between the current memory access and the one to the same address that preceded it. More precisely, an ideal cache (one that always keeps the right address ranges) whose size = **reuse distance** would enable it to capture the memory access by holding data from the previous access. In short, it is possible for the ideal cache to hold the data for this address until this subsequent memory access to the same address. Typical reuse distance graphs start high at short distances and fall

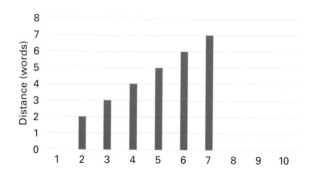

Figure 5.26 Reuse distance for A[] in the bubble sort program, using an array of size 8.

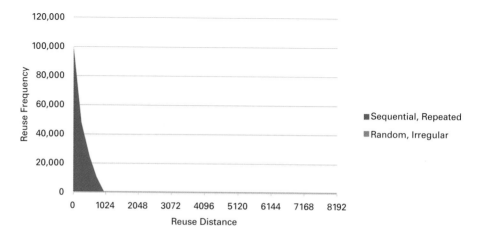

Figure 5.27 Reuse distance graph for the sequential, repeating program and the random, irregular program in Figure 5.25. The sequential, repeating program (blue) is close to an ideal reuse distance profile, while the random, irregular program (orange) is close to the worst.

as the distance increases. Many decline smoothly, but some have a more jagged shape, with the sharp features reflecting important thresholds for cache sizes.

An ideal reuse distance plot would have all the memory references occurring clustered at low reuse distances, such as in the sequential, repeating program shown in Figure 5.25. The histogram for that program would start out high and drop off sharply after a short reuse distance, dropping to a very low, nearly zero value to the right. We illustrate the reuse distance plot for such a program in Figure 5.27. Specifically, the sequential, repeating program has high data locality, making all A[] references within $8 \times 1,024 = 8,192$ bytes.

In contrast, a poor dynamic locality reuse distance graph would be lower on the left side, with a long, heavy-weight tail to the right. That graph would reflect many operations accessing memory that has not been accessed for a very long time. For example, the poor locality, random references program in Figure 5.25 would have a graph that extends far to the right, and has a much lower peak (or none at all) at the left, with low reuse distances as shown in Figure 5.25. With the intuition from what is a good vs. poor reuse distance graph, let's consider what profiles can be supported well by a given memory hierarchy system.

Principle 5.9: Reuse Distance Is an Application-Oriented Characterization of Dynamic Locality

A reuse distance is a portable characterization of an application's dynamic locality. It depends only on the application's behavior, not the computer, and thus is a portable characterization of program execution.

5.6.3 Modeling an Application's Memory Performance Using Reuse Distance

Given a reuse distance graph, we can estimate the effectiveness of a cache memory hierarchy. We can leverage the reuse distance data to estimate how effectively specific caches with known sizes will filter the memory operation stream. However, estimating with reuse distances assumes that the ideal filter entry management (cache block management) occurs, thus simplifying cache behavior such as block structure, associativity, replacement, and more. In practice, real cache designs do a pretty good job of approximating ideal behavior, so we can use the combination of cache sizes and reuse distances to accurately estimate memory hierarchy performance for the application program.

We use the simplifying assumption that a cache of size X captures all reuse of distances $<X$. This is not strictly true, but depends in turn on the assumption that the computer architect–designed cache policies are good, and their behavior is close to ideal. With this assumption, we can annotate the reuse distance graph to indicate the memory operations that should be captured at each level of the cache. We indicate these with a set of red boxes in Figure 5.28.

For each red box in Figure 5.28, the width corresponds to the size of a cache, and there is one box for each level of cache. What indicates good performance? By looking at the reuse distance graph with the boxes for the memory hierarchy superimposed, we want to look at the weight of the histogram captured in each box. This weight corresponds to the fraction of memory references captured by the cache. It is desirable for the graph to be high on the left; that reflects a large amount of data locality that will be captured by the smallest, fastest cache. For the performance to be good, ideally the number of memory operations serviced by each level should be 90 percent or more of the remaining references. That is, the box should capture at least 90 percent of the references to the right of the previous box. The red boxes shown correspond to a three-level memory hierarchy with cache sizes of 16 KiB, 256 KiB, and 1 MiB, respectively.

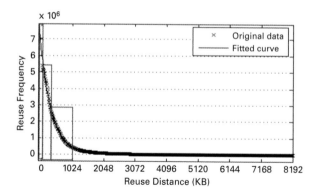

Figure 5.28 Reuse distance graph for the OLTP (database program). Annotated with red squares for each cache's ability to capture reuse (width = cache size). References beyond the red boxes are modeled as served by DRAM.

Reuse distance plots can also be used to estimate memory system performance. For example, using the weight outside the boxes, starting from the right, one can estimate the number of memory accesses to DRAM. Multiplying this number with the DRAM access time can be a good first-order estimate of memory penalty in execution time.[4]

5.6.4   Tuning a Program for Dynamic Locality

Another important goal is to enable application programmers to tune for dynamic locality and thus higher performance. Loop nests or chains of procedure calls can often be reorganized to improve data locality. Reuse distance is a good way to assess whether program changes are effective by looking for a shift of the distribution to the left. For example, Figure 5.29 shows a simple matrix multiply based on dot products and a tiled matrix multiply – reordering the computation for dynamic locality. The value **k** determines the size of a tile k^2, and directly shapes the reuse distance profile.

Introducing tiling, small values of k shifts the reuse distance profile leftward, and typical program tuning chooses the value of k to keep the knee of the curve just less than the corresponding cache sizes. However, for a fixed-size matrix multiply, at some point the reuse distance increases again as the number of tiles decreases. Such changes in reuse distance graph are a clear sign by which to track progress. Further, because the reuse distance is a portable characterization, tuning reuse distance may be both easier and more robustly portable than direct performance tuning on different machines. This portability is important, as over the lifetime of a large application the memory hierarchies of computers continue to evolve. Consequently, reuse distances turn out to be a good way to think about progress in improving data locality. That is, improving the reuse distance profile of a program will generally provide robust improved performance on modern memory hierarchies.

---

[4] This works well in many cases, but can be wrong if an application is not memory-intensive and prefetching is very effective.

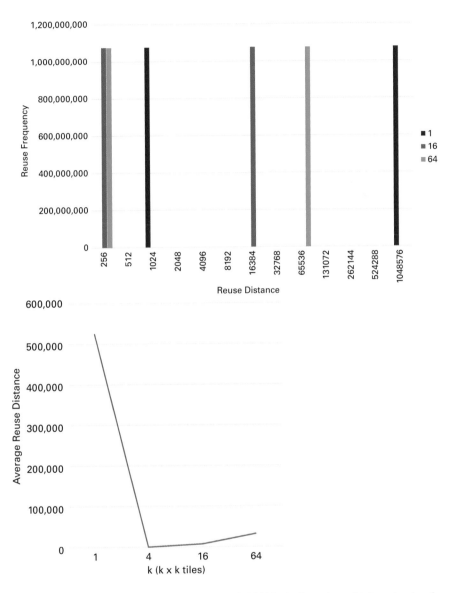

Figure 5.29 Reuse distance graphs for a $1,024 \times 1,024$ blocked matrix multiply, using $k \times k$ tiles. $k = 1$ matches the dot product program. Successively larger tiles shift the bars closer due to repeated use of one tile, and a second bar the repeating of a row of tiles. For a given filter size, there is an optimum tile size for a given matrix size beyond which larger tiles increase average reuse distance (right).

Principle 5.10: Reuse Distance Is a Useful Tool for Estimating Application Performance on Memory Hierarchies

Reuse distance profiles can be used to estimate application dynamic locality and the performance impact of a memory hierarchy on a specific program. Thus, it can be used to tune application dynamic locality for performance.

5.7   Access Rate and Parallel Memory Systems

The sequential state abstraction for program execution requires memory operations to occur in sequential order (as in Chapter 4). The execution of a sequence of memory accesses is difficult to achieve at very high rates. Further, to provide high-capacity, low-cost memory, computers use slow semiconductor DRAM memory.

Caches filter memory accesses, serving many of them well before they reach the DRAM memory system. However, even with high hit rates in filters, the resulting access rates can be high. For example, consider the three-level Intel Skylake cache hierarchy discussed in Sections 5.4.6 and 5.4.6. With the average hit rates shown for the SPEC 17 benchmark suite of 97, 78, and 88 percent, a single processor (core) that can generate two billion accesses/second would generate 1.5 million accesses per second. If the CPU chip has multiple cores, perhaps as many as 32 or 64, as described in Chapter 7, it will need a correspondingly higher access rate. Even for SPEC rate 17, well known as not demanding of the memory system, 45 or even 90 million references per second will be needed. Further, cache misses are generally expected in bursts, so the peak burst rates of misses could be as much as 5–10 times higher. Because a single DRAM bank cannot support such a high access rate, computers use a parallel memory system to achieve these high rates.

As in Chapter 4, computer architects have created techniques that preserve the **illusion of sequence**, while enabling parallel execution of memory operations. These techniques create memory system parallelism – a parallel memory system. The core idea is to exploit the fact that different memory addresses are independent – they do not affect each other. This means that operations on different memory addresses can be executed independently.

To increase memory operation rate, a memory system can partition the memory address space into disjoint ranges, using parallel memory banks to implement each range. Each of these memory banks implements access to a range of addresses, and thus allows many memory accesses to be executed concurrently. The idea of concurrent processing of memory requests is depicted in Figure 5.30, where contiguous ranges are implemented by each memory bank. More sophisticated designs are possible which interleave the addresses across banks, allowing adjacent words of memory to come from different memory banks, accelerating common memory access patterns such as reading an array sequentially.

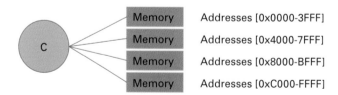

Figure 5.30 A parallel memory system distributes memory references to independent memory banks that operate concurrently. Each bank owns a subrange of the address space.

With a parallel memory system, a high level of parallelism is possible. To ensure correct program execution (sequential memory abstraction), if two memory operations attempt to access the same memory location (e.g. a store to address 0x0088FF00 followed by a load of 0x0088FF00), the accesses are serialized by the single memory bank, ensuring that both memory operations produce the correct result. Also, if a store to an address ZZ is followed by another store to the same address, they must also be executed in order to ensure that the resulting value in memory contains the correct value in the end. However, all of the concurrency in memory can be tricky for a software program – particularly if it is being executed out-of-order – so computers have a **memory-consistency model**, a which is set of guarantees the parallel memory system makes to the software [105]. This model serves to simplify programming. It reduces the situations that a program has to manage to ensure correct and repeatable execution. Examples of allowed and prohibited memory access reordering (concurrency) are depicted in Figure 5.31 for a memory consistency model called **total store ordering (TSO)**. The program order (sequential abstraction) generates the sequence of operations shown in the leftmost column. The TSO example is allowed because interchanging the store to X3 and the load from X2 does not produce any observable differences.

The second column shows a correct order, based on Intel's TSO memory consistency model. This model does not allow stores to pass each other nor does it allow loads and stores to the same address to pass each other. The rightmost column depicts an incorrect order where the Store X4, B passes a store to the same address, B, producing the wrong final value. That is, interchanging the Store X4 and Store X5 operations is not allowed because it changes the order of the stores.

In modern main memory systems, a high degree of parallelism is used to increase the operation execution rate. These units of parallelism are called "banks" and "channels" in DDR systems. But not only is there parallelism across channels, but a high performance processor typically includes multiple memory controllers of double data-rate synchronous DRAM or SD DDR. For example, the AMD Zen 2 can support eight-channel DDR, each of which can support a stream of memory requests. However, as we will see, Zen 2 servers have many cores sharing that memory system.

Sequential (Program) Order	Allowed Order (TSO)	Not Allowed Order
lw x1, A(x0)	lw x1, A(x0)	lw x1, A(x0)
lw x2, B(x0)	sw x3, A(x0)	lw x2, B(x0)
sw x3, A(x0)	lw x2, B(x0)	sw x3, A(x0)
sw x4, B(x0)	sw x4, B(x0)	sw x5, B(x0)
sw x5, B(x0)	sw x5, B(x0)	sw x4, B(x0)

Figure 5.31 Memory accesses and ordering requirements; the green order changes are correct, but the red ones are not.

In practice, memory parallelism is limited by interface and control overheads with access rates in the ten of millions of requests per second, far lower than the instruction processing rates of modern computers. As covered in Chapter 3, miniaturization enabled each processor to execute instructions at tens of billions per second. So, computer architects created novel techniques that both reduce memory access latency and increase memory operation rate.

Principle 5.11: Memory Access Performance Is Critical for Computer Performance

The large memory capacity required by application software creates both the memory access bottleneck and memory latency. Fortunately, most software has ample dynamic locality, and multiple levels of caches (memory hierarchies) can efficiently exploit it, providing the illusion of a fast memory. Reuse distance is a valuable application concept for estimating and tuning application memory hierarchy performance.

5.8   Summary

With the miniaturization of electronics over seven decades, a processor and memory have shrunk from building-sized (as in the ENIAC) to a fraction of a silicon chip. However, over the same period, application demands for memory capacity have grown over 128 million-fold, causing a major imbalance in the size of processors and memory. As a result, memory is physically much larger than the processor, necessitating the use of approaches such as magnetic cores and capacitors in DRAM.

While most of the memory must be far away, physics allows a small amount of memory to be close to the processor and thus it can have low access latency. To exploit this idea, computer architects invented the idea of warping space, enabling a small address range to be both fast and close. Using this capability to exploit dynamic locality, caches filter memory operations, servicing accesses in the selected address range with low latency. These address ranges can be managed with a simple set of rules that effectively capture dynamic locality.

Effective exploitation of dynamic locality allows programs to execute with low-latency memory access while computers are built with large memory capacities. The memory capacity of typical computers has grown from 1 megabyte in the 1980s to 1 gigabyte in the 1990s, to tens of gigabytes in the 2000s, and now 512 gigabytes to terabytes in 2020. These large memory capacities allow computers to handle ever-larger computations, massive scientific data sets, and the "big data" arising from Internet-scaling, as well as the pervasive rise of video and other rich data sensors. The exploitation of dynamic locality allows these large data sets to be consumed without slowing the fast computing engines operating with clock periods of less than a nanosecond – not even enough time to get a signal off the compute chip, much less reach the farthest corners of a terabyte memory.

The idea of caches (filters) can be applied recursively, reducing access latency of the original memory operations, the filtered set of operations, and so on. These multi-level approaches are a key element of memory systems in all commercial computing systems. While much discussion of caches focuses on reducing memory access latency, equally important is their effect on increasing feasible access rates. Without these benefits, computer performance would be dramatically lower.

For software architects and developers, understanding the dynamic locality in their programs is critical to increasing performance. Reuse distance is a portable characterization of data locality and captures dynamic locality in program behavior. It forms a useful intellectual framework for characterizing and optimizing dynamic locality in an application, independent of a specific machine.

5.9   Digging Deeper

Memory technology has evolved dramatically from the 16-kilobit mercury delay lines [17], the magnetic cores invented by An Wang [44] and exploited by Whirlwind [95], and a nearly 40-year run with semiconductor DRAM as the dominant technology. Jacob's excellent book on DRAM technologies and systems is the canonical reference for memory [50]. Recent developments around phase-change memory reflect the end of DRAM scaling and the tremendous continuing pressure (a 128 million-fold increase!) for larger memory capacities at low cost [101] to support memory systems well beyond 20 terabytes. Radical approaches such as DNA memory [9] continue to emerge.

The memory wall has been famously highlighted [64, 114], but existed for many years before. The slower growth of memory bandwidth compared to the faster growth of compute processing speed has been documented by McCalpin [62]. As the mainstream technology, DRAM continues to evolve rapidly in packaging to meet system needs. The last five years have seen branching from DDR DIMM formats to a variety of in-package formats for smartphones (LPDIMM) and GPUs (HBM) [57]. These formats forgo the modular pluggable memory architecture (DDR) that had dominated the industry for four decades.

Dynamic locality is exploited by caches, and computer architects have developed and refined caches for decades ranging from the caches of the 1970s [92], the multi-level cache hierarchies of the 1990s [76], and beyond. While caches are generally effective, the rise of graph analytics and other sparse computations on massive data have created interest in architectures that can perform well even without data locality. Although instruction access locality is typically high, the negative performance impact of poor dynamic locality is even greater for instruction references than for data references. For example, in a recent International Symposium on Computer Architecture (the leading research conference on computer architecture), a paper examining datacenter workloads characterized miss rates of 11 MPKI – about 1.1 percent – as problematic [1]. The authors then proceeded to propose a set of techniques that could reduce the miss rate by a further 90 percent, to about 0.1 percent.

The notion of reuse distance was pioneered in program analysis [25, 118], and captures the fundamental structure of memory references. Recent work has sought to extend this to parallel programs, providing a temporal notion of distance in such programs and exploiting information about this for the design of caches and memory systems. Reuse distance has become popular as a portable characterization of the data locality in program execution, and is widely used in performance programming and modeling.

5.10   Problems

5.1   Section 5.1 describes several different memory technologies. Each of these exploits a different physical phenomenon to encode information. Let's explore these and how they meet the objectives of memory.

Mercury delay lines encoded a sequence of bits into "waves" that traveled down a tube filled with mercury. Because the speed that these waves propagate in mercury is slow (a physical property), a sequence of 1,000 bits could be stored in an delay line of 1 meter. Each bit was about 1 mm long!

(a)   The speed of sound in air is slower, 243 meters per second; could we build an *air delay line* memory?

(b)   How long would it have to be to hold 1,024 bits?

(c)   How fast would the electronics need to be in bits/second to store and read bits from the new memory?

5.2   Magnetic core memories each store a single bit in the magnetic polarization of a ferrite core. Thus, writing to such a memory requires changing the polarization of the core (a small ferrite ring), and these memories retain their values even after the computer is turned off – the memory is persistent. Shrinking and efficiently manufacturing core memories progressed slowly and they were overtaken by semiconductor memories. However, magnetic random access memory (MRAM) uses electron spin to encode information in magnetic polarization. While growing in density, they are still trailing charge-based memories such as DRAM and NAND flash. Look up information on current MRAM products; how do their densities and read/write speeds compare to DRAM?

5.3   Charge-based memories such as SRAM DRAM, and NAND flash, encode information by storing electrons. This is easier than many other memories because the molecular bonds don't need to be reorganized. However, extreme scaling of these memories to high densities has reduced the number of electrons used for each bit to remarkably small numbers. Do a little research; how many electrons are used to encode a bit in state-of-the-art SRAM, DRAM, or NAND flash? Given that electrons are statistical entities, speculate on how much lower this number can go. Explain.

5.4 Phase-change memories such as Intel's 3D Xpoint encode bits in the crystalline state of a small lump of material. By controlling heating and cooling rate, the material can be made into an amorphous or crystalline state. Material in these states differ in their resistance, a property that electronic circuits can easily read. What kind of phase-change memories are available in the market today? How does their capacity compare to DRAM? NAND flash? How does their cost/gigabit compare?

5.5 In Section 5.1 we discussed four different memory technologies for storing bits of information: acoustic waves, magnetic polarization, electric charge, and phase-change. Think about other "technologies" that could be used to store bits in a computer.

(a) Describe three different ways in which binary information is stored in your everyday life. For each, describe what a "1" and what a "0" represents, whether it is persistent, and what causes changes in the value of a bit.

(b) Think about the different ways we have seen to store information for computers, such as punch cards, paper tape, magnetic tape, CDs, DVDs, bubble memory, and more. It is important for bits to be small, so that storage can be small. What is the smallest thing way to store bits that you can think of? Are there fundamental limits?

(c) Beyond small size, one of the important properties of memory in a computer is fast read and write operations. For some you proposed above, how long would it take to read a bit? Write a bit?

5.6 Some have proposed the use of DNA (deoxyribonucleic acid) that commonly encode genomic information to store information [9]. Given what you can find about modern sequencing and DNA encoding technology, answer the following questions.

(a) What density can be achieved with a single strand of DNA?

(b) A single strand of DNA might not be the most reliable way to store data. Describe a few ways to create redundancy that might make DNA storage reliable? How much do they cost in storage capacity?

(c) Modern DNA sequencing typically depends on amplification (copying) of the DNA strand before sequencing snippets. What would the read time be for DNA storage?

5.7 Memory scaling has benefited from the same microelectronic miniaturization as the computing electronics. Using the data in Table 5.1 that describes the size of computer systems and the memory capacity, what is the size of a bit of memory for each system (ignore the size of other parts of the system)? How has it changed over time?

5.8 The original 64-bit SRAM memory was approximately 4 cm^3. Compute the density of this semiconductor memory, and compare to a modern stacked DRAM memory such as HBM2 (see https://en.wikipedia.org/wiki/High_Bandwidth_Memory).

(a) How much has the density increased?

(b) Some forecasters project that stacked DRAM will only be able to achieve two more doublings of density. If that is true, what will be the final density of stacked DRAM per stack?

(c) As you have seen, stacked memory is typically deployed around the periphery of a GPU chip; this limits the number of stacks and therefore the total memory capacity. Explain how this idea supports the 3D latency model we have discussed.

5.9 The original 64-bit SRAM memory was approximately 4 cm^3. In this problem we will compare it to flash memory technologies.

(a) How does this compare to early NAND flash memories introduced in 1987?

(b) Compare its density to modern NAND flash memory chips such as Samsung's 136-layer 256-Gbit v-NAND technology (2019). How much has density increased?

5.10 Despite the rapid increase in memory density, the even faster growth of software's appetite for memory has caused memory latency to increase. In fact, the growth of application memory use is the key reason for exploiting dynamic locality. In this problem, we will explore several reasons for memory demand growth. For each, estimate how much application memory size may have increased as a result, and explain your estimate.

(a) Larger computer word sizes (16-bit to current x86_64).

(b) Larger programs – dozens to billions of lines of code.

(c) Higher precision scientific models, for example progress in modeling climate from 256 × 256 km tiles to 1 × 1 km tiles.

(d) Larger data sets driven by much higher computer transaction rates – purchases, web clicks, web searches, cameras, etc.

(e) Larger data sets due to aggregating these very large data sets by internet powerhouses such as Google and Facebook.

5.11 A modern laptop processor has three levels of cache, with the largest one approximately 16 MB. Take a picture with your smartphone and check the size of the file.

(a) How many photos from your smartphone would be required to fill the cache?

(b) The chances are your estimated size is based on the compressed version of the photo. This is convenient for storage, less ideal for modification. The uncompressed version might be five times larger; how many uncompressed photos from your smartphone would be required to fill the cache?

5.12 A modern smartphone processor has three levels of cache, with the largest one approximately 8 MB. The download size of a typical web page (including photos) has grown from 4 KB in 1995 to approximately 1.3 MB in 2020). How many web pages can fit into the cache?

5.13 A modern smartphone such as the iPhone 12 has a display with 2,532 × 1,170 resolution of full color (perhaps 3 bytes per pixel).

(a)   How much data are required to represent the full image on the screen?

(b)   Clicking on a web page often produces nearly a full new image (and more if you scroll). Given a 1.3 MB average download size for a page, how much data is presented? (Hint: it's more than 1.3 MB.)

(c)   When using multiple applications, users often "flip back and forth," how much data has to be moved by the computer for each screen "flip"?

5.14   The idea of dynamic locality, described in Section 5.4.2, depends on the structure of memory addresses generated by typical computer programs. This locality comes from many sources. We explore several of them below; give an example of each, and then explain why a similar effect would occur in most programs.

(a)   Program execution dynamic locality includes linearly increasing addresses, and repeated addresses. Give an example. Explain why this phenomenon would occur in many programs.

(b)   Procedure code reuse, such as in a recursive program or a commonly used procedure such as Python's "substring in fullstring." Give an example. Explain why this phenomenon would occur in many programs.

5.15   The idea of dynamic locality, described in Section 5.4.2, depends on the structure of memory addresses generated by typical computer programs. This locality comes from many sources. We explore several of them below; give an example of each, and then explain why a similar effect would occur in most programs.

(a)   A consecutive set of data accesses of regularly increasing memory addresses. Give an example. Explain why this phenomenon would occur in many programs.

(b)   A consecutive (in time) set of data accesses clustered together in memory space. Give an example. Explain why this phenomenon would occur in many programs.

(c)   A nearby set of memory references, repeated with the exact same structure, thousands or even one million instructions apart. Give an example. Explain why this phenomenon would occur in many programs.

5.16   In modern processors, the caches are large, as much as 16–64 MB. In this question, we will explore what happens to programs that use only a small amount of data. (Hint: this is a good way to make your program go fast!) Assume you have a processor with the three-level cache hierarchy described in Section 5.4.6, and you want to execute a program that sums the values (long integers) in an array with the following numbers of elements. Considering only the memory references, how long will the program take to execute for an array of the following sizes:

(a)   1,024 elements. The first time? Twice? Explain why.

(b)   8,192 elements. The first time? Twice? Explain why.

(c)   65,536 elements. The first time? Twice? Explain why.

(d)   524,288 elements. The first time? Twice? Explain why.

(e)   4,194,304 elements. The first time? Twice? Explain why.

5.17 Cache design researchers defined the three "C"s of cache misses (capacity, compulsory, and conflict). The idea is that compulsory misses reflect the first time data are used. Capacity misses arise from the limited size of the cache, so it cannot capture the full working set of the program. Conflict misses are due to limited flexibility in placing data in the cache – making it impossible to keep several items in the working set in the cache together. Consider the following program:

```
long A[1024], B[1024];
long sum = 0; sum2 = 0; sum3 = 0;
for (i= 0;i++;i<1024){
   sum += A[i] + B[i];
}
for (i= 0;i++;i<512){
   sum2+= A[i] + B[i+256];
}
for (i=0;i++;i<256){
   sum3 += A[i] + B[1023-i];
}
```

For the A[ ] and B[ ] arrays and a 8 KB direct-mapped cache with 64-byte blocks, explain how the references to the arrays produce compulsory, capacity, and conflict misses. Be specific.

5.18 We described two simple rules in Section 5.4.2 for selecting the addresses that should be in the fast set.

(a) Explain what common program structures these rules exploit to identify dynamic locality. Give two specific program examples, and explain how their behavior is captured by the rules.

(b) It is difficult to write a program with poor instruction locality using structured programming constructs such as for, while, if–then–else procedures. Explain why. Give an example of a program with poorer locality and make the case that it has the worst instruction fetch locality possible.

5.19 While filters/caches are highly effective in capturing dynamic locality in computer programs, there are cases where their behavior does not capture software behavior. A number of researchers have proposed that software can explicitly manage the small, fast memories. Typically, this is done by making one part of the address space fast (small memory) and allowing the software to control speed by moving data between parts of the address space. For the following programs, assume there is a byte array of fast memory, and the rest of the memory is slow. Write a program that moves the frequently accessed data into this fast memory.

```
char* FastMemory[32768];
```

(a) Consider a small program, say a bubble sort of an array long A[4096]. Rewrite the program to make maximum use of FastMemory[]. What fraction of the references are to the fast memory? What are the difficult things in writing a program in this fashion?

(b) Consider a larger program, a matrix–matrix multiply for a 16×16 matrix of floats. Rewrite the program to make maximum use of `FastMemory[]`. What fraction of the references are to the fast memory? What are the difficult things in writing a program in this fashion?

(c) Consider an even larger program. Perhaps a procedure that calls your bubble sort and matrix–matrix multiply programs. How would applying this idea of software-controlled locality exploitation scale up to larger software applications?

(d) The power of microarchitecture (hidden memory hierarchies) is to deliver benefits of dynamic locality without explicit software effort. Think about what you learned in writing a set of software-managed locality examples. Do you think this approach is feasible for large-scale software? Give several reasons why or why not and explain.

5.20 Take a full cache implementation description from a computer architecture textbook, such as Hennessy and Patterson [40].

(a) Analyze the features in the cache structure, including block size, associativity, replacement policy at each level, and explain how each corresponds to our two simple rules in Section 5.4.2.

(b) Pick two features that cause cache behavior to be less than ideal compared to our fast set and two simple rules. Can you give an example of a sequence of memory operations (addresses) in which the actual cache will give poorer performance than our simple filter (cache)?

5.21 Calculate the average memory access time (AMAT) of the following cache configurations and hit rates. The latency given for each level is that *experienced by a software program* when a hit occurs at that level, not that of an internal hardware structure as used in some textbooks.

(a) L1: latency $= 2$ cycles, hit rate 90 percent; main memory latency $= 300$ cycles.

(b) L1: latency $= 2$ cycles, hit rate 90 percent; L2: latency $= 12$ cycles, hit rate $= 90$ percent; main memory latency $= 300$ cycles.

(c) L1: latency $= 2$ cycles, hit rate 90 percent; L2: latency $= 12$ cycles, hit rate $= 80$ percent; L3: latency $= 30$ cycles, hit rate $= 70$ percent; main memory latency $= 300$ cycles.

(d) How much does the addition of the L2 cache improve performance? The L3 cache?

5.22 Using a local machine with a performance tool such as *perf*, write a program that achieves the highest cache hit rate you can for each of the following. Turn in your code and the perf report for each.

(a) The instruction cache.

(b) The L1 data cache.

(c) The L2 cache *and* maximizes the fraction of memory operations serviced by the L2 cache.

(d) The L3 cache *and* maximizes the fraction of memory operations serviced by the L3 cache.

(e) Describe the changes you made to increase the hit rate in each case. What limits the hit rates?

5.23 Using a local machine with a performance tool such as *perf*, write a program that gets the lowest cache hit rate you can achieve for the following. Turn in your code and the perf report for each.

(a) The instruction cache.

(b) The L1 data cache.

(c) The L2 cache.

(d) The L3 cache.

(e) Describe the structure of references you used to produce low hit rates in each case. How likely are these to occur in a realistic application? Can you imagine an example? (Hint: think about randomized data structures.)

5.24 Take a common suite of benchmarks such as the PARSEC benchmarks (https://parsec.cs.princeton.edu). Run the benchmarks on a modern microprocessor using a performance tool that gives you access to cache performance counters, such as perf ("perf stat [program]"). Further information can be found at the perf wiki: https://perf.wiki.kernel.org/index.php/

(a) Present the cache performance statistics for each benchmark. How well does each cache (L1, L2, L3) work for each benchmark. Are all of them necessary for all benchmarks?

(b) Compute the AMAT for each application kernel.

(c) What is the geometric mean for the average memory latency? How well do the caches work?

5.25 Take the matrix multiply example from Figure 4.18. We will analyze reuse and cache performance for a variety of matrix sizes. For all parts of this problem, consider only the memory references for the matrix access.

(a) Calculate the reuse distance for matrix sizes (N values) of 16, 64, and 128. You can assume that the values in the A[ ], B[ ], and Result[ ] matrices are 64-bit quantities. The reuse distance on the x-axis should have units of memory references, words, or bytes, but make sure it is labeled clearly. How does the size of the matrix affect the reuse distance graph?

(b) Consider the performance of a cache hierarchy with L1: latency $= 4$ cycles; L2: latency $= 12$ cycles; main memory $= 300$ cycles. For each size, calculate AMAT, estimated from the reuse distance profile. How does the matrix size affect the AMAT for the memory hierarchy?

(c) Matrix multiplication is considered a very friendly application for caches. Can you rewrite the application to give even better cache results (and reuse distance graph) than we saw above in the earlier parts of this question?

5.26 Extend the idea of optimizing reuse distance in an application for better dynamic locality. Consider two sorting algorithms, the bubble sort discussed in Chapter 2, and a Hoare's Quicksort (a recursive sorting program) that you may have seen in an algorithms class, or can quickly find on the web.

(a) Consider reuse distances for reference to the array being sorted (let's call it A[ ] for convenience). For bubble sort, plot the reuse distance for references for an array of size $N = 1,024$. For simplicity, you can assume that the algorithm always swaps items when there is a conditional test.

(b) Consider reuse distances for reference to the array being sorted (let's call it A[ ] for convenience). For the recursive quicksort, plot the reuse distance for references for an array of size $N = 1,024$. For simplicity, you can assume that the algorithm always swaps items when there is a conditional.

(c) These two sorting algorithms compute the same result (a sorted array). How much of a difference does the choice of algorithm make for the reuse distance profile?

(d) Pick some larger, more realistic sizes of arrays, say one million entries (8 megabytes). Mapping these data sets onto realistic memory hierarchy sizes and latencies such as the Skylake processor, use the reuse distance model you created to estimate the average memory access time (and therefore performance) in sorting a one million element array for each algorithm. What is the difference between them?

5.27 Many programs have poorer reuse distance behavior than matrix multiply. Pick one of your favorite algorithms and repeat the three steps in Problem 25. Be sure to pick a variety of data set sizes that are large enough to really work the memory hierarchy. How do the results compare to those of matrix multiply?

5.28 Programs can often be modified to improve their reuse distance behavior. Take one of your favorite algorithms, code it naively, and perform a reuse distance analysis. How does the graph look? Then, optimize the program for the reuse distance – characterize quantitatively, how does the graph change? Using a model hierarchy from Problem 25, evaluate how much performance difference these changes might make.

5.29 Pick another commercial processor's memory hierarchy, such as an ARM processor on an iPhone or Android phone. Find the best technical description that you can, and compare it to the system described in Section 5.4.6.

(a) What are the differences in the design?

(b) How are these differences likely to affect the relative performance of the two memory hierarchies?

(c) Can you come up with the reasons behind the different choices designers made for these two systems? Explain. (Hint: these decisions often arise from different application requirements or system design or operating constraints.)

Credits

6   The General Purpose Computer

What is computable? There is a practical answer to that question that is defined by the processors and associated memory hierarchies that we have discussed. This state-of-the-art varies over time with the progress of computer architecture and computing technology (as covered in Chapter 3). We refer to this level of computing performance as a general purpose computer. There is also a theoretical answer to that question, which we will address in Section 6.4.

At any point in time, the state-of-the-art for processors and memory hierarchies embedded in commercial CPUs defines what is practically feasible in computing applications and more generally computing. What do we mean by that? If all computers were 100 times slower or faster at today's costs, that would change qualitatively what applications are practical. Likewise, if computers were 100 times more expensive or cheaper at current performance, that would also change qualitatively what applications are practical. This "state of the art" or general purpose computing is defined by the most widely used building block, a processor (core). The performance of a single core, commonly called single-thread performance, broadly defines the level of computing capability. While the performance of a single core has increased rapidly for decades, its greater arc has been similar across the major computing hardware designs. In short, the rising tide of computer performance is not specific to one company, but rather to a general purpose, what we'll call a practically universal computing processor. We provide evidence to support this observation, and then contrast this notion to the crowning jewels of computer science theory – computational complexity of algorithms and computability theory, which puts even orders of magnitude increase in computing performance in perspective. The objective is to provide a user of computing and computing hardware a practically useful classification of the computing hardware landscape, and thereby a notion of practical general purpose computing.

6.1   A Commercial Processor: Intel Skylake

Before we compare them, it would be good to talk about a full-blown commercial processor design in some detail. As you will see, it has a strong connection to all of the architecture concepts we have covered.

Modern CPUs are composed of a set of "cores," each a complete processor. We describe the design and performance of a single commercially designed core that supports good performance across a broad range of algorithms and data structures. Such cores form the basis for general purpose computing; they can be used for all types of applications. An architect might call these processors practically universal – in an analogy to the notion of universal computing in complexity theory. Since 2005, modern CPUs have included explicit parallelism (multiple cores) – a topic we address in Chapter 7. We focus on a single core (processor) and associated memory hierarchy here.

Each of these processors employs the out-of-order, speculative execution techniques described in Chapter 4. In a modern CPU design, each of these cores embodies an extraordinary complexity, involving more than 100 million transistors and pipeline depths as much as 20 stages. We show the logical structure of a modern CPU core from Intel in Figure 6.1. It has two key parts, the "front end" and the "back end."

The front end fetches the x86 instructions that are of variable length – for the format, operation, and operands – ranging from one byte to as many as 17 bytes. It decodes the complex format of each part and prepares the instruction for execution by translating it into special "u-ops" – simple operations that match the hardware back end well. Each x86 instruction can turn into multiple u-ops, and the instruction predecoder processes 16 bytes at a time, which can correspond to one or several x86 instructions and generally produces a larger number of u-ops.

After that, the front end employs a number of instruction-level parallelism (ILP) techniques, including parallel instruction (u-op) scheduling and peephole optimizations such as u-op fusion. The u-ops are scheduled as many as six at a time for execution by the back end. Because the front end is connected to instruction fetch, it is the place where branch prediction (see Section 4.3.1) is performed. The predictions enable the instruction fetch engine to follow the speculation path, fetching the correct instructions for that path and filling the queues with those instructions. The queues are then used by the back end, exploiting the ILP across basic blocks that arises from speculative execution (see Section 4.3), and includes recovering from misprediction when necessary.

In the back end (execution engine), u-ops are executed in a pipelined and out-of-order fashion with as many as 50 operations executing simultaneously. The back end implements register renaming, and then maps operations to the yellow boxes in the EUs region. Each box is a function unit that can execute in overlapped fashion. The collection is diverse, including four integer units, four floating point units, numerous vector units (AVX), and a set of special functions. These operation results are all orchestrated by the scheduler, which performs renaming/reorder buffer (ROB) management with 224 registers. It also includes the architecture physical registers, where values eventually land (pink boxes). The back end includes a register–alias table (our map from Figure 4.15), and also reservation stations that were originated in the IBM 360/91 in 1968. The back end also manages cleanup when branch prediction/speculation turns out to be incorrect, as discussed in Section 4.3, by flushing the ROB entries beyond the incorrect speculated branch. Two other critical features are the instruction fetcher's connection to the instruction memory (logically through the instruction cache at the top of the front end), and a second interface to data memory (logically through the data cache at the bottom, in the memory subsystem block). The interface to data

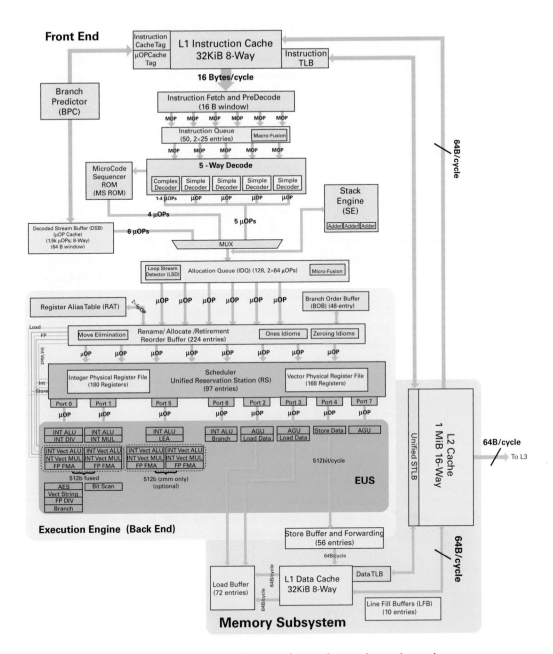

Figure 6.1 Intel Skylake microarchitecture: front end, execution engine, and memory subsystem. The microarchitecture corresponds to over 100 million transistors.

memory is complicated, including a load buffer that pairs the results with the right outstanding load instruction and a store buffer that coalesces small writes into larger blocks, and also provides loads that match store addresses with the new data values. Both the instruction and data caches connect to a unified L2 cache – the next topic of discussion.

> **Principle 6.1: Commercial Processors Use ILP to Achieve High Performance**
>
> *State-of-the-art, commercial processors employ the techniques for ILP described in Chapter 4 to achieve good sequential performance across a variety of algorithms and data structures.*

6.2   A Commercial Memory Hierarchy: Intel Skylake

The memory hierarchy of the Intel Xeon Skylake-SP is deep and exploits the address filtering ideas discussed in Chapter 5. The memory hierarchy has three levels of caches backed by a dynamic random-access memory (DRAM) layer, as depicted in Figure 6.2. The first two levels of the cache hierarchy are also depicted in the block diagram we described in Figure 6.1, but the caches are much larger than depicted there. The third level of cache, the L3 cache is also known as last-level cache, or LLC for short. The L1 caches are closest to the processor, and consist of two separate instruction and data caches of 32 KiB capacity each. Each of these caches has the same cache organization of 64 sets of 64 byte blocks. This means that the fast set of addresses is divided into 64 different sets, each of which can keep 8 address ranges. The address ranges are 64 long, corresponding to the 64 bytes of memory. Access latency is usually four cycles, and both of these caches allow one access per cycle, implying multiple requests are processed concurrently. Furthermore, even when there is a cache miss at this level, in many cases subsequent accesses can be processed while the miss is being serviced by the L2 cache and beyond.

At the next level, there is a unified L2 cache, with 1 MiB capacity, and 1,024 sets. Each of these fast sets can keep 16 address ranges, and as before each range is 64 addresses (64 bytes). Access latency is 14 cycles. *Unified* is a term used to describe caches that include both instructions and data. So, in effect, if we think of the L2 cache as an address range filter (see Section 5.4.1), it can hold 16,000 address ranges of 64 bytes. The L2 and L3 caches in the Skylake memory hierarchy are unified caches.

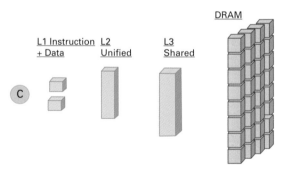

Figure 6.2 The Intel Skylake has a three-level cache hierarchy backed by DRAM; 32 KiB separate instruction and data caches, a shared 1 MiB L2 cache, and a very large L3 cache (1.375 MiB/core, as large as 38 MiB).

The L3 cache for Skylake is shared across multiple cores, and in the largest multi-core server chips can be as large as 38 MiB (see Chapter 7). So, one might think of it as 1.375 MiB per core. However, a single program can use the capacity of the entire L3 cache, so we describe its characteristics here. It has $28 \times 2,048 = 57,000$ sets, each with 11 entries. Again, entry in these fast sets is 64 addresses/64 bytes. The L3 cache has an average of 60 cycles latency. I effect, if we think of the L3 cache as an address range filter (see Section 5.4.1), it can hold $57,000 \times 11 = 627,000$ address ranges of 64 bytes.

The final DRAM system is six channels $\times$ 2666 Mhz, with an aggregate bandwidth of 128 GB/s and estimated latency of 500 cycles (150 ns) for a processor at 3.5 GHz. The six channels provide a parallel memory system to service the requests coming out of the three-level memory hierarchy.

At each level of the cache, set selection is done by using a subset of the address bits – effectively a very fast and cheap hash function. Operating uniformly on 64-block addresses-bytes makes the memory hierarchy simple and fast. We have 8 and 11 entries in each set, which is sufficient to capture flexible data locality, and avoids complex bookkeeping for large caches. Replacement algorithms are simple in both L1 and L2 caches because of their high speed of operation. The LLC has complex tracking of usage patterns that not only inform replacement, but also support intelligent prefetching of data from the DRAM. This is possible because the LLC is far from the processor and at 60 cycles latency there is time for more complex logical function and even some bits of state for bookkeeping. Furthermore, the power and latency cost of a miss at L3 typically goes off-chip (and in many cases off-package) to DRAM. The high cost of DRAM access makes it worthwhile to be as smart as possible to avoid that overhead as frequently as possible.

6.2.1 Caches and Power

A practical consideration of commercial processors is that they must run at modest power – to limit their need for supply and also the heat they create. Any increased power directly increases the cost of the infrastructure and operating cost for computing. We have seen that small filters (caches) can be used to satisfy most memory operations by exploiting dynamic locality (Chapter 5). It also turns out that the same filters (caches) dramatically reduce the power consumption required for memory access. Because the filters use small memories that can be packed close to the processor, if they can satisfy a memory access, the request and response need only travel a shorter distance. The information for these is transmitted across a shorter distance, reducing both latency and memory access energy.[1] This idea is illustrated in Figure 6.3, which depicts each level of the memory hierarchy drawn to scale for their capacity and physical size. The L1 cache (green) fits quite close to the processor. The blue L2 cache (blue) is 1 MiB, and because of its size must be some distance away.

---

[1] If you dig deeper into the technology, some of the technologies used for cheap, high-capacity memory such as NAND flash or phase-change memory can require more energy for access as well.

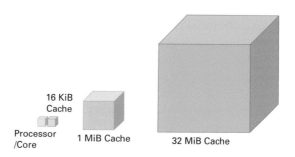

16 KiB
Cache

Processor
/Core

1 MiB Cache

32 MiB Cache

Figure 6.3 Three-level memory hierarchy drawn to scale for both capacity and physical size. Small capacity caches can be close to the processor. The smaller memory size and shorter distance reduces the energy per memory operation, and thus power consumption.

The 32 MiB L3 cache is even larger, and a DRAM memory of perhaps 16 GiB or more would be dramatically larger (not shown).

While often overlooked, caches, ability to reduce the power consumption of computing is critical to the viability of computers. Let us analyze the impact of caches on power consumption, using the commercial memory hierarchy we described earlier. In Table 6.1, we enumerate the capacities, latencies, and read access energies for the memory hierarchy in the Intel Skylake microprocessor core. Note that nJ denotes nano-joules (10^{-9} joules) and pJ denotes pico-joules (10^{-12} joules). The energy required for read memory access for a 64-bit word is reported for each level of the hierarchy, and can be seen to increase rapidly as a function of the memory capacity (and physical size). The smaller-capacity memories consume lower energy per access as well as having lower latency. We will see from this example that the computing performance that we take for granted would be infeasible from a power-consumption perspective without the use of caches.

To reveal the impact that caches have on power consumption, we first consider the power required if all processor memory accesses were served by DRAM. Then, by successively adding caches, it is possible to calculate how much power is saved by each level of caches. Consider a 3 GHz processor core. The instruction fetch rate for a single core is approximately four bytes per instruction, with an average of 15 percent memory instructions, then additional memory data accesses are $0.15 \times$ 8 bytes $= 1.2$ bytes/instruction. Overall, this produces a total requirement of 5.2 bytes per instruction $\times$ 3 GHz $\times$ 3.3 instructions per clock $= 52$ GiB per second of memory access requirement. At this access rate, the power required to service from DRAM would be:

$$\text{ALL DRAM POWER} = 52 \text{ GiB/s} \times 80,000 \text{ pJ/8 B} = 520 \text{ W}.$$

This is excessive power for memory! In general, the processor chips themselves are no more than 25 watts in a laptop, and perhaps up to 150 watts in a server. If we have a multicore chip (see parallelism in Chapter 7) with 28 cores, the power requirement

Table 6.1. Intel Skylake memory hierarchy parameters.

Name	Capacity	Access latency	Access energy
L1 instruction and data	32 KiB each	4 cycles (1.3 ns)	8 pJ/word
L2 unified	1 MiB	12 cycles (4 ns)	32 pJ/word
L3 shared	27–38 MiB	40–60 cycles (13–20 ns)	400 pJ/word
DRAM	1 TiB	500 cycles (150 ns)	80,000 pJ/word

for memory would be $28 \times 520 = 14.6$ kilowatts! For the rest of the analysis, we will focus on meeting the needs of just a single core to keep the numbers less outrageous.

With a decent hit rate in the L1 caches, say 90 percent, we can reduce this power dramatically, as shown below:

$$\text{L1 Power Savings} = 52 \text{ GiB/s} \times 0.9 \times (10 \text{ nJ} - 8 \text{ pJ}) = 468 \text{ W}.$$

This reduces the power requirement by 90 percent from 520 W to only 52 W. The two tiny 32 KiB caches reduce the memory access power by 90 percent, saving over 460 W! The remaining power of 52 W is still far too high, but adding another layer of caches, L2, produces further savings. If the L2 cache has a hit rate of 80 percent, it reduces the memory access power as follows:

$$\text{L2 Power Savings} = 52 \text{ GiB/s} \times 0.1 \times 0.80(10 \text{ nJ} - 32 \text{ pJ} - 8 \text{ pJ}) = 42 \text{ W}.$$

This reduces the memory hierarchy power from 52 W to only 10 W. A further saving from a similar hit rate at the LLC or L3 cache is as follows:

$$\text{L3 Power Savings} = 52 \text{ GiB/s} \times 0.1 \times 0.20 \times 0.80(10 \text{ nJ} - 400 \text{ pJ} - 32 \text{ pJ} - 8 \text{ pJ})$$
$$= 8 \text{ W}.$$

This reduces the actual DRAM access power to around 2 W, a remarkable reduction of 260 times through the three levels of memory hierarchy! This is still high, but could be manageable. If we have 28 cores on the CPU chip (this is possible!), then this would still amount to nearly 50 W of power, which is quite a lot. There are several reasons that we do not see quite such a high number for memory power. First, the hit rates are often higher than the rates we assumed. Second, if the resulting DRAM memory access rate is too high, the DRAM cannot service the requests at that rate, and slows down the computer's execution. This reduces the rate of energy consumption, reducing power consumption. For example, the hit rates we assumed would produce a 40 million DRAM accesses/second rate and that's per core, still pretty high for a memory system.

So, the results are very clear. Filtering addresses (caches) is a magic bullet in multiple dimensions. Cache hits not only reduce access latency, but also increase access rate (addressing the memory wall) and reduce the power consumed due to memory accesses. What a trifecta!

> **Principle 6.2: Commercial Processors Exploit Deep Memory Hierarchies to Achieve High Performance at Low Power**
>
> *State-of-the-art, commercial processors employ the techniques for address filters (cache hierarchies) described in Chapter 5 to reduce average memory latency and low power.*

6.3   CPUs Are General Purpose Computers

If you read the press releases of leading computer companies, you might think that each new product heralded revolutionary advances, and that the consequence of all of their innovation is that their products are incomparable. This impression would be wrong. First, a definition. Among computers, the definition of a general purpose computer is one that works well on a wide range of applications. The differences in performance of computers are "constants" from the perspective of mathematical notions of computational complexity. But in the context of processors, despite a performance increase of billions over the past seven decades, its is rare for a computing product to have even as much as a two-fold advantage compared to another brand. This performance parity is largely true for computers of today; however, this does not mean that every processor you could buy is within twice the performance of all others. Rather, because performance can be increased by simply adding more processors (and consuming more power), there are larger performance differences, that it can be attributed to factors such as larger chips, a newer semiconductor process, faster memory chips, greater power/heat budget, super-cooling (gamer systems!), and so on.

When talking about computers (or processors), we have meant a traditional processor (one core) or a CPU (a collection of cores). These processors are computing engines designed to execute programs written for the sequential state abstraction as fast as possible. These systems typically include a miniaturized processor (Chapter 3), aggressive ILP techniques including speculative execution (Chapter 4), and aggressive memory hierarchies to exploit dynamic locality (Chapter 5). All of these characteristics seek to execute a single sequential program (thread) as fast as possible. As a result, some have termed these classical computers "latency" engines, since they focus on executing the program path with the lowest latency possible.

While modern instances of such machines include collections of cores (e.g. multicore) that can process a set of threads at the same time, these collections bring with them the ability to minimize the time along a critical path or thread of execution. This is done without any help from the programmer in identifying parallelism, although the implementations often exploit parallelism for performance.

As shown in Figure 6.4, computing systems span a range of different operating power levels. Because these systems are scaled up by adding parallelism (post-Dennard scaling), computing throughput can be increased for each unit of power. Unfortunately, single-thread performance is more difficult to increase. For example,

Smartphone   Laptop   CPU
3 W   15 W   75 W

Figure 6.4 Differences in power account for most of the differences we see in computer performance. Higher-power systems can deliver more computing.

Figure 6.5 Comparable classes of computers have similar performance.

smartphones are limited to less than 3 W by the ability to get heat out of the system. Note that these systems are dynamically regulated, so if you find your phone running too slow (and it is hot in your hand), you can speed it up by putting it onto a cold surface or even in your freezer. Laptops are generally limited to about 25 W, and many users people have experienced a warm lap from the power coming out of a laptop. In a server setting, CPUs can be 75–200 W; one might think about general purpose (effectively universal) computers at each of these power levels, as shown in Figure 6.5.

Focusing on server-class CPUs as a comparable class of processors, in this group are Intel's x86 processors, AMD's x86 processors, and ARM's emerging server processors, all with comparable performance across their varied instruction set architectures (ISAs). That is, given the same power budget, area budget, cost, and other technology features, you would be able to build processors with similar performance. A good way to see this is to look at the highest-performing processors delivered by several companies over time.

In Table 6.2, we show the Passmark benchmark performance for single-thread CPU performance across a range of desktop and server CPUs. The examples shown include the highest-performing models of the CPUs available from Intel and AMD as of early 2020. Interestingly, in many cases the single-thread performance of the desktop CPUs is as high or higher than that of the servers. Note that across the six years, the difference between processors from Intel and AMD was never more than 25 percent; they have been in virtual performance parity.

Table 6.2. Single-thread processor performance (Passmark Benchmark).

Processor	Clock speed	Year	Passmark performance
Intel Core i5-4440S	2.8 GHz	2013	1,863
AMD FX-6350	3.9 GHz	2013	1,485
Intel Core i7-7700	3.6 GHz	2016	2,342
AMD A12-9800	3.8 GHz	2016	1,861
Intel Core i9-9900KS	4 GHz	2019	2,991
AMD Ryzen 9 3950X	3.5 GHz	2019	2,982

The highest-performing processors are usually the best indicator of what is possible because they are the least constrained by power, cost, etc. The lower-performing parts are often designed for a lower-power operation, such as a laptop or smartphone, or designed for lower cost as required by that product.

> **Principle 6.3:** Commercial Processors Use ILP and Memory Hierarchies to Achieve High Performance
>
> *State-of-the-art, commercial processors employ the techniques for ILP and cache hierarchies described in Chapters 4 and 5 to achieve good performance across a variety of algorithms and data structures. This breadth of performance makes CPUs general purpose computing engines. More hardware and power allow integration of multiple cores or accelerators, increasing computing throughput but not sequential performance.*

6.4   Perspective: Mathematical Universality and Complexity

It's important to understand that these tangible computers span a range of general purpose computing with similar computational capability. This is a much smaller range than the crowning jewels of computer science theory – computational complexity of algorithms and computability theory. The latter, computability theory, addresses things that are computable and those that are uncomputable. The former, complexity theory, divides things that can be computed into those that are practically computable and those that for most purposes cannot be computed precisely.

The fundamental underlying theory of computability posits that according to Church's Thesis, a function on natural numbers can be calculated by an effective method if and only if it is computable by a Turing machine. In effect, this means that all interesting computable functions can be computed by a Turing machine. Now, complexity theory divides the computable functions into polynomial time (class P) and non-deterministic polynomial time (class NP), the latter thought to require exponential

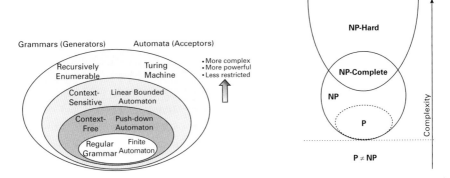

Figure 6.6 Complexity: machine classes and languages (left); polynomial algorithms, exponential for general purpose computers (right).

time. Computations are in class P if they are polynomial time reducible to P (a polynomial × a polynomial = a polynomial). This is illustrated in Figure 6.6, which depicts both machine types and their power with respect to these classes.

However, implementers of practical software systems are focused on finer, narrower distinctions in capability. Linear algorithms are practical; quadratic algorithms are practical for small problem sizes, but probably infeasible for larger problems; and N log N algorithms or poly-log algorithms are much preferred. Sublinear algorithms are considered a must for certain classes of big data problems such as data mining or sampling. Exponential algorithms are too expensive for any real use on problems of any size. All computers we discuss are Turing-complete, with the caveat that they do not have an infinite tape (or infinite anything), but rather a large but finite memory and storage system.

> Principle 6.4: Asymptotic Theory Complexity Governs a Far Greater Range Than the Differences Between Practically General Purpose Computers
>
> *Asymptotic complexity governs growth rates that range from linear to polynomial to exponential. These divide a vast range of performance, far larger than the constant factor differences among commercial computers*

6.5 Summary

The design of commercial processors (microprocessors) is built on the ideas of parallel implementations of sequential abstraction (see Chapter 4) and layers of address filters (memory hierarchy) that exploit dynamic locality (see Chapter 5). These powerful concepts, combined with technology scaling, are the drivers of computing performance. The industry realizations are quite complex and aggressive, but notably focus on innovations that hide that complexity from the software. Lucky applications! These techniques provide the rising foundation of commercial processors' performance that continues to advance computing across the economy and society.

If we compare state-of-the-art processors, we find that while there is healthy competition, the long-term differences in performance between the CPU cores from Intel and AMD remain small, within 25 percent, and leadership varies over time. Larger differences in capability come from constraints of product and deployment – how much power, price point for product, etc. – that determine how many of the cores can be employed, and how fast they can run. So, despite aggressive marketing, all of these products have approximate performance parity. Further, these CPU cores are designed for good performance across a broad range of algorithms and data structures, so they are practically universal general purpose computing engines. These basic engines underlie the revolution across the computing spectrum – from smartphones to laptops to cloud datacenters and even the growing invisible computing world – Internet of Things (IoT) smart infrastructure, micro-satellites, and more.

Computer architecture exists in the larger landscape of computing, complexity, and computability. Algorithmic complexity theory divides algorithms into linear, polynomial, and exponential. It is important not to confuse these with the large increases in computing power that have been achieved with the steady progress of microelectronics miniaturization that have yielded an exponential rate of improvement over time of both processors and larger computing systems. Our computers of today are more than 100 million times more capable than ENIAC, but applying an exponential or even polynomial complexity algorithm can quickly take us from a manageable time of one second to thousands of seconds (hours) to millions of seconds (months). It would take the computing power of millions of cores an entire cloud datacenter to match this, and then the next increase in size would overwhelm even that.

6.6   Digging Deeper

A wealth of information is published about new microprocessors and leading designs in a variety of online resources that review the newest offerings [85], and do extensive benchmarking for a wide range of common applications. For a little more in-depth view, particularly looking at internal design choices, limitations, and challenges, researchers in the field often refer to the Microprocessor Report or the annual Hot Chips Symposium [35, 46]. There is a wealth of information from leading companies in the field directly, including Intel, AMD, ARM, and a new open-source hardware community around the RISC-V architecture.

On the topic of general purpose universality, there is a long history of the competition between computer companies for the accolade of the highest performance. Some good resources are the Computer History Museum's "Intel and the Microprocessor Wars" [16] and "Great Moments in Microprocessor History" [102]. The rapid increase in microprocessor performance is well documented in CPU DB [21]. A broad view of accelerators can be found in several articles [8, 15, 27].

For a deeper dive into computational complexity, see the classical book by Garey and Johnson on complexity theory [30].

6.7   Problems

6.1   We explored the opportunities for ILP underneath the sequential abstraction in Chapter 4. Where are each of the following functions realized in the commercial processor design?
(a)   instruction fetch;
(b)   instruction decode;
(c)   register read and register write;
(d)   register renaming;
(e)   branch prediction: and
(f)   speculative execution. (Hint: this is in more than one place.)

6.2   In Section 6.1, we saw a commercial example, the Intel Skylake, a general purpose processor used in many laptop computers and cloud servers. This processor included a set of features that speed up general program features. For each of the features below, give an example of the program feature it exploits, and how it is exploited to increase performance (we leave caches to the next question):
(a)   front-end instruction fetch and predecode;
(b)   instruction decoders – four for simple instructions and one for complex instructions;
(c)   renaming engine and register alias table; and
(d)   execution units (various types).

6.3   In Section 6.2 (and in the diagram for the processor in Section 6.1), the three-level cache hierarchy of a commercial processor was laid out. Explain the rationale for each of these features of the Skylake memory hierarchy, and how they improve performance. They are common in other processors.
(a)   Two separate instruction and data caches at L1.
(b)   Cache sizes L1 smaller than L2 smaller than L3.
(c)   Cache latencies L1 shorter than L2 shorter than L3.
(d)   Complex, sophisticated replacement policies at L3.

6.4   Let's explore the idea of a practically general purpose computer.
(a)   What range of algorithms would you expect it to execute well? Explain.
(b)   Computers all have a finite memory capacity, and that capacity does limit the range of programs that can be executed. What is a fair way to compare whether computers are practically general purpose with respect to memory capacity?
(c)   In Section 6.3 we saw that the level of power that a computer consumes can increase its capability. Given what you know about power consumption of processors, how much faster (more compute capability) would you expect a computer that consumes twice as much power to be? Five times as much power?

6.5 In Section 6.2, we analyzed how caches can reduce the fraction of memory accesses that reach the DRAM, and therefore reduce the energy consumed by the DRAM. Recompute these power values for a program where the caches are less effective.

(a) Hit rates of L1: 80 percent, L2: 70 percent, L3: 70 percent. How much is the power? How much did it increase?

(b) Hit rates of L1: 95 percent, L2: 85 percent, L3: 85 percent. How much is the power? How much did it decrease?

(c) One interesting property of programs/computers is that as the cache hit rate decreases, so does the program execution speed. Assuming that the program's execution rate decreases with **average memory access time**, as defined in Section 5.4.7, and the reduction equally reduces the memory reference rate (from the program), what happens to the DRAM power?

6.6 The commercial memory hierarchy described in Section 6.2 not only has three levels of varied sizes, it has different sharing properties for the cache storage. Let's explore those properties.

(a) The first-level cache **separates** the memory references for instructions and data. As processors operate at high clock rates as high as 3–4 GHz, it is difficult for L1 caches to provide a high enough rate of accesses. Explain how separating the instruction and data caches helps with this problem.

(b) At the second-level cache, the Skylake system uses a **unified** cache, holding both instructions and data, and servicing the misses from the two L1 caches from a single L2 cache. Explain why this is possible.

(c) Assuming decent L1 hit rates for instructions (95 percent) and data (90 percent), for a 3 GHz processor, what is the average access rate for the L2 unified cache?

(d) The third level of caches is **shared** across all of the cores on a multicore CPU (see Chapter 7). This is possible because although the parts of the L3 cache (banks) are distributed across the chip, the L3 cache memory is slow enough that the time for signals to travel across the trip do not dominate L3 access time. Explain how sharing this capacity could help performance of a single core.

(e) If we had a 16-core processor, and each of the cores were operating on a completely different set of program and data, would the shared L3 structure increase performance? Explain why or why not.

6.7 Dig back into the early days of digital electronic computers. As commercial computer emerged in the 1950s, how much did their performance vary by design? At any point in the 1950s, what was the biggest gap in performance between computers from different companies?

6.8 By the mid-1960s the industry was dominated by IBM and the "BUNCH," an acronym for Burroughs, UNIVAC, NCR, and Honeywell. Among this group, what was the largest gap in their fastest computer performance? Plot the relative performance from say 1963 to 1969. In what year was the biggest difference in performance?

6.9 As discussed in "Digging Deeper" in Chapter 4, through the late 1980s and 1990s there was a long competition between "RISC" (reduced instruction set) microprocessors and Intel's x86 processors. Plot the performance ratio between the fastest x86 and RISC processor each year from 1985 to 1995.

6.10 Complexity theory separates computations into different classes that grow at significantly different rates. We will explore how different these classes are. For simplicity, we will ignore constant factors and explore only the growth rates.

(a) Plot the runtime for a computation that has $O(1)$ – constant time, $O(n)$ – linear growth, $O(n^2)$, $O(n^4)$, $O(n^8)$ – all polynomial, and $O(2^n)$ – exponential. Make the plot for the values of $n = [1, 4, 16, 64, 256, 1,024]$. (Hint: make both a semi-log and then a log–log plot.)

(b) How large does n have to be for the classes of constant, linear, polynomial, and exponential to be well separated?

(c) Consider the idea of a general purpose computer, as we discussed in Section 6.3. How large a change in n would we need to overcome the difference between the Intel and AMD CPUs? The ATI and Nvidia GPUs?

(d) Explain how to relate the notions of computational complexity and different performance among CPUs of the same year. Is one more important than the other? Explain briefly why.

6.11 Recently, there has been much excitement about the prospect of **quantum computing**. This is because quantum bits (qubits) can represent complex computations and structure through the entanglement of qubits. The coupling between qubits makes it impossible to reason about them separately.

(a) This property means that quantum computers may be able to solve problems with exponential complexity in constant time. Unfortunately, it's difficult to build quantum computers and the largest today have perhaps 32 qubits. Thinking about the complexity theory trade-offs, for what sizes of problems and complexity classes could a 32-qubit quantum computer have better performance?

(b) What about a 64-qubit computer? 128-qubit?

(c) One of the problems with quantum computers is that they suffer from a large constant "disadvantage" due to noise, input/output, and other issues. Suppose that makes their "clock rate" one million times slower than conventional computers, how does this change your assessment for the various numbers of qubits?

(d) What would be the properties of a general purpose quantum computer?

Credits

Figure 6.4 (centre) setthaphat dodchai/iStock/Getty Images Plus, (right) Javier Zayas Photography/Moment/Getty Images.

7 Beyond Sequential: Parallelism in Multicore and the Cloud

Sequential abstraction has enabled software to manage the complex demands of constructing computing applications, debugging software and hardware, and program composition. However, with the end of Dennard scaling (see Section 3.3.4), we have been unable to create sequential computers with sufficient speed and capacity to meet the needs of ever-larger computing applications. As a result, computer hardware systems were forced to adopt explicit parallelism, both within a single chip (multicore CPUs) and at datacenter scale (supercomputers and cloud computing). In this chapter, we describe this shift to parallelism. In single-chip CPUs, the shift has produced multicore processors with first 2 or 4 cores, but growing rapidly to 64 cores (2020) and beyond. Understanding of multicore chips, parallel building blocks used in even larger parallel computers, provides an invaluable perspective on how to understand and increase performance.

At the datacenter level, the rise of internet-scale applications drove the creation of scale-out datacenters (1990s) that can contain 25,000 processors and millions of cores! These massively parallel computing resources are accessible to companies and ordinary people as "cloud computing," and are used for the largest computations humanity undertakes today. We discuss these massive ensembles as another form of parallel computers, and show how they can be utilized for internet-scale services and data analytics computations.

7.1 The End of Dennard Scaling and the Shift to Parallelism

Around 2006, Dennard scaling ended as the benefits of voltage scaling were largely played out (see Section 3.3.4). Feature scaling to smaller sizes enabled Moore's Law of increasing numbers of transistors by increasing density (reduced area). However, without voltage scaling, power limitations prevented further clock speed increases, as shown in Figure 7.1. This led to a new age in single-chip computers, generally known as the "Age of Parallelism" or the "Multicore Era."

At the end of Dennard scaling, computer designs shifted to the use of the bounty of Moore's Law, increasing numbers of transistors to make a single processor faster or creating multiple cores on a CPU chip. This produced CPUs with 2 or 4 cores at first, but this is now growing past 64 cores per chip. This shift has had a major impact on applications and software, forcing them to adopt explicit parallelism in programming and execution.

Table 7.1. Dennard scaling and post-Dennard (parallelism) scaling.

	Dennard 1975–2005	Post-Dennard 2006 to present
Size (linear)	$0.7\times$	$0.7\times$
Voltage (linear)	$0.7\times$	$1\times$
Clock rate	$1.4\times$	$1\times$
Transistors/die	$2\times$	$2\times$

The resulting multicore CPUs are parallel computers, providing a parallel abstraction of multiple threads executing simultaneously against a shared memory. With multiple threads, each executing a program (which may or may not be the same program), the sequential abstraction breaks down in both software and hardware, presenting the challenges of concurrency, coherency, and consistency. Furthermore, the multiplicity of cores produces multiple loci of computation, requiring shared data to be communicated from one core to another. If software can solve these problems, the capability of multicore systems to compute (e.g. transform data) increases with the number of cores, giving them tremendous potential computing performance. But the price of this is new challenges in how to write, debug, and tune parallel programs. We will consider how to program these systems a little later.

Another way to think about it is that under Dennard scaling the quality of computing increased with each generation – as clock rates increased the speed of existing software with no programmer effort at nearly 40 percent per year. In fact, the empirical evidence has shown that the net benefit was over 50 percent per year (Figure 7.1)! In the post-Dennard era, the quality increase has not quite stopped, but rather slowed to 20 percent per annum. With a continued exponential growth in the number of transistors available, multicore parallelism uses the additional transistors to increase **quantity** in proportion to the additional number of cores, and thus an opportunity for a large performance increase with a substantial software effort (Figure 7.2).

Principle 7.1: Slowing Sequential Performance Improvement Triggers a Shift to Parallelism

Improvement of single-thread performance in the post-Dennard era is slow, so the rapid advance in computing performance comes from parallelism, which can be thought of as an increase in quantity (capacity or throughput).

The potential of multicore chips lies in the growing computing capacity, not core processing speed. In an ideal case, a computation could be divided across the multiple cores with little required communication and coordination. If such were true, employing parallelism in hardware effectively could produce close to **linear speed-up**, as shown in Figure 7.2. That is, the application would achieve a performance improvement in accord with the growth in computing capacity.

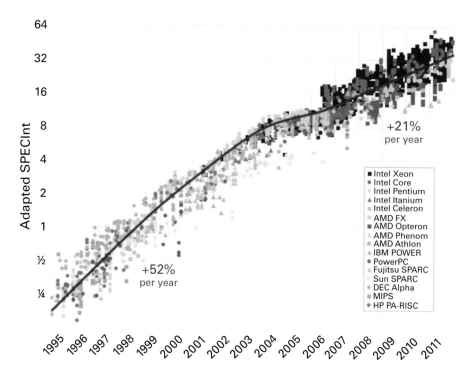

Figure 7.1 With the end of Dennard scaling (2005), annual improvement in single-thread performance has slowed down by over 30 percent per annum.

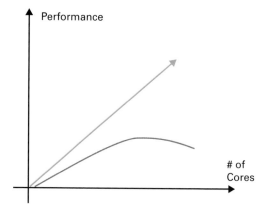

Figure 7.2 Post-Dennard scaling produces increases in the number of cores, providing the hope of linear speed-up (green). However, communication and coordination can reduce the effective speed-up for parallel execution (blue). This decreases the benefit of additional cores.

On the other hand, if significant communication and coordination is required, performance often suffers. This is because such work is required only in the parallel execution, not the original sequential program (and hardware) with only a single locus of computation. This produces poorer increases in performance with the addition of multicore resources, as shown in Figure 7.2. These poorer improvements are called **sublinear speed-up**, and reflect a lesser return on the additional hardware for additional cores.

7.2 Parallel Single-Chip Computers: Multicore CPUs

To explain what form the transformation to parallelism takes, we start by describing several features of multicore CPUs. We then shift to discuss the biggest change this shift to parallelism requires: parallel programs. First and foremost, multicore chips have multiple cores. That is, they include multiple complete processors, each capable of executing a computer program at high speed designed with the full set of features we have seen in Chapter 4, and miniaturized as described in Chapter 3. Together these provide as many as 64 powerful cores on a single CPU chip (in 2020). First, let's begin with a 28-core Intel Skylake CPU design, depicted in Figure 7.3. The repeating pattern of colored boxes together comprise a core (processor and caches), and the array of cores is laid out in two dimensions and connected together by a mesh communication fabric. The fabric sends messages between the caches (labeled LLC), allowing them

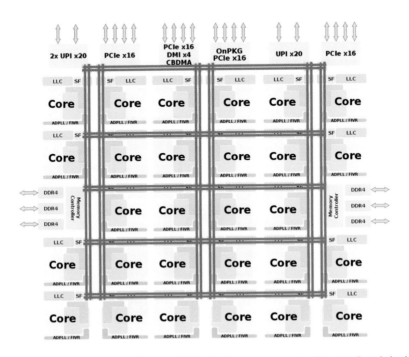

Figure 7.3 High-level structure of server CPU with 28 cores, connected by a mesh and sharing memory controllers.

to present a coherent view of memory. Another use for the mesh is to send messages from the caches to the memory system when cache misses occur.

> **Principle 7.2: Multicore Chips Provide Thread-Level Parallelism**
>
> *Multicore CPUs are parallel sets of processors integrated on a single silicon micro-chip.*

In addition to the 28-core server chip, the same Skylake core is used in smaller computing systems such as laptop computers. As illustrated in Figure 7.4, these laptop (or client) computers employ fewer cores, 2–8, and add a graphics processing unit (labeled EUs) to perform 2D and 3D graphics on the high-resolution display. The reuse of the core across different CPU products shares the costs of design, but also ensures software and performance compatibility. These smaller chips are designed to operate with less power, usually less than 25 watts (servers consume 150–300 watts).

Equally important to the cores, perhaps a quarter of each CPU chip is dedicated to a large multi-level cache hierarchy. These caches supply the processors with data at high speed and have private cache memory hierarchies (separate L1 instruction and data caches plus a unified L2 cache) at the top, as we covered in Section 6.1. As depicted in Figure 7.5, these caches provide high-bandwidth, low-latency access to the core, and, equally important, reduce the memory access rate requirements by filtering the stream of memory references down dramatically. The next level is the last level of cache memory on the CPU chip; there, it is important to maximize the chance of avoiding a memory operation going to the off-chip DRAM as the energy cost and latency of accessing DRAM are much greater. For that reason, most multicore chips share capacity across all cores, creating a very large shared L3 (sometimes called last-level cache or LLC) of as much as 38 MiB on the chip [109]. The cores also typically share

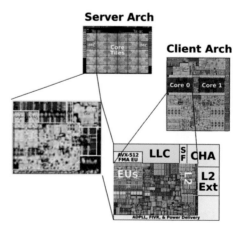

Figure 7.4 Server CPUs (top) include numerous cores (lower right) that are combined in either a dual-core client chip (upper right) with the addition of a graphics processing unit (EUs). Each core is a complete compute engine.

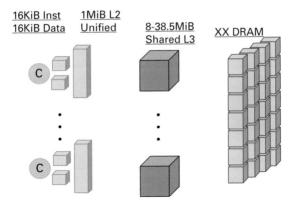

16KiB Inst   1MiB L2
16KiB Data   Unified   8-38.5MiB
                         Shared L3   XX DRAM

Figure 7.5 Hierarchy of a Skylake multicore tile. Each core has private 16 KiB L1 instruction and 16 KiB L1 data, as well as a 1 MiB L2 unified cache per core. The L3 cache is shared across all cores, and typically is 1.375 MiB × number of cores. Product CPUs range as large as 28 cores and 38.5 MiB L3.

the DRAM memory controllers. All of these structures are depicted in Figure 7.5. All of the cores, L3 cache banks, and memory controllers are connected by an on-chip interconnection network, often called a network-on-chip.

The caches on a multicore chip provide a coherent interface to memory for all of the cores. Changes made by one processor are assured to quickly become visible to all other processors. This enables the collection of cores to be programmed as if they shared a single memory, despite the fact that 100 or more caches on the chip may contain copies of a datum. These caches are critical to make the processors deliver high performance. However, if the copies were allowed to disagree – become incoherent – it would be very difficult to write parallel software. To avoid this, cache coherence protocols are combined with memory consistency models (see Section 5.7) and synchronization operations such as atomics, locks, and semaphores to enable the parallel threads running on the cores to quickly coordinate their computing effort.

Important Fact: Cache Coherence Protocols

Multicore CPUs employ caches to support the performance of each core (processor), creating multiple copies of data items, giving rise to cache coherence and synchronization challenges. All modern multicore CPUs employ cache-coherence protocols that detect potential incoherence and prevent it from becoming visible to the software [40].

7.2.1 Example: AMD Ryzen Multicore Chip and System

Let's consider a leading multicore server CPU, introduced by AMD at the end of 2019. This CPU is called "Rome" and comes from the Ryzen line. Rome includes 64 cores with a massive 64 MiB of L3 cache memory, and can connect as much as 4 TiB of

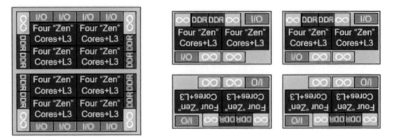

Figure 7.6 AMD Ryzen CCDs include eight cores, associated L1 and L2, and shared 8×4 MB L3 caches. Each of the four chiplets is 213 mm^2, and together comprise an area of 852 mm^2. They are packaged together into a "Rome" CPU, producing a 64-core CPU (single package as at right).

DRAM (eight memory channels and >200 GiB/s bandwidth). The implementation is illustrated in Figure 7.6, packaging two four-core modules into a CCD (core chiplet die) then eight of those CCDs into a single package. Such a single package is what we commonly call a single CPU (or sometimes "socket") and corresponds to what we used to call a single-chip CPU.

Multiple Rome CPUs are packaged into a server, as shown in Figure 7.7. Two server CPUs are packaged onto a small computing card (printed circuit board); this card contains the two CPUs and as much as 8 TiB associated DRAM. This layout is designed to keep the computing as close together as possible (small is fast!). The remainder of the space within the 2U-high 19-inch rack server is consumed by storage (typically solid-state disks) and networking that usually is connected at the back (currently 40 GiB/s, increasing to 100 GiB/s in datacenters). In addition, a substantial amount of space is consumed by power and cooling for the server.

Servers such as these are the workhorse building block of both enterprise datacenters and the hyperscale cloud providers such as Amazon, Google, and Microsoft. With slight modification, they are also used in supercomputers such as those in the USA's Exascale Compute Project (ECP) [98].

> **Principle 7.3: Server Multicore Parallelism Is Large, More than 100-fold**
>
> *Multicore servers are highly parallel machines with over 100-fold parallelism within a single two-CPU server. It's a substantial software challenge to exploit even one server effectively.*

7.3   Programming Multicore Computers: OpenMP and pthreads

The shift to increasing numbers of cores, rather than faster single cores–requires a dramatic change in software: parallelism. As in earlier chapters of the book, we continue from the perspective of a single program, asking the question: **How can we write a parallel program for a single application?** While this topic has been the subject of much research over 40 years, two approaches are most widely used: pragmas (annotations) to sequential programs, and explicit software threading. We consider leading examples of each of these approaches, **OpenMP** and **pthreads**.

7.3.1 OpenMP: Pragma-Based Parallelism

OpenMP is a popular approach to writing parallel programs that adds **pragma**s to traditional sequential programs. The idea is that adding pragmas to sequential programs, allows them to be ignored when compiling for a single-threaded implementation. This approach provides for a single source compatibility between sequential and parallel (multicore) implementation. Most pragmas, such as OpenMP, focus on loops because they account for most of the computation time in most programs. OpenMP adds a set of pragmas to declare that iterations within a loop can be executed in parallel – with no concerns of correctness. An OpenMP program example is shown in Figure 7.7.

The OpenMP pragma parallelizes only the outermost loop of the matrix multiply program, creating the ability to exploit up to n parallel threads. For matrix multiply this parallelism is safe because the program only reads the a and b matrices, and only one of the iterations of the i loop updates c[i]. Computations within a single i loop iteration will be done sequentially. If fewer than n threads are available in the computer, they will execute the iterations in turn. If a programmer wanted to further increase the amount of parallelism, they could add nested pragmas on the j or k loops. Note that increasing parallelism beyond the hardware's ability to exploit (e.g. more than m threads on an m-core machine) can lead to reduced performance due to contention for both computing and cache resources.

```
# pragma omp parallel for
for ( i = 0; i < n; i++ ) {
    for ( j = 0; j < n; j++ ) {
        c[i][j] = 0.0;
        for ( k = 0; k < n; k++ ) {
            c[i][j] = c[i][j] + a[i][k] * b[k][j];
        };
    };
}
```

Figure 7.7 OpenMP example for matrix multiplication. The omp parallel for pragma indicates that all iterations of the outer loop (index i) can be executed in parallel, creating the potential for n parallel threads.

7.3.2   pthreads: Explicit Thread-Parallelism

pthreads take the basic sequential execution model and extend it with multiple active program threads, each an independent locus of program control (and therefore parallelism). Thus, each thread can be thought of as an independent program, but it shares the global variables and heap with other threads. The stack variables (automatics) are private to each thread of execution (pthread). As shown in the example in Figure 7.8, explicit operations are used to create new threads (`pthread_create`) and to join two threads together (`pthread_join`) – for example, synchronizing their completion. These operations must be composed correctly for the desired program result to be achieved; however, doing so is often quite tricky.

Our pthread program spawns a helper thread that increments a variable x 100 times, producing the final value of x = 100. At the same time, the original thread increments the variable y 100 times, producing the final value of y = 100. Both variables are visible to the original as well as to the helper thread, requiring care in coordination to ensure they do not interfere with each other. For example, consider what program changes would be required to swap the roles of the original and helper threads with respect to the variables x, y. Perhaps that is simple, but what if alternative even and odd increments were to be done in different threads? What synchronization would be required? pthreads are used in many server programs to support both asynchronous

```
void *inc_x(void *x_void_ptr){
  int *x_ptr = (int *)x_void_ptr;   /* increment x to 100 */
  while(++(*x_ptr) < 100);
  return NULL;   /* the function returns */
}

int main(){
  int x = 0, y = 0;
  pthread_t inc_x_thread;      /* create 2nd thread which executes inc_x(&x) */
  if(pthread_create(&inc_x_thread, NULL, inc_x, &x)) {
    fprintf(stderr, "Error creating thread\n");
    return 1; }

  while(++y < 100);   /* increment y to 100 in the 1st thread */

  if(pthread_join(inc_x_thread, NULL)) {
/* wait for 2nd thread finish */
    fprintf(stderr, "Error joining thread\n");
    return 2;
  }

  /* show results - x is now 100, courtesy 2nd thread */
  printf("x: %d, y: %d\n", x, y);
  return 0;
}
```

Figure 7.8 A pthreads example for parallel counter incrementing. The thread spawn creates a separate thread that executes concurrently in the same address space (variables). The programmer must coordinate the threads correctly.

interaction and scalability, it is generally considered to be more difficult and error-prone than OpenMP programming.

Principle 7.4: Parallel Programming Is a New Abstraction for Parallel Computers

Multicore chips break the sequential abstraction. New software that provides explicit parallelism is required to exploit this hardware parallelism for higher performance. This software is more difficult to develop, incurring greater complexity for correctness and performance.

7.3.3 Challenging Parallelism in a Single Multicore CPU

With some idea of how parallel programs can be written, it is worth considering the challenge of creating enough parallelism to achieve good performance on a modern multicore CPU – that is, to utilize an entire multicore CPU effectively with only a single program. A single multicore CPU may have as many as 64 cores, 256 MiB cache, and 4 TiB of DRAM, as shown in Figure 7.9. To make full use of the 64 cores, that number of parallel threads will be required, each with a large chunk of independent computation.

If we use the matrix multiply example from Figure 7.7 expressed with OpenMP, and assume $n = 64$, each of the parallel threads will compute 1/64th of the N^3 operations.

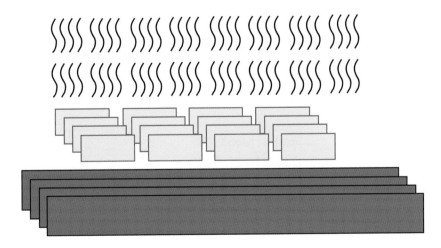

Figure 7.9 A single Rome 32-core CPU supports 64 threads. In order to fully utilize a Rome CPU, an application must provide ample parallelism. These threads are supported by 16×16 MiB L3 caches and up to 4 TiB of DRAM, each server CPU thus supporting a vast amount of computation and data.

This means that each thread would be responsible for 4,096 multiply-accumulates and associated instruction overhead, so about 40,000 instructions. For parallel threads that share 500-cycle latency DRAM, this granularity can achieve good performance. However, for larger configurations, multiple CPUs, and multiple compute nodes in a cloud datacenter, much larger chunks of computation will be required.

7.3.4   Simpler Use of Multicore: Libraries and Servers

In many widely used programming environments, such as Python, R, and JavaScript, it is common to encapsulate parallelism in libraries – making the performance of multithreading available to library users without any programming effort. For example, multithreaded versions of matrix and computer vision libraries are available in Python, and many R implementations have multithreaded operators.

Many of the multicore servers in enterprise and cloud datacenters are filled by a simpler model. The simplest of these is called **server consolidation**, in which the computation tasks from formerly discrete computers is consolidated onto a large multicore server. In such cases, no reprogramming is required, and the compute capacity of the new computer replaces several slower computers formerly required to do the job, presumably at a cost saving. This idea is illustrated in Figure 7.10 (left); different jobs are run on the multicore server in a timesharing fashion. New applications can be added to the workload run on the server as they arise. This approach is also typical on a laptop computer – use your performance monitor to check how many processes are running.

Another common approach to utilizing the growing capacity of multicore servers is data parallelism. Here, the same program is run over larger quantities of data, requiring an increase in the computation and memory. If the computation done over different parts of the data do not interact strongly, then the chunks of work over independent chunks of data can be handled by different cores, as shown in Figure 7.10 (right). This approach is common in databases and data-intensive applications that are of growing importance in data analytics and artificial intelligence (AI). Many of these applications

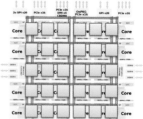

Figure 7.10 On servers, found in a corporate or cloud datacenter, multicore parallelism is often used to (1) consolidate multiple jobs, allowing them to be run on fewer servers as illustrated on the left; or (2) execute uniform computations in, for example, a data analytics task over large amounts of data, as illustrated by a set of green blocks on the right.

are built with Spark or Hadoop, or naturally arise from request-level parallelism for internet services such as web search, social media requests, or even GPS directions.

> **Principle 7.5:** Workload-Level Approaches Can Utilize Multicore Server Parallelism
>
> *There are many different approaches to utilize the capacity of multicore servers, including server consolidation, data parallelism, and writing new parallel software. There will be more approaches over time.*

7.4 Million-Way Parallelism: Supercomputers and the Cloud

Today's single multicore CPU has remarkable computing resources, including capacities of perhaps 640 billion instructions per second, and 4 TiB (terabytes) of memory. However, for a growing number of applications, and for a class of internet-scale applications such as web search or global social networks, one or even a few dozen servers are not enough to handle these extreme-scale applications. While internet application companies such as Google, Facebook, Microsoft, Alibaba, Baidu, and Amazon have needed extreme-scale computing resources since the late 1990s, the need for scale has grown to many enterprises and applications beyond in the past decade. The demand has given rise to cloud computing in which massive datacenters of 25,000 CPUs or more provide computing services to thousands of customers and corporations (Figure 7.11). These datacenters can be as much as 20,000 square feet. The image in the figure depicts a floor plan of approximately 500 racks, accommodating perhaps 16,000 servers and the corresponding two million cores. There are larger datacenters, some as large as 3,000 racks. In these datacenters, the servers are divided between compute and storage and are connected by high-speed networks (40 GiB/s in 2019, shifting to 100 GiB/s), with dense Clos network–based topologies, as shown in Figure 7.13.

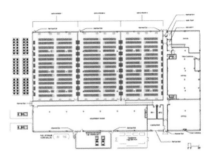

Figure 7.11 Open Compute standard 19-inch wide, 2.25-meter compute rack, and a floor plan with hundreds of racks (pink squares, top view).

Cloud services can be provided under long-term contract or on-demand. While these datacenters serve thousands of customers, some of the applications operate at extreme scale, employing 10,000 cores or more simultaneously, the equivalent of 1,000 CPUs. We first describe the compute hardware structures in these so-called hyperscale datacenters, and later, we will discuss the software structure of the applications that fill them.

While datacenters are often shown with a glamorous front view of colored lights and long aisles, their networking, power, and cooling requirements require construction of extensive infrastructure to feed them, which are often well hidden. The front highlights the computing and networking equipment – which can be easily related to the exciting internet and cloud services that we – and all companies, governments, and more – use everyday. The contrast between the front and the underside of the datacenter is illustrated in Figure 7.12. The hidden infrastructure includes reliable power supply, cooling, and physical support for heavy racks of computing equipment. The infrastructure is often larger than the compute equipment itself, and is critical to reliable operation of the datacenter. However, the computing equipment is by far the most expensive part.

As can be seen in Figure 7.12, cloud datacenters include large numbers of servers mounted in standard racks – approximately 500 racks, accommodating perhaps 16,000 servers, and the corresponding 2 million cores. In these datacenters, the servers are divided between computer and storage and are connected by high-speed networks (40 gigabits per second in 2019, shifting to 100 gigabits per second), with dense Clos network-based topologies.

In Figure 7.13, the network for Facebook's F16 datacenter network topology is depicted, illustrating the three levels of networking – rack, fabric, and spine. The F16 network includes 100 gigabit and even 400 gigabit connections [119]. These Clos network topologies provide the highest bandwidth within a rack and a reduced bandwidth along the racks in a row. Finally, the bandwidth is reduced even further when going across the datacenter through the spline planes. However, as shown in the figure, despite this drop-off, there are a very large number of connections across the center of the datacenter. Desirable properties of these topologies include redundant paths for reliability and load balance, the ability to add more network bisection at any

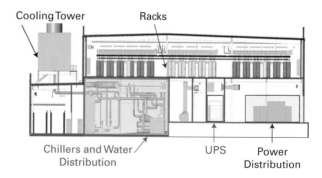

Figure 7.12 The glamorous "front side" of a datacenter (left) and the extensive networking, power, and cooling infrastructure needed to make it work (right).

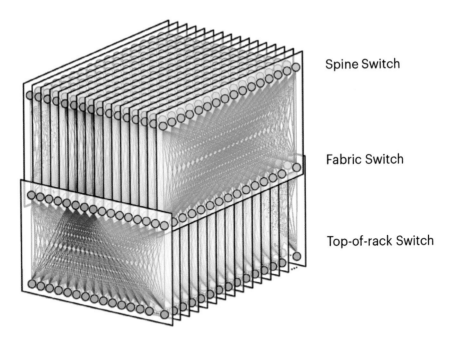

Spine Switch

Fabric Switch

Top-of-rack Switch

Figure 7.13 Clos network topology used in hyperscale datacenter networks [87, 119]. (Image Courtesy Facebook).

time, and low latency (few hops). With the growing importance of analytics and other data-intensive computations, the need to move data fast and at massive scale makes these high-speed networks one of the key costs in a datacenter.

> Principle 7.6: Scale-Out Parallelism in the Cloud is over ONE Million-Fold Parallelism
>
> *Cloud datacenters use multicore servers as building blocks of vast computing resource pools with millions of cores. Cloud resources support internet-scale, government-scale, and enterprise-scale computation. They also support some of the lowest-cost and highest-productivity computing environments.*

7.5 Efficient Parallelism: Computation Grain Size

The major challenge in parallel computing is to divide the work into "grains" for parallel execution. These grains are often called tasks. Ideally, the grains can be executed in parallel with as little synchronization and data sharing as possible. With a larger number of parallel grains, the software will be able to utilize more hardware parallelism (e.g. more cores). The detailed structure of synchronization and data sharing is application-specific, and thus difficult to address broadly here. But the key challenge for efficient parallel execution is that the grains (or tasks) should be large enough

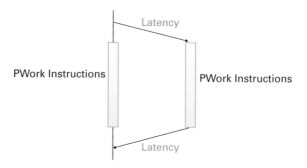

Figure 7.14 Efficient parallelism requires that the grain size be large enough to compensate for the latencies and overheads of creating the parallel execution. Each grain must be large enough to execute efficiently as in a single-threaded computation.

to overcome the overheads of creating and minimally synchronizing with the rest of the program. And because the cost of creating parallelism, synchronizing, and data sharing varies for each type of parallel system, the computation grain size that can be efficient is different on each type of system. In the rest of this subsection, we discuss this problem of efficient parallel "grain size."

In Section 7.3, we outlined a parallel program for matrix multiply using OpenMP, and chose a degree of parallelism and grain size that provided efficient parallel execution. In that case, each of the parallel tasks computed one row of the output matrix, a large quantity of computation including many dot product operations.

Let's consider more generally how the latency for communication and the bandwidth available affect the coordination cost for each parallel task. Consider the following rule of thumb for efficient parallel execution:

$$PWork > latency \times 4 \times 10,$$

where *PWork* is the grain size, and *latency* represents the one-way communication latency between the two loci of parallel execution. This rule of thumb works because 4 scales the one-way latency up, and 10 ensures that *PWork* achieves 90 percent efficiency relative to the round-trip overhead. This idea is based on the simple analysis shown in Figure 7.14. This rule of thumb ensures that the *PWork* instruction is large enough to dominate the overheads of communication and synchronization (the latency).

We can apply this rule to several different types of hardware parallelism. For example, in a multicore CPU the parallel threads share data using the L3 (or LLC) caches. This means that the latencies for communication and synchronization are determined by the speed of interaction of each core with the L3 caches. Thus, for efficient sharing through the L3 caches (i.e. the three matrices fit in the L3 cache easily) this produces a minimum grain size of $40 \times 4 \times 10 = 1,600$ cycles. Then, the estimate of 40,000 instructions, which might take 15,000-20,000, cycles is large enough to achieve good efficiency for parallel execution.

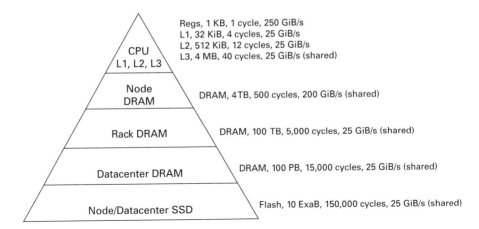

Figure 7.15 Access latency pyramid for increasing scopes of cloud computing resources. The pyramid latencies determine the cost of sharing and of coordination, thereby determining the grain size required for efficient parallelism. Multicore processors can share the L3 cache within the same chip, node DRAM within the same node, rack DRAM within the same rack, and datacenter DRAM and datacenter SSDs (flash storage) within the same datacenter.

In order to consider efficient parallel grain sizes for larger-scale systems in the cloud, one must have some key performance statistics for these systems. Figure 7.15 summarizes the access latency and bandwidth at each level of storage, working from the processor outward. The first level is most complicated, but only the L3 couples between cores, and it determines the grain size for efficient task parallelism within a CPU chip.

Taking this idea further, we can estimate the grain size of parallelism needed to achieve efficient parallelization at the node, the rack, and the datacenter level with DRAM. Using the latencies in Figure 7.15, these correspond to 20,000 cycles within the node, 200,000 cycles within the rack, and 600,000 cycles across the datacenter. Assuming 2.5 instructions executed per processor cycle on average, the estimated number of instructions needed correspond to parallel grains of 50,000 instructions (node), 500,000 instruction (rack), and 1,500,000 instructions (datacenter). By comparison, an entire 64×64 matrix–matrix multiply is only about 2.5 million instructions, so trying to distribute across any nodes beyond a rack in the datacenter is unlikely to result in improved performance. Using the rule of thumb, parallelization of a 64×64 matrix multiply within a rack might give a little benefit, but it is definitely beneficial within a node or chip. The conclusion is clear – efficient parallel execution across these scales of hardware requires much larger computations – billions of instructions or more. Thinking more broadly, it's fortunate that many cloud applications exceed that cost greatly (imagine the number of instructions to execute a web search, or update your social network feed). Further, many of these applications have coarse-grained parallelism (hundreds of millions of instructions) and require high degrees of parallelism (thousands of cores), making it possible to spread such applications across a datacenter.

> **Principle 7.7: Computation Grain Size for Efficient Parallelism Model**
>
> *For efficient parallelism, the parallel grains (tasks) must be large enough to overlap communication latency. We can estimate this as four times the one-way latency multiplied by 10 (for 90 percent efficiency).*
>
> *In modern systems, these thresholds are 50,000 instructions within a node and 1.5 million instructions across a datacenter. In a cloud environment, scalability, reliability, and robustness are also important.*

7.6   Programming Cloud Computers: Coarse-Grained Parallelism

As we have seen, while the cloud can reach a vast scale of computing resources, bringing these resources to bear on a single application is challenging. The overheads associated with coordinating these resources can limit scalability and efficiency. Fortunately, several major application styles have been developed that coordinate large quantities of cloud resources scalably: three-tier web, scale-out map–reduce, microservices, and the newest addition, function-as-a-service (aka serverless).

7.6.1   Three-Tier Web: Scalable Web Services

Early web applications experienced major challenges in scalability and reliability. Through rapid experimentation, and many failures and successes, the industry converged on a simple three-tier architecture as the canonical approach (Figure 7.16). This architecture provides scalability for clients while ensuring strong data consistency in the back end, a critical requirement to support actions with financial consequences, such as e-commerce.

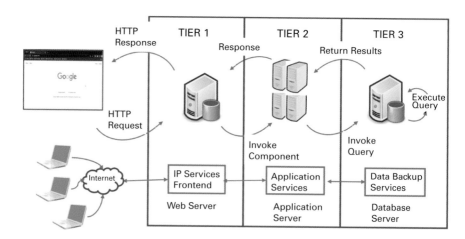

Figure 7.16 Nearly all scalable e-commerce and internet services are built on a three-tier web architecture with layers for web presentation and connection, application logic, and data services.

In the three-tier architecture, the first layer – the web – is responsible for maintaining connections to clients and creating the presentation – the web pages – used for interaction with the client program (or the human user). In the second layer – the application or business logic – the computation and services needed by the application are implemented. Both the first and second layers are stateless, meaning the connection and state can be dropped at any time. This allows internet-scale services to manage their resources flexibly, focusing on the most valuable customers and shedding demand when overloaded. The third tier is an implementation of reliable data services, usually a scalable, serializable store such as a database. This allows the three-tier web architecture to support business services such as e-commerce, reservations, email, and other first-generation web services. Three-tier architectures were scaled to thousands of processors and millions of clients.

7.6.2 Scale-Out Map–Reduce (Hadoop and Spark)

In the late 1990s, the rise of internet-scale services such as web search created a need to process large amounts of data, far more than could be accommodated by any database system of the time. In fact, a major problem was that the computations, such as computing a search index, required so many machines to host the data that one of them would crash before the computation could be completed. This would destroy the results of the computation, wasting all of the work to that point.

To solve this problem, in the late 1990s Google internally built a map–reduce system based on the concept of a map pioneered in the LISP programming language [63]. The idea was to apply a function to a set of objects, and then reduce the collection of answers to a single-value answer. This approach allowed scale-out to large quantities of data (terabytes then, petabytes now). Google generalized this to allow general computation in both map and reduce operations, retaining the ideas of parallelism in the application of the function (the map function) across the set of objects while also applying the reduce operations in parallel. This is possible when the reduce operation is associative and commutative. As important, the map–reduce framework was tolerant of failures, allowing their unreliable cluster with thousands of machines to finish computation of the web search index correctly, despite many individual machine crashes. This enabled map–reduce to organize and complete larger computations than had ever been accomplished.

Shortly after Google published its map–reduce paper [22], Hadoop was created as a clone, written in Java and open-sourced. Hadoop has been widely used for research, and also in a number of companies. We depict a Hadoop map–reduce execution in Figure 7.17. All of the data come from the Hadoop filesystem (HDFS), are read/written to the HDFS, and finally written to the HDFS at the end. The map phase is parallel across subsets of the input data, as is the reduce phase after the data have been shuffled (sorted) between the map and reduce. Finally, the reduce produces a small amount of data as the result of the entire map–reduce. The reads and writes to HDFS are the most expensive part of a map–reduce, because they involve input/output. However, they are critical because they provide map–reduce with the ability to survive machine crashes, as the data written to disk are safely preserved.

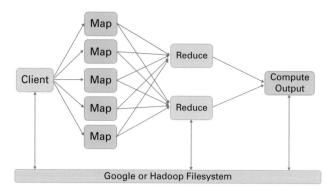

Figure 7.17 Google's map–reduce enabled internet-scale iterative computation. Hadoop is an open-source clone of map–reduce (shown above), and Spark enabled map–reduce to be fault-tolerant while run in-memory, dramatically speeding up its execution.

Spark recently took the idea of map–reduce further, using a novel approach to enable fault-tolerant implementation wholly in memory, eliminating the expensive writes and reads from disk that were at the center of every map–reduce operation. Because these input/output operations are so expensive, eliminating them allowed Spark to speed up map–reduce computations dramatically. Thus, it caught on as a parallel composition framework [117]. These three frameworks, map–reduce, Hadoop, and Spark are used to create many scale-out parallel computations for the cloud, particularly large-scale data analytics. All of these frameworks (and the applications implemented on top of them) are subject to the performance constraints of efficient "grain size" for parallelism, discussed in Section 7.5.

7.6.3   Microservices: Modular Reliability and Evolution

In the aftermath of stateless web applications served by the three-tier architecture, more complex applications began to emerge. One important class of applications, video streaming, involved long-running, complex interactions, but also needed highly reliable and scalable service. These applications had complex workflows and dependences that were not easily mapped into the three-tier architecture. Netflix has become one of the business leaders in this space, and consequently its teams created a long string of novel cloud software architectures to support rapid software evolution, extreme scalability, and high reliability. Their approach has come to be called a "microservices" architecture. A 2018 snapshot of the microservices communication graph is shown in Figure 7.18.

The drive for extreme resilience led Netflix to take this radical new approach. Their microservices architecture includes hundreds of distinct microservices, each of which can be independently started, stopped, and upgraded (each of the circles in Figure 7.18). These microservices all execute in parallel, and may even have internal parallelism, exploiting the bounty of parallel hardware in the cloud datacenter. With a microservices application architecture, Netflix not only can achieve modularity and separate microservice reliability/failure domains, at an operational level they exercise it regularly. Within their ChaosMonkey framework they not only routinely crash pro-

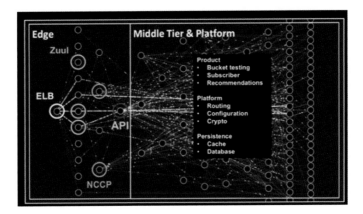

Figure 7.18 Netflix pioneered a **microservices** approach to cloud applications. This approach factors a service into a large collection of independently failable, restartable, versionable, and upgradeable microservices. It also includes a provision for autoscaling the microservices. As can be seen in the image, their microservice architecture includes hundreds of distinct processes with a complex communication structure.

cesses, but also groups of processes and even entire datacenters intentionally to test the robustness of services and service deployments. This aggressive approach produces robust service deployments – despite both high failure rates and correlated failures of processes, compute resources, and networks.

The same modular architecture and independent start, stop, and upgrade gives Netflix a major advantage in rapid software evolution. This modularity, akin to "hot-swappable" hardware such as USB devices that can be plugged and unplugged without rebooting the operating system, allows Netflix to add functionality, fix problems, and revert out of accidentally introduced bugs quickly. In fact, these improvements can be made without disruption of even currently connected customers. Today, microservices, combined with containers, is viewed as one of the dominant software architectures for cloud applications.

7.6.4 Serverless (Function-as-a-Service)

Recent years have seen the rise of a new model of computing for the cloud – function-as-a-service (Figure 7.19). Clouds have always been complicated to use because they required explicit management of resources (e.g. virtual machines, containers, etc.). And because the billing was per resource-hour used, cloud developers undertook complex schemes to ensure service availability without overpaying. Serverless (aka "cloud functions" or "function-as-a-service", or FaaS) takes the radical step of eliminating the explicit provisioning of resources by applications. Instead, applications can register functions (serverless functions), attaching them to events within the cloud or even those coming from an external network (for example, an incoming HTTP request). When the event occurs, the underlying FaaS implementation ensures that the registered function is invoked, which transfers the job of efficient resource management and dynamic scaling (many invocations in parallel) to the cloud operator. In one bold stroke, the FaaS model eliminates the need for an application to implement resource

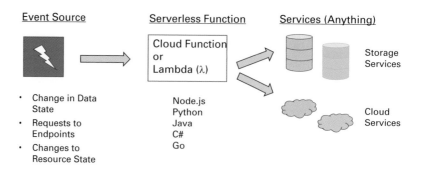

Event Source   Serverless Function   Services (Anything)

- Change in Data   Node.js   Storage
  State   Python   Services
- Requests to   Java
  Endpoints   C#   Cloud
- Changes to   Go   Services
  Resource State

Figure 7.19 The idea behind serverless is to eliminate the explicit management of resources, thereby simplifying application development. Applications can attach **cloud functions** to any event in the cloud or even an incoming HTTP port, and that function is executed every time the event fires, implicitly allocating resources and releasing them. The serverless model is a pay-as-you-go model, in which one pays only for the function invocations actually run.

management by providing automatic invocation and, as requests scale, autoscaling (aka rightsizing). That is, if 100 requests arrive for a given serverless function, the FaaS implementation will create 100 parallel invocations! This illusion of plentiful resources depends on the high degrees of hardware parallelism in the cloud. In effect, each invocation is at least one new thread – so if a service garners hundreds or thousands of concurrent invocations, they give rise to a bounty of software parallelism.

Critical to making the model work, serverless shifts from a resource-hour billing model to a pay-as-you-go model based on GiB-seconds. That is, the application is charged per-invocation, and how many GiB of memory it uses and the number of seconds these FaaS invocations consume. Not only does this make cost proportional to use, but it also creates a low cost of entry for applications. That is, a new application costs little to deploy, and costs only increase if the innovator is successful in attracting use. This enables both aggressive innovation and deployment of new ideas, but also opens the door to new classes of applications with low and bursty loads, such as novel Internet of Things (IoT) applications. Serverless makes it much easier to build applications, and has led to an explosion of new mobile and IoT applications.

> Principle 7.8: Cloud Applications Use Coarse-Grained Parallelism to Scale-Out
>
> *Cloud applications use coarse-grained parallelism in a wide variety of software architectures (three-tier, map–reduce, microservices, and serverless) to increase total application capability for internet-scale applications (number of users and functions).*

7.7   Summary

The end of Dennard scaling produced stagnation of processor clock rates, slowing improvement of single-thread performance. With the much slower increase for single threads, and the investment in Moore's Law increase of transistors in multiple cores (i.e. parallelism) and cache capacity, software has experienced dramatic disruption, forced to look beyond the sequential state abstraction to parallelism.

- **Parallelism in multicore CPUs** requires new programming approaches. Software must provide parallel threads to utilize the ever-growing capacity of multicore CPUs and multicore server nodes, which as of 2019 had grown to 128 threads, 512 MiB of L3 cache, and 8 TiB of memory. Single-program approaches include OpenMP (pragmas in a sequential program), explicitly parallel threads (pthreads), and many others, but programming is much more difficult without the foundation of sequential abstraction. Therefore, many systems hide parallelism in libraries, or limit it to data parallelism, doing the same work over ever-larger quantities of data, and depending on the growth of data to utilize these ever-larger servers. Another common approach is server consolidation, simply taking the work from many independent servers and putting it together on the new, larger-capacity server. Regardless of approach, greater computing capability is accessed through parallel computing.
- **Parallelism in the cloud.** The cloud represents a scale-out of parallelism to tens of thousands of highly parallel multicore servers. This hardware has potential parallelism of as many as 10 million cores or threads, and correspondingly vast quantities of memory (100 petabytes!). Modern cloud datacenters are connected with high-speed networks, typically with several 100 gigabits/s Ethernet connections per server, allowing data to be accessed at over 25 GiB/s across the datacenter, but at growing latencies of up to 15,000 cycles (compared to 500 cycles for local DRAM).
- **Efficient parallel computation.** In all these parallel systems, applications must have certain characteristics to tap the full power of the computing hardware. Within a node, a latency of 500 cycles and bandwidths of 200 GiB/s enable parallel tasks to be efficient at about 50,000 instructions. At the datacenter level, with a latency of 15,000 cycles and 25 GiB/s (but shared), efficient parallelism will require parallel tasks more like 1,500,000 instructions. This may seem too large to be useful, but many cloud applications achieve this quite nicely!

The driver for the creation of cloud datacenters is the rise of internet-scale applications (since 1999) and cloud computing (since 2007). To utilize these massive facilities, software architects have created new application structures that harness large quantities of coarse-grained parallelism. That is, coarse enough to be executed efficiently on cloud hardware. These models include the three-tier architecture (scalable web applications) and map–reduce (scalable analytics) that date back to the late 1990s. In the past decade new models, such as microservices and serverless, have arisen to meet the needs of ballooning complexity, extreme reliability, and the needs of a new generation of cloud application developers to tap these parallel resources at effective cost and scale. All of these models are enabled by the million-fold parallelism and massive compute power of cloud datacenters, and the innovation continues–surely there is more to come!

7.8   Digging Deeper

The shift to multicore at the end of Dennard scaling began a new epoch for computing – parallel computing as the mainstream. With many publications heralding the challenge, many new government research programs were started to address parallel programming [99], with the common perspectives that nearly all software had be parallel, and that the degree of parallelism needed to increase steadily if computing performance were to continue to grow rapidly.

However, it's important to realize that traditional measures of parallel efficiency, while intellectually sound, posed far too demanding a standard for successful parallel software. These traditional models of parallelism assumed a linear cost for parallelism, and therefore demanded good parallel speed-ups. However, with Moore's Law, the increased hardware parallelism comes at a relatively small incremental cost, so even modest speed-ups (e.g. 1.3 or 1.5 out of 2) could be cost-effective [14]. Investing those same transistors in an even larger core would, according to Pollack's rule, only produce a return as little as the square root of the increase (1.4 per doubling of transistors) [107]. For years prior to the end of Dennard scaling, these Pollack's rule benefits were considered by most architects to be a good return on transistors.

Multicore processors originated in the late 1980s, originally built from multiple CPU chips, then later turned into collections of multicore processors in the mid 2000s with multiple processors per chip. All these systems had to solve the cache coherence problems; today systems typically use directory-based systems [19]. Early multi-level systems used **inclusion**, but this approach wasted cache capacity with redundant copies of data at multiple levels, so recent systems have used directories that span multiple levels of cache to eliminate this waste [109].

Google was an early leader in cloud computing software, including map–reduce [22], a parallel filesystem [31], both of which were later cloned in open source as Hadoop. Barroso coined the term "warehouse-scale computers" and was the architect of the early Google datacenters [4]. Early cloud datacenters used inexpensive, low-performance networks, but recent designs have been aggressive, expensive networks reflecting the increasing compute-intensity of their workloads and the need to move massive amounts of data [86].

Cloud software has developed a large and growing set of application architectures to harness the scale of parallelism available in datacenters with as many as 100,000 servers and meet the demands of ever-growing numbers of users and data scales. These include three-tier web, scale-out map–reduce (Hadoop and Spark), microservices [71], and most recently FaaS [43]. There is a wealth of literature – and software – written on these approaches.

7.9   Problems

7.1   While single-thread performance increased rapidly under Dennard scaling through 2006 (52 percent per year, as shown in Figure 7.1), the rate of increase dropped to only 21 percent per year after 2006.

(a) Calculate the "lost" single-thread performance due to the end of Dennard scaling from 2006 through today. If Dennard scaling had continued, how much faster would single-thread performance be today?

(b) Instead of faster single-thread performance, Moore's Law has yielded parallelism over the past 15 years. Supposing that the number of cores doubled every three years since 2006, starting with one, how many cores would we have today? What parallel efficiency would we have to achieve across those cores to deliver the same total compute performance of a single thread in (a)?

(c) Discuss how likely it is that a set of applications can achieve greater or lesser parallel efficiency than the threshold in (b). Give an example for each of one that is less, equal, and greater than the threshold and give a plausible explanation why.

7.2 In multicore chips, there are often large, shared L3 (or last-level) caches. These caches can account for as much as half of the CPU chip area.

(a) Give two reasons why it might be a good idea to have such a large cache (the kinds of benefits that justify the cost).

(b) Multicore chip designers need to think about whether to dedicate silicon area to more cores or larger caches. Can you formulate this trade-off? How can we relate both to performance? And to cost? (This is a difficult problem.)

7.3 Size and latency in cloud systems.

(a) Estimate the size of the CPU chip relative to a 2U server, a common building block for cloud datacenters. For simplicity, do this computation in two dimensions, and you can assume that the CPU chip is in a 1 × 1-inch package (the standard server is 19 inches wide and 42 inches deep). How do the latencies in Figure 7.15 compare to projections from our physical size and clock period model (Section 3.3.1)?

(b) Estimate the size of a rack. How do the latencies in Figure 7.15 compare to projections from our physical size and clock period model (Section 3.3.1)?

(c) Estimate the size of a datacenter. How do the latencies in Figure 7.15 compare to projections from our physical size and clock period model (Section 3.3.1)?

7.4 Using the OpenMP pragmas used in Section 7.3.1 (or you can find the full standards at www.openmp.org), write a dot product program for two arrays: A[16384] and B[16384].

(a) Explain how many elements of the A[ ] and B[ ] arrays will be computed by each thread on an 8-core machine. A 32-core machine?

(b) Look at the worksharing-loop construct. Can you change the number of elements that will be computed by each thread? Explain when and when not doing this would increase performance.

(c) A common element critical to efficiency is how OpenMP parallel loops do reductions. Using the dot product example, explain why this is, and how much difference it could make in parallel performance.

7.5 Using the OpenMP pragmas used in Section 7.3.1 (or you can find the full standards at www.openmp.org), write a matrix multiply program for two 256×256 matrices of double precision floating point numbers.
(a) Write a parallel version that assigns entire dot products to each of the threads.
(b) Describe which dot products wind up on each of the threads in a 32-thread (core) system.
(c) Look at the worksharing-loop construct. Can you change the number of dot products that will be computed by each thread? How many different mappings can you create? Explain why they might help or harm performance.

7.6 Using the OpenMP pragmas used in Section 7.3.1 (or you can find the full standards at www.openmp.org), write a matrix multiply program for two 256×256 matrices of double precision floating point numbers.
(a) Write a parallel version that assigns entire dot products to each of the threads.
(b) A critical factor in parallel performance is sharing of data across the caches. Assuming the 32-core system has private L1 and L2 caches for each core, as we saw with the Intel Skylake CPU in Section 6.1, what parts of the matrices have to go into multiple L2 caches? Count how many copies of each, and indicate where they go.
(c) Explain how these copies of the dot products access the matrix, and the bytes of data implied for each dot product on a cache system. Remember, a typical commercial processor moves data in units of 64-byte blocks.
(d) For better cache performance, highly optimized matrix multiply algorithms will use tiles (perhaps 16×16) and decompose the matrix multiply into a set of block $\times$ block multiplies. Explain how this improves memory hierarchy behavior (fewer cache misses).

7.7 Using the OpenMP pragmas used in Section 7.3.1 (or you can find the full standards at www.openmp.org), write a matrix multiply program for two $N \times N$ matrices of double precision floating point numbers.
(a) Write a parallel version that assigns entire dot products to each of the threads.
(b) Describe which dot products wind up on each of the threads in a 32-thread (core) system.
(c) What happens to the work distribution to threads if we increase the size of the matrix $(2N, 4N, 8N, \ldots)$?
(d) What happens to the cache behavior if we increase the size of the matrix $(2N, 4N, 8N, \ldots)$? Are there more or fewer cache misses per compute operation (a multiply or add)? Explain.

7.8 Consider the cache behavior in Problem 7.7 for the matrix multiply program based on dot products. When the program is parallel, the reuse distance structure of a program gets spread across multiple cache hierarchies.
(a) Consider a small matrix multiply, where $N = 16$, and one core. What does the reuse distance profile look like? Explain.

(b)   Now consider executing that program using OpenMP. What does the reuse distance profile for each thread look like? Explain how parallelization changed the reuse distance profile.

(c)   Consider four cores, then eight cores. Explain how the reuse distance profile changes.

(d)   Now consider how the matrix multiply was parallelized. Is there a better way to parallelize it so that the resulting reuse distance profiles for each core will produce higher cache performance?

7.9   Python has two kinds of support for parallelism: threads (concurrency) and processes (scale-out). In this problem, we will explore scale-out because it is a little simpler to reason about. It can be effective when you are dividing up large chunks of work across cores.

(a)   Look up the **joblib** package for Python and read about how it can create "embarrassingly parallel" loops to exploit a multicore system. Write a simple loop that divides up a large dot product computation of two vectors of floating point numbers: A[16384], B[16384].

(b)   Using joblib, write a simple loop that searches a large text document of 10 megabytes for a particular substring, "University of Chicago", and returns a list of the offsets where it appears.

(c)   Using joblib, write a simple loop that creates a list of all possible strings of length 6 ASCII characters.

7.10   Parallel programming is considered to be a challenging task. Find a commonly used benchmark suite that has both sequential and OpenMP versions, such as the NAS Parallel Benchmarks (NPB). For example, see www.nas.nasa.gov/publications/npb.html.

(a)   Run the sequential and parallel versions on a multicore machine. How does the performance differ?

(b)   Using a tool such as perf, characterize the performance of the suite. Where can you see parallelism increasing performance? Are there any hidden costs to the parallelism? (For example, is the total number of instructions the same?)

(c)   Examine the sequential and OpenMP versions of the source code for each of the benchmarks. How many lines are different? Why is it this few/many?

(d)   Think about some programs you have written or worked on. Is it likely to be a similar or different fraction? Why?

7.11   Parallel programming is widely considered to be a challenging task. Find a commonly used benchmark suite that has both sequential and OpenMP versions such as the PARSEC Benchmarks suite. For example, see https://parsec.cs.princeton.edu

(a)   Run the sequential and parallel versions on a multicore machine. How does the performance differ?

(b)   Using a tool such as perf, characterize the performance of the suite. Where can you see parallelism increasing performance? Are there any hidden costs to the parallelism? (For example, is the total number of instructions the same?)

(c) Examine the sequential and OpenMP versions of the source code for each of the benchmarks. How many lines are different? Why is it this few/many?

(d) Think about some programs you have written or worked on. Is it likely to be a similar or different fraction? Why?

7.12 Consider the volumetric efficiency of a cloud datacenter. Use the calculations from Problem 3 and assume that a 2U server is 3.5 inches high.

(a) Compute the volumetric compute efficiency of a 2U server in terms of the fraction occupied by the two CPU chips.

(b) Compute the volumetric compute efficiency of a rack of 2U servers, assuming there are 12 per rack, and a row of racks occupies a space that requires three-quarters of the depth of the rack both in front and behind it.

(c) Datacenters also consume space above and below the machine racks. They also consume space for a lot of plumbing, heat radiators on the roof, etc. For now, ignore that and consider only the basic space above and below for power, wires, and cooling. So, assuming we need 72 inches above and 36 inches below the rack for these, what is the final volumetric efficiency for computing in the datacenter?

7.13 Take a simple program and explore scaling and efficiency across three dimensions of "size": data, thread parallelism, and node parallelism. One possibility is the NPB (NAS Parallel Benchmarks).

(a) Run and tune at multiple scales. Start with a small problem size, then gradually increase the data size to exercise the memory hierarchy (caches).

(b) Get a parallel version, and explore a range of parallelism, using one of the larger data sizes. Exercise the overhead of parallelism and efficient grain size.

(c) Get/build a cloud parallel version – coarse-grained parallelism (cloud) – perhaps using map–reduce (Hadoop or Spark). On-demand versions are available. Analyze your application size and performance data (timing and more). Connect the performance to the general architecture features and overheads discussed in Section 7.5. Analyze what is required to amortize the cost of communication and other task overheads to get good scaling and efficiency. Characterize quantitatively and explain what you have achieved.

7.14 Using the package for Jupyter Notebook and Spark available from www.jupyter .org, perform the following exercises.

(a) Create a vector of ascending integers from 0 to 2^{20}. Next, create a complementary vector of squares of these integers, and create a complementary vector of fractions.

(b) Create a complementary set of vectors for each of those above, each of which is the current number divided by its successor. For example, from [0, 1, 2, 3, ...] you would generate [0, 0.5, 0.667, ...].

(c) How long does it take to do these computations? How much speed-up can you get by increasing the number of workers?

7.15 Using the package for Jupyter Notebook available from www.jupyter.org, perform the following exercises.
(a) Find a data set on the web in CSV form of at least 10 MB. Load it as a dataframe.
(b) Compute a `select` analytic query.
(c) Load another related dataframe of at least 10 MB which has a common column.
(d) Execute a `join` query.
(e) How would the scalability of the application change if we used 100 MB of data? 1 GB? Explain.

7.16 Here, we compare OpenMP and Spark for parallel computation. Consider the matrix multiplication for $N \times N$ matrices. We will explore the ability to achieve good parallel speed-ups with these two parallelism models.
(a) Using OpenMP, write a parallel matrix multiplication program. Make sure it has at least N-fold parallelism, and run it on a range of T threads, and for various values of N. Specifically, let T range from 1 to the maximum number of threads on the server node (typically 20–64), and vary N from 16 to 512 in powers of two. Characterize the parallel speed-up by plotting T on the x-axis and performance on the y-axis. There should be one line for each value of N.
(b) Do the same thing using Spark.
(c) Compare their speed-ups. Which system gives better performance? Does this change as N increases? Explain.

7.17 A common application for serverless (function-as-a-service) is a client–server application that accesses information in the cloud.
(a) Create an S3 bucket with a set of records from your address book.
(b) Create a serverless function to access records in the address book, based on last name. Consider whether you should return all names from the address book that match, or just one. How hard is it to make this change?
(c) Create a serverless function that searches the address book, using substrings of the last name. How hard is this change?
(d) Change your serverless function to do "last name completion," calling a serverless function each time you type a character and returning all of the possible completions. How fast can this function be performed?

7.18 One common use of FaaS or serverless is to trigger an analysis pipeline, to keep a set of data structures and metadata consistent.
(a) Create an S3 bucket with a set of images, each with a key of its filename. Feel free to find a public domain set or you can experiment with a set of photos you have taken.
(b) Write a serverless function that iterates through all of the images in the bucket and creates a list of their sizes (e.g. 4 MB, 2 MB, etc.), and adds it to the bucket under the name "list-of-lengths."
(c) Write a serverless function that adds an image to the S3 bucket, then updates the metadata for "list-of-lengths."

(d)   Write a serverless function that retrieves an image, based on a size range.
(e)   Write a serverless function that retrieves an image, based on its name.

7.19   Serverless systems support dynamic scaling, allowing parallelism to grow and get a large job done quickly.
(a)   Create an S3 bucket with a set of 100 images, each with a key of its filename. Feel free to find a public domain set or you can experiment with a set of photos you have taken.
(b)   Write a serverless function that iterates through all of the images in the bucket and creates a list of their sizes (e.g. 4 MB, 2 MB, etc.), and adds it to the bucket under the name "list-of-lengths." How long does it take?
(c)   Write a serverless function that iterates through all of the images in the bucket, doing a complex image transformation, such as recoloring it 100 times, and then putting the transformed image into a second S3 bucket. How long does it take?
(d)   Rewrite your serverless function to launch a parallel set of serverless functions to do the complex image transformation. How long does it take?
(e)   Was it difficult in the iteration case to detect when all of the complex image transforms were done? What about in the parallel case? Explain.

Credits

Figure 7.1 Jeff Preshing; **Figure 7.6** S. Naffziger et al., Pioneering Chiplet Technology and Design for the AMD EPYC^{TM} and Ryzen^{TM} Processor Families: Industrial Product, in 2021 ACM/IEEE 48th Annual International Symposium on Computer Architecture (ISCA), Valencia, Spain, 2021 pp. 57–70, doi: 10.1109/ISCA52012.2021 .00014; **Figure 7.11** Open Compute Project; **Figure 7.12** (right) P. Sharma, P. Pegus II, D. Irwin, P. Shenoy, J. Goodhue and J. Culbert, Design and Operational Analysis of a Green Data Center, *IEEE Internet Computing*, 21(4):16–24, 2017, doi: 10.1109/MIC.2017.2911421; **Figure 7.13** Courtesy of Facebook.

8 Accelerators: Customized Architectures for Performance

The end of Dennard scaling forced a shift to explicit parallelism, and the adoption of multicore parallelism as a vehicle for performance scaling (see Chapter 3, specifically Section 3.3.4). Even with multicore, the continued demand for both higher performance and energy efficiency has driven a growing interest in accelerators. In fact, their use has become so widespread that in many applications effective use of accelerators is a requirement. We discuss why accelerators are attractive, and when they can deliver large performance benefits. Specifically, we discuss both graphics processing units (GPUs) that aspire to be general parallel accelerators, and other emerging focused opportunities, such as machine learning accelerators. We close with broader discussion of where acceleration is most effective, and where it is not. Software architects designing applications will find this perspective on benefits and challenges of acceleration essential. These criteria will shape both design and evolution, as well as use of customized accelerator architectures in the future.

8.1 The Emergence of Accelerators

Recent years have seen a growing interest in accelerators for computing. If we have practically general purpose computers, then what is an accelerator? An accelerator is a specialized computing device that exploits the structure and operations of a focused class of computations for higher performance or efficiency. For example, GPUs are designed to run computations with high levels of fine-grained parallelism that fit into small memories (even recent compute-optimized GPUs typically have only 8–16 GB of memory). Accelerators often require tedious low-level programming in order to deliver their benefits. Furthermore, when stretched beyond their area of specialization, accelerators are much slower than general purpose processors, especially when sequential programs with good algorithms and data structures (or even parallel threads) are effective. For example, a GPU running single-thread programs can produce 10-fold or lower performance compared to a CPU thread. As a result, accelerators typically complement traditional processors in a system with the computing workload distributed across processor and accelerator often based on performance, but also software convenience.

8.1.1   Accelerator Hardware Opportunities

Why can accelerators be so much faster than general purpose processors? In most cases, this can be attributed to a few simple attributes and a specialized niche of computation. We enumerate the key features that enable accelerators to outperform general purpose processors below:

- more hardware (applicable to the computation);
- higher degree of parallelism; and
- efficient, customized communication structure.

First, accelerators typically have many more operation units (add, mul, shade, etc.) that match the specialized computation domain. This greater quantity of hardware that matches the specialized domain provides high throughput for those critical operations. One could add such units to a CPU, but they might not be cost-effective. That is, for many users of the CPU, the additional hardware might provide no benefit. Second, exploiting higher degrees of parallelism is an important source of throughput and energy efficiency in most accelerators. Because traditional CPUs start with a sequential state expression of the program, they must "discover" opportunities for parallel execution. And of course, this higher degree of parallelism does depend in part on having more applicable hardware. In contrast, GPUs and many recent deep neural network (DNN) accelerators get high degrees of parallelism directly from the programmers or the software; they do not have to do any of the discovery work! Third, accelerators add efficient communication structures, matched to the algorithms and required data movement and synchronization for the specialized domain. These structures speed up computation and reduce energy costs. For example, the fast-Fourier transform (FFT) is a commonly accelerated computation, and explicit butterfly networks can avoid many load, store, and index computation operations.

By exploiting more operation units, specialized communication structures, and high degrees of parallelism, accelerators can achieve 10–100-fold increases in performance at the same silicon area or power. We will explore two types of accelerators, the relatively general, but highly parallel GPUs, and two examples of machine learning accelerators – the Google TensorFlow processing unit (TPU) and the Cerebras CS-1.

8.1.2   Programming and Software Challenges

To outperform CPUs, accelerators typically make several choices that make programming challenging. First, most accelerators use a high degree of parallelism to gain higher performance. Well beyond the 64 threads required by a multicore chip, accelerators such as GPUs may require parallelism of 4,096-fold to even 128,000-fold or more to achieve full performance. Second, accelerators often use specialized operations, limiting the flexibility of computation operations to enable much higher parallelism or low-energy implementations. For example, many accelerators for machine learning focus on 16-bit floating point formats and even 8-bit integer formats. This enables much higher degrees of parallelism and energy efficiency, but precludes

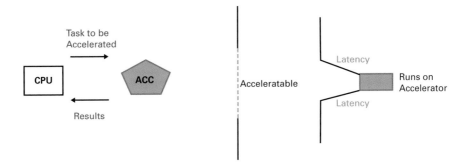

Figure 8.1 Tasks are sent to the accelerator. Performance benefit depends on having a large enough grain size to overcome the overheads for data movement and latency.

general purpose performance. Third, accelerators often specialize their interconnection structure and data movement for a narrow class of computational operations – such as matrix–matrix multiplies. Specialized hardware structures eliminate the overhead of many instructions (fetch, decode, execute, etc.) at the cost of applying only to applications that match that fixed structure.

The peculiarities of accelerators mean in general that custom programming (or reprogramming) is required. That is, the use of existing CPU software is not possible. To manage the complexity of accelerator programming, many software systems use libraries to encapsulate the complexity or even a special domain-specific language or accelerator-specific language introduced just for the accelerator (e.g. Tensorflow or CUDA). Further, since most accelerators apply to only part of the computation, large software applications become complex patchworks of traditional software and accelerated subroutines. Because the encapsulation of software incurs an overhead, and data may need to be moved from the processor to the accelerator and back again, each use of the accelerator needs to be a large "grain size" of computation. This idea is similar to the idea of grain-size for parallelism. As shown in Figure 8.1, the grain size must be large enough to overcome the accelerator overheads.

Typically, the traditional program sends tasks to the accelerator. This sending is similar to a procedure call to the accelerator. Along with the control information, data must be transferred for the arguments (e.g. copying arrays or data structures to the accelerator). For a given latency or invocation overhead, a rule of thumb applies for efficiency:

$$\text{Accelerator work} > \text{latency} \times 4 \times 10.$$

The accelerator work should be greater than the round-trip latency (overhead) and then multiplied by 2 and then 10 to ensure 90 percent efficiency. For example, if the latency/overhead is 100 instructions, then 4,000 instructions of work are required to achieve high efficiency.

> **Principle 8.1: Accelerators Apply to Narrower Types of Computations**
>
> *Accelerators exploit higher degrees of parallelism, specialized computation operations, and specialization computation structures to achieve higher performance and energy efficiency.*

8.2   Parallelism Accelerators

Graphics processing units represent a fundamentally different approach to computing. They abandon the sequential abstraction and require programmers to express explicit parallel computation and manage data locality. This radical departure forfeits the benefits of the sequential abstraction for composition, debugging, and more, as discussed in Chapter 4. They also share the key properties of accelerators, including higher density of units for domain operations and much greater parallelism to achieve performance. Unfortunately, GPUs are difficult to program. We discuss the differences below, then continue with the notion of practically general purpose GPUs, and GPUs as general parallel accelerators.

8.2.1   The Architecture of GPUs

Graphics processing units were shaped by the different and extreme performance demands of graphics computation. Graphics has thousands-to million-fold parallelism due to the many pixels in a display and across the many objects displayed on a computer screen. To meet these demanding performance requirements, GPUs gave up sequential state abstraction. Furthermore, graphics applications demand low, fixed latency for rendering with 24 or more frames per second (FPS) desired. This hard deadline in the FPS requirement was a critical driver. For example, 15 FPS is an important threshold for smooth animation and interactive response in games, scientific visualization, and more. Higher frame rates and pixel resolutions are also desirable. This natural and easily accessible graphics parallelism shaped GPUs as throughput engines for thousands of closely coordinated threads (nearly the same or single instruction, multiple-thread, or SIMT). These systems exploit programming languages that are specially focused on expressing these forms of parallelism, such as OpenCL, CUDA, and SyCL [51, 72]. The latency requirements drove the investment in hardware to create massive computing throughput, enabling both increasingly rich graphics effects (recently physics, translucency, smoke, hair, etc.) and extremely high resolution (HD, 4K, and more).

Single-instruction Multiple Thread   The building block in an Nvidia GPU is the streaming multi-processor, called SMX. This building block is already parallel, with

32 CUDA cores, each of which have an arithmetic-logic unit (ALU) and a register file. The idea of SIMT plays out across the group of cores. The threads have limited autonomy, as all cores see the same instructions, but can diverge in their computation based on values, conditional branches, memory indirection, and communication indirection. However, the best performance is realized when the threads operate in lock-step. The SMX construct from the Fermi microarchitecture (2008) is shown in Figure 8.2 (left).

Even a single SMX presents a significant parallel programming challenge. Designing a program to make effective use of 32-way parallelism with near-identical execution in each thread is generally achieved by exploiting data parallelism. Programming tools such as CUDA or SyCL [51, 72] exploit large arrays or data collections, and given the low performance of individual CUDA cores, programs can only achieve good performance when these 32 CUDA threads perform similar instruction sequences. Control or task parallelism is not exploited at this level.

A full GPU has a number of SMXs – for example, there are 16 in the 2008 Nvidia Fermi GPU (see Figure 8.2 (right)), but as many as 160 in the Nvidia Volta V100 GPU (2017), and more in the A100 (2020). This means that utilizing a full GPU will require a large amount of task-level parallelism, a need that some applications satisfy with further data parallelism or resort to task parallelism. Programming to utilize multiple SMXs is comparable to programming for thread parallelism in multicore CPUs. But, current-day multicore CPUs need perhaps 32- to 64-fold parallelism, whereas a GPU with 160 SMXs and 5,120 CUDA cores has an extreme parallelism requirement to achieve peak performance. And just as in a multicore CPU, these must be orchestrated to achieve good data reuse in the caches.

GPU applications express huge quantities of parallelism explicitly, exploiting GPU designs with large numbers of ALUs. This enables them to achieve much higher operation rates than conventional CPUs. The number of parallel execution units has increased steadily, growing more than 10-fold from 16 SMXs in 2008, and adding machine learning features such as tensor cores. The resulting increase in peak throughput performance is highlighted in Table 8.1.

Table 8.1. GPU peak performance (single precision floating point).

Processor	Year	Performance	Power	GF/watt
Nvidia V100	2019	14.9 TF SP	300 W	49.6
AMD Radeon RX 5700 XT	2019	10.1 TF SP	235 W	42.9
Nvidia M60	2016	9.65 TF SP	300 W	32.2
AMD Radeon RX 480	2016	5.8 TF SP	150 W	38.7
Nvidia K40	2013	5.0 TF SP	235 W	21.3
AMD Radeon R9 290X	2013	5.6 TF SP	250 W	23.8

GF, gigaFLOPs; SP, single precision; TF, teraFLOPs.

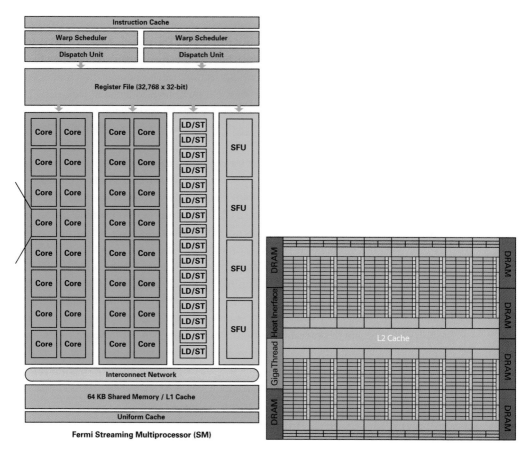

Figure 8.2 At left, the compute building block of an Nvidia Fermi GPU is a 32-thread parallel SIMT execution engine, called an SM or SMX. The cores share a single register file, and the larger special function units. At right, Nvidia's Fermi GPU combines 16 SMXs that share an L2 cache, accounting for 512 CUDA cores.

8.2.2   Diverse GPUs and Performance

As parallel accelerators, Nvidia and AMD GPUs, and presumably Intel's upcoming GPUs [110], are practically universal parallel computer architectures. For example, in the current generation, the gap in peak performance per watt between the top-end Nvidia and AMD GPUs is about 16 percent and has historically been less than 20 percent. For most, this difference is too small to justify rearchitecting software or selecting new algorithms.

> **Principle 8.2: GPUs Are Data-Parallelism Accelerators**
>
> *GPUs exploit fine-grained data parallelism to deliver higher performance on applications. With new programming models and programmer efforts, they exploit 1,000-fold application parallelism, to deliver 10–30-fold performance increase on many highly parallel applications. However, GPUs can suffer 10 times worse performance if there is insufficient parallelism.*

The rise of GPUs has produced a range of new programming languages that enable expression of fine-grained data parallelism. These include OpenCL, CUDA, and SyCL. To illustrate this programming style, we present an example of an Nvidia CUDA program for dot product in Figure 8.3. CUDA is only supported on Nvidia GPUs, while other models such as OpenCL and SyCL are supported across platforms.

The example shows fine-grained parallelism on elements of a vector, and the special keyword `threadIdx` indicates that the program will be run using an array of threads – perhaps dozens to as many as hundreds. This CUDA program expresses that all of the multiply operations in the dot product can be executed in parallel. However, it serializes the sum, using a single thread. A more aggressive, but more complicated, program might also parallelize that reduction. GPUs, origin was based on graphics parallelism for the millions of pixels in each frame, and even across multiple frames, which means that at the CUDA level, GPUs can execute millions of operations at the same time. Among the first areas beyond graphics to adopt GPUs was engineering design and simulation (aka ECAD), which benefited from the higher potential performance. Optimized circuit and physical simulations could be run on

```
#define N 512
__global__ void dot( int *a, int *b, int *c ) {
    // Shared memory for results of multiplication
    __shared__ int temp[N];
    temp[threadIdx.x] = a[threadIdx.x] * b[threadIdx.x];
    // Thread 0 sums the pairwise products
    if( 0 == threadIdx.x ) {
        int sum = 0;
        for( int i = 0; i < N; i++ )
        sum += temp[i];
        *c = sum;
    };
};
```

Figure 8.3 An Nvidia CUDA dot product program that illustrates a fine-grained data parallel programming style. This CUDA procedure creates a CUDA thread for each element of X1 [], and thus can express 2,048-way parallelism.

a single deskside GPU, replacing a cluster of CPUs. Next, GPUs were adopted for high-performance computing, and at present are becoming the platform of choice for the fastest single computers – exascale systems [98]. As their software ecosystem has matured, allowing many applications to benefit from their high performance on fine-grained data parallelism by using libraries, GPUs have become more widely used in data analytics, and particularly machine learning (deep neural networks, or DNNs).

8.3   Machine Learning Accelerators

Machine learning has exploded into prominence because of its effectiveness in addressing a wide range of computational tasks in artificial intelligence and in other areas of computing. A narrower area in which there is much interest in acceleration is DNNs. In such networks (Figure 8.4) there is substantial computation for inference (one multiply-accumulate for each neuron input) and even more for training (stochastic gradient descent for backpropagation). Further, there is ample parallelism across the neurons, and the communication pattern is static once the network topology is defined. Interestingly, these are the exact characteristics that support the design of efficient accelerators. Given these, machine learning accelerators also exploit operation density, parallelism, and optimized communication structures to achieve high performance. These properties should be becoming familiar (they are the same for GPUs).

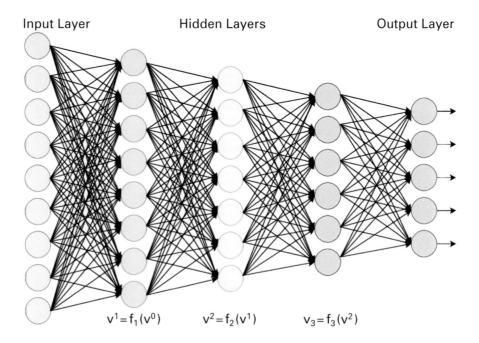

Input Layer   Hidden Layers   Output Layer

$$v^1 = f_1(v^0) \qquad v^2 = f_2(v^1) \qquad v_3 = f_3(v^2)$$

Figure 8.4 Deep neural networks have plentiful parallelism and are computationally intensive. Each circle represents a neuron, and each line a connection.

One advantage the machine learning accelerators have is that much of the machine learning community has converged on a single computational model, deep learning, and a few software programming frameworks. These include Tensorflow and Pytorch. Because the vast majority of machine learning users and application developers use these frameworks, accelerator designers for ML can often avoid supporting general purpose software.

8.3.1 Google's Tensor Processing Unit

The Tensor processing unit (TPU) is an example machine learning accelerator that accelerates high-level operations such as matrix multiplication and convolution. It operates on large data items (matrices, for example), that typically capture the state of one level of a DNN and therefore can have thousands of values. The TPU is implemented on a PCIe card that can be hosted in a CPU-based cloud node, and each TPU chip integrates the functions shown on the top in Figure 8.5a – two large matrix multiply/convolve units, a transpose unit, a vector unit, a large local memory, and some smaller FIFO (first in, first out) and buffer memories. The host queue accepts instructions for the TPU (commands) from the host processor. Other elements provide high bandwidth access to stacked HBM2 DRAM, and connectivity to the host CPU via the PCIe bus. The TPU is used for both inference and training in the datacenter, but actually supports a flexible high-level language, called TensorFlow, that can express computations on vectors, matrices, and tensors with higher dimensions. There have been three generations of TPU, and as of December 2018 the deployed TPU in Google datacenters was TPUv2, shown on the bottom in Figure 8.5b, which includes two cores per chip and four chips per PCI board. Each core can deliver approximately 4 teraops and therefore the PCI board delivers a total of 180 teraops.[1]

Because some of the larger DNNs can involve 200 million parameters and take up to 10^{20} compute operations to train [100], the TPUs can be aggregated together to achieve higher total performance, as shown in Figure 8.6. The TPUs are connected directly to each other using a three-dimensional torus topology, so messages can be sent between them with both lower latency and higher bandwidth than through the regular datacenter network. These ensembles can achieve 100 petaops performance, approaching the capability of supercomputers.

Google has also designed a low-power engine for inference, called the Edge TPU, with a similar matrix-oriented acceleration architecture, which implements only 8-bit and 16-bit integer operations, requiring DNN models to be quantized for deployment.

---

[1] We refer to these as teraops because deep learning accelerators typically operate on small number representations such as FP32 or Google's Bfloat16. These smaller representations reduce data movement and operations cost, while preserving much of the application value.

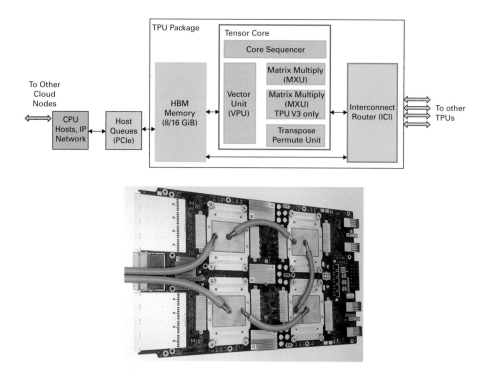

Figure 8.5 Google's TPU accelerates computation on DNN layers annd thus DNNs. The logical architecture (top) and their embedding (two cores/chip, four chips/card) in a TPUv2 PCIe card (bottom) for each cloud node. Each PCIe card achieves 180 teraops.

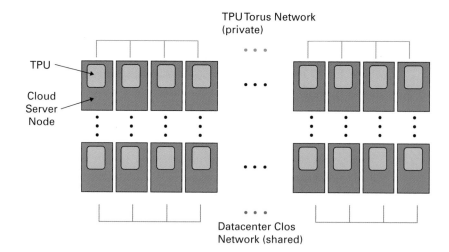

Figure 8.6 Each TPU is hosted in a cloud node. Its backside torus network is private and can couple 2,048 TPUs to create a 100 petaflop computer.

However, the energy benefits of this limited set of datatypes enables the Edge TPU to operate in low-power environments such as a smartphone or Internet of Things (IoT) device.

8.3.2 Cerebras CS-2: A Wafer-Scale Machine Learning Accelerator

Google is not the only builder of aggressive machine learning acceleration hardware, with Microsoft, Alibaba, Huawei, Nvidia, and Intel as the other players. We present one of the most novel accelerators, the Cerebras CS-2 here, and detail several other efforts in the *Digging Deeper* section.

A CS-2 system includes 850,000 processing elements connected in a two-dimensional array. Whereas traditional chips are formed by cutting a wafer into perhaps 100 silicon die, Cerebras leaves them connected, connecting over 8,000 processing elements in the area of a die to their neighbors with a two-dimensional mesh network. With a total of 40 GiB of memory, it has a phenomenal computing to memory capacity ratio. Sean Lie. Multi-million core, multi-wafer AI cluster. In *Proceedings of Hot Chips 33*, Stanford, CA, August 2021. Equally impressive is its power consumption, estimated at 15–20 kilowatts.

Novel features of the CS-2's processing elements (see Figure 8.7) include a fast local memory with no hierarchy! Because it has only 48 KB of memory per processing element, access is fast and uniform – there are no memory hierarchy delays. Further,

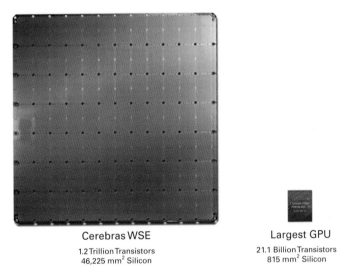

Cerebras WSE

1.2 Trillion Transistors
46,225 mm^2 Silicon

Largest GPU

21.1 Billion Transistors
815 mm^2 Silicon

Figure 8.7 Cerebras CS-2 is an array of processing elements, each highly capable, but connected by a two-dimensional mesh of high-speed, low-latency interconnect. While the overall system can exceed 1 petaflops, its primary limit is a memory of only 19 GiB for nearly 400,000 processing elements.

each processing element can communicate in all four directions in the mesh in parallel, and with low latency. Finally, the CS-2 has dataflow synchronization, enabling computation by communication actions with low overhead. While many things are still secret about the Cerebras machine, we already know enough that makes it unique among computing systems, and even among machine learning accelerators.

While the Cerebras hardware technology makes it difficult to compare fairly to other chips and systems, in the future we expect to see interesting results in MLPerf (a leading industry benchmarking association for machine learning accelerators and software [67]), showing training times for large DNNs that allow direct comparison to clusters of GPUs. Other results show the fastest *strong scaling* performance on conjugate gradient, a difficult scientific computing kernel. On an 18 GiB problem, the CS-2's predecessor, the CS-1, was over 200 times faster than any other computing system – of any size! This is only true for the optimum problem size (18 GiB) – one that both fits in the memory and has sufficient computation to use all of the processing elements.

Principle 8.3: Machine Learning Accelerators for Deep Learning Specialize Compute Operations, Communication, and Datatypes

Machine learning accelerators for deep learning focus on matrix and vector operations, as well as high compute density and parallelism. They can match or surpass GPUs on training and inference, and their narrow focus enables delivery of high DNN performance with low programming effort.

8.3.3   Small Machine Learning Accelerators (Edge)

Not all accelerators are large and powerful. The two machine learning accelerators discussed so far are high-powered datacenter accelerators, but machine learning is increasingly used in devices at the edge of the Internet, such as in smartphones or video cameras. These devices have both limited power (heat) and battery life (energy), so such edge machine learning accelerators focus on extreme energy efficiency, at an acceptable level of performance. For example, most smartphone cameras use a DNN to identify faces in the view of the camera, marking them with a rectangle for convenience. Every Apple iPhone since the iPhone 11 in 2017 includes a **neural engine** [112], which is a special processor for machine learning applications, and is used by applications such as Face ID, Animoji, and Facetime. This DNN accelerator and several others like them on Android phones are close to the size of a single processor core, but can achieve 600 billion operations per second (typically 8- or 16-bit integer operations) with well below a single watt of power. This performance is as much as 50 times greater than the processor core, but only for DNN applications.

8.4 Other Opportunities for Acceleration

There are many other opportunities for accelerated computing. Many of these involve high degrees of parallelism over large quantities of data that enable easy offloading of the computation or data encoded in unusual ways that CPUs do not find easy to manipulate.

One important area for acceleration is media processing – playing videos on your phone or recoding them for multiple resolutions and streaming rates in the cloud for YouTube or Netflix. Additional examples include compressing your photo libraries or scanning them for face-recognition based "tagging." Video and image encodings use complex structures and algorithms designed to reduce their size dramatically while maintaining quality. As a result, bytes and even bits are manipulated extensively, again a weak spot for CPUs, and images and video have extensive parallelism – across pixels and across frames. Accelerators in your smartphone for video decoding allow you to watch streaming video for as much as 30 times longer using less energy than would be possible with a CPU.

A common area for acceleration involves encryption, such as the advanced encryption standard (AES) [33]. Classical encryption algorithms such as the AES employ lots of bit-level rearrangements of blocks based on keys. Because processor operations are typically word-oriented (64 bits) or perhaps subword oriented (32 bits), manipulating individual bits not only reduces performance dramatically, but also fails to exploit the significant parallelism available in the bit rearrangements. For that reason, cryptography accelerators (and even special cryptography instructions in general purpose processors) are popular and can achieve 40 times or better performance and energy improvement.

Accelerators are being studied for many other areas, and there are doubtless many more areas of opportunity that have not yet been identified. While accelerators have significant advantages, they also have significant drawbacks. Only time will tell how the balance between general purpose and specialized accelerators will turn out.

8.5 Limitations and Drawbacks of Accelerated Computing

Accelerators can provide as much as 100-fold increases in computing performance and energy efficiency for a narrow computational domain. However, they have significant drawbacks as well. Accelerators represent a fundamental challenge to the structure of both hardware and software. For hardware, first, accelerators take up resources and dedicate them to specialized and narrow computational domains. They can give terrific performance for that narrow domain, but no benefits for other domains. They just consume silicon area that translates to increased cost for hardware. It is not unusual for a mobile chip to have 75 percent of its silicon area inactive. The second challenge is that if the standards change – for example a new type of encryption (i.e. post-quantum crypto) or new video encoding standard (H.264 a few years ago) – the accelerator design may not be flexible enough to support the new algorithms and data structures. In such a case, the accelerator will provide no benefit to the new algorithms. This is a problem we rarely have with CPUs! Finally, accelerators take resources away from the general purpose processors. This may be the most disruptive hardware characteristic, as it decreases the number of general cores available for general parallel software and thus the performance accessible to a much broader class of applications. This makes is just a little harder for new applications to catch on.

For software, the situation is even worse; accelerators:

- are difficult to program;
- often require reprogramming with each new generation; and
- are disruptive to software architecture.

First, most accelerators are difficult to program, requiring more effort to create the same functionality, albeit at higher performance and energy efficiency. Second, that software effort often has limited durability, since a revision in the accelerator design or computation structure can render it unusable. This is a continual problem with accelerators; in fact, so much so that the mainstream open-source packages such as Android OS are not tuned for specific hardware and accelerators by the open-source community. Rather, they are tuned for the accelerators on chips from Qualcomm, Samsung, and others by the respective hardware vendors. This is because these companies want to showcase the performance of their chips, and thus have the greatest incentive to deliver high-performance software libraries for media, etc. Finally, perhaps the largest long-term problem with accelerators is that they disrupt the software architecture of large applications, siloing[2] parts of the system and preventing better large-scale designs and refactoring. Further, accelerators can actually encourage the use of worse algorithms that require more operations if the structure of that algorithm better matches the parallel computation and communication structures of the accelerator. This is discouraging, because if the accelerator is removed, remedial algorithm design and implementation may be required. These sorts of challenges have become known in the software community as **technical debt**, where design decisions create an ongoing increased support and opportunity cost for the system [11].

Principle 8.4: Accelerators Can Increase Programming Effort and Incur Technical Debt in the Software Architecture

Accelerators' performance advantage is based on parallelism, density, and values. By exploiting special properties of a narrower domain and significant programming effort, higher performance can be achieved, but the software **technical debt** *incurred is significant. A key challenge is that accelerators are typically unable to run conventional software at competitive speed (10 times slower).*

---

[2] Locking into a closed module without interaction with the rest of the system.

8.6   Summary

In 2005, CPUs alone would have been the entire story for computing architectures, but the past decade has seen the rise of "accelerators" as a mainstream hardware and software approach. Important among these are:

- **GPUs** which, with their explicitly parallel programming model and highly parallel architectures, have grown from high-performance computing niches such as graphics, engineering modeling, and scientific computing toward the mainstream. These GPUs exploit extreme parallelism to achieve higher compute density and energy efficiency – at the cost of programmability and memory capacity. Within the class of GPUs there has been a long-running competition between Nvidia and AMD, yet in this parallel accelerator niche, again performance parity has emerged. Despite significant differences in architecture across the leading vendors, GPU performance is mostly limited by power and chip area in each successive generation.

- **Machine learning (DNNs):** Beyond parallelism, DNN accelerators exploit special domain datatypes and compute operations to great effect in increased efficiency. As machine learning applications have proliferated in video, photos, speech, natural language, and more, machine learning accelerators have not only garnered great excitement and investment (over 100 venture-funded startups), but have found their way into all kinds of computing systems from large-scale cloud datacenters down to smartphones and even IoT devices such as smart doorbells, intelligent assistants, and web cameras.

- **Other accelerators** that exploit special datatypes and operations to achieve high efficiency and performance on domains such as media computing (video, images), cryptography, and search ranking.

The primary downside of accelerators is their narrow applicability. When taken outside of their chosen domain of specialization, accelerators typically give little benefit, and can often be 10 times slower than traditional processors. In short, when they do not apply, they are of little use. Further, as discussed in Section 8.5, accelerators pose important challenges to software architecture, calcifying software architecture and incurring technical debt.

8.7   Digging Deeper

Graphics processing units evolved over two decades, starting as little more than VGA controllers in the 1990s to become powerful computers able to drive multi-million pixel displays with 24-bit color, and producing images derived from rich three-dimensional models. Key drivers for computing power came from the growing resolution of computer displays from 640×480 to today's near paper-quality displays. Much of the early graphics architecture work was developed at Silicon Graphics Inc. [108], founded by Jim Clark. SGI pioneered the graphics pipeline, and its proprietary IRIS GL system formed the initial design of Open GL, the major competitor to Microsoft's Direct X. GPUs emerged to support these graphics APIs on PCs. These PCs later evolved into powerful gaming platforms and engineering design workstations. GPUs evolved into more generally programmable machines, called "general purpose" GPUs (GPGPUs). This idea, and its emergence, is described by John Nickolls and William Dally [73]. The core ideas behind GPGPUs were brought to Nvidia by Nickolls from Maspar [59, 106], and in turn borrowed from Thinking Machines [81]. GPU programming tools for data parallelism, such as CUDA or SyCL [51, 72], have become quite popular, and are used in increasing numbers of high-performance and graphics-intensive applications.

The rise of machine learning is well described in Hinton, Bengio, and Lecun's Turing Award talk and article [41], describing how long years of work painstakingly created the understanding of how to make backpropagation work for training, and how the availability of large data collections such as ImageNet, combined with fast parallel computing in the form of GPUs, enabled this breakthrough [56, 79]. Beyond Google's TPU, other machine learning accelerators include academic work such as Eyeriss2 and EIE [13, 37]. Other leading cloud machine learning accelerators have been built by Alibaba, Huawei [36, 39], and a GitHub page documents over 100 machine learning hardware accelerator vendors [93]. Notable systems among these are the Cerebras CS-1 and CS-2 [78]. Sean Lie. Multi-million core, multi-wafer AI cluster. In *Proceedings of Hot Chips 33*, Stanford, CA, August 2021.

With the rise of accelerators and the popularity of **co-design**, where the hardware is optimized to match particular application domains or software packages, designers of large-scale systems have become concerned about **technical debt**. The idea here is that local optimization can provide some benefits, but constrains larger-scale refactoring and application progress. If such techniques are employed, they incur a debt for their maintenance and perhaps slow forward progress [11].

8.8   Problems

8.1   Explore the role of an accelerator in computing systems.

(a)   The notion of an accelerator is in contrast to a general purpose computer, as discussed in Chapter 6. Explain how a narrower domain of an accelerator might be defined, and why an accelerator with such a narrow applicability would be attractive.

(b)   In order to be viable, typically an accelerator needs to deliver a 10 times improvement in performance or energy efficiency. Explain why.

8.2   Accelerators are typically applicable to a narrower domain of computing; they are specialized for that domain. Within the universe of computation, several dimensions are important for creating an accelerator that gives a large performance benefit.

(a)   Define a narrower set of datatypes and operations that are useful for a computing domain. Describe the domain.

(b) Describe some important computation and data movement patterns for that domain, and how an accelerator could be customized for them.

(c) Are there memory structures that could be customized to increase accelerator performance? Describe them.

8.3 In 1967, Gene Amdahl, a famous computer architect, formulated a performance law that captures limits on the benefits of accelerators. **Amdahl's law** defines the execution time of the whole task before acceleration as T. This execution time can be divided into a part that benefits from acceleration p and a part that would not $(1 - p)$. Then:

$$T = (1 - p)T + pT = (1 - p)T + pT.$$

If the accelerator provides a benefit of s, then the improved execution time $T(s)$ can be written as

$$T(s) = (1 - p)T + \frac{p}{s}T.$$

(a) Compute the improved execution time $T(s)$ if $T = 100s$, $p = 0.5$, and $s = 10$.

(b) What value of p is required to achieve a speed-up (runtime improvement) of eight times?

(c) What value of p is required to achieve a speed-up of 25 times if $s = 50$?

(d) Amdahl's law is often considered a limit on performance benefit, given a particular accelerator (defines both p and s). Explain why this is true.

(e) For designers of programmable accelerators, it is possible that Amdahl's law does not provide a strict limit. Explain how programmability affects the achievable p and s for an application.

8.4 One long-studied computing algorithm for acceleration is the Fast-Fourier transform (FFT).

(a) Explain what the FFT algorithm is, and the datatypes on which it is computed.

(b) Since an FFT can be run on user applications of arbitrary size, it's important to be able to decompose such an application into a unit of computing suitable for an accelerator. Explain how a large FFT could be decomposed into smaller FFTs of, say, size 256 or 1,024.

(c) Composition of accelerated functions is often a critical bottleneck. What operations need to be implemented efficiently to compose these smaller FFTs efficiently? Would implementing them with a loop on a CPU be sufficient to achieve high performance?

8.5 One rich domain for accelerators is bioinformatics (genomics), with computations over strings of characters (GCAT, representing DNA chemical bases). In this space, accelerator designers have argued that in order to achieve radical performance advantages, the algorithms for analysis must be changed. This is a significantly different view, because the design (and limitations and challenges) of the hardware is reshaping the computation.

(a) Read the paper on the DARWIN accelerator [97]. Describe the programming interface for the application.

(b) Summarize the motivation for changing the algorithms. How do the algorithms change the achievable performance from acceleration? How much performance increase can be expected?

(c) Summarize the changes to the algorithms. What kind of expertise or knowledge would be required to decide if these changes are a good idea? (Trade the performance for the change results.)

8.6 One rich domain for accelerators is computer graphics. In fact, this domain gave rise to special machines as early as the 1980s in companies such as Silicon Graphics. Classical graphics pipelines have a series of stages that take a three-dimensional model to a rendered two-dimensional image (frame in a video).

(a) Look at the OpenGL framework and classical rendering pipeline. What are the stages? What data are passed between stages, and how much (quantity)?

(b) Digging a bit deeper, look into the operations in each stage. Why is it suitable for acceleration? How much faster do you think it could be made to run with special hardware (accelerator) compared to a CPU? Explain.

(c) The early computer graphics accelerators defined a class of high-end computers from Silicon Graphics, and then later became a central element of PCs and smartphones. In the past 10 years, these "graphics processing engines" have been programmed more generally as GPUs. Can you explain how they achieved this "reverse evolution"? That is, to create a more general capability – general purpose GPU – from a specialized GPU accelerator.

8.7 GPUs claim to be general purpose parallelism accelerators. Based on what you have learned about GPUs, define the acceleration domain.

(a) What is the computing domain? What datatypes and operations? What computational structure?

(b) How much benefit (performance increase) can be achieved on programs that match this structure?

(c) One other corollary change for GPUs is the need to use a small, but high-bandwidth memory (first GDDR and later HBM). This restriction first limited GPUs to 4 GB of memory, then later 8 GB. How does this restrict applications? How significant is this restriction?

8.8 Nvidia GPUs group a set of threads and execute them together in a "warp." These units of 64 threads are the building blocks of performance in a larger GPU. If we try to execute a sequential thread on a warp, we get the performance of a single CUDA core, with a rather unusual memory hierarchy. Looking at several of the white papers at www.nvidia.com for the Maxwell, Pascal, or Turing microarchitectures, compute how single thread performance might compare to an Intel Skylake core. How much slower is it? Can you explain why this is so?

8.9 Google's TPU accelerates DNN operations with its matrix multiply array. Tensors are a mathematical concept similar to vectors and matrices, but more general.

For this problem, you may need to refer to Google's web pages on the TPU, or perhaps the TPU paper [52].

(a) Why can a specialized matrix multiply array do these operations faster (and more efficiently) than a C program on a CPU core? (Hint: think about how many instructions are required on a CPU.)

(b) To quantify this, consider a matrix–matrix product for a 64×64 matrix, which can be done in a single instruction on the TPU. How many instructions does it take on a CPU?

(c) Of course, the TPUs single-instruction matrix multiply is not quite the same cost as a simple add, xor, or load/store instruction. However, it is much cheaper than the number of instructions you just computed. Give three specific costs that are reduced by the TPU accelerator formulation of matrix multiply.

(d) The downside of accelerators is that they suffer from narrow performance. That is, failing to accelerate computations that just slightly miss their focus. Can you describe a variation of the matrix multiply computation that is *very close*, but not quite acceleratable by the TPU? Try to describe one that is as close as possible.

(e) Now consider a CPU version of your "near-miss" example from the previous part of the question. How much would the performance vary between the matrix multiply and your near-miss computation? Be as quantitative as possible.

8.10 Google's TPU gives little performance benefit for many software programs such as a word processor, Python interpreter, or graphical user interface.

(a) Why is this? Explain.

(b) Think about the applications that you use every day. Can you think of any that can be accelerated by a TPU? What does this tell you about the domain of applications that the TPU can accelerate?

(c) Of course, as we discussed in Chapter 1, the variety of applications and their behavior is constantly changing. What change would it take for a TPU to be valuable for these applications?

8.11 One exciting example of an accelerator for machine learning model training is the Cerebras (see https://cerebras.net), a wafer-scale machine learning accelerator. This system combines all of the silicon area of an entire "wafer" to create a giant computing surface, with several hundred times the transistors of the largest GPU or CPU.

(a) How many transistors, computing units, does it have? How much silicon area? What is its peak performance?

(b) Given what we know about the power consumption of GPUs, use the transistor count to estimate the power required for a Cerebras wafer-scale system.

(c) One of the radical aspects of the wafer-scale Cerebras system is that it does not adopt a hybrid technology approach (no separate technology for memory, such as DRAM). Based on the information you have, how much memory does the Cerebras machine have per compute core? How does this compare to systems we have studied?

(d) What implications does this memory size have for the types of applications for which it can be used?

(e) Brainstorm some ideas for how to add DRAM to the Cerebras design. Can it be done in a way that preserves the unique advantages of the system?

8.12 Cerebras CS-1 employs an array of processing elements, each simple and flexibly programmable. Given the numbers in Section 8.3.2, estimate the following properties for a GPU system such as the Nvidia A100, Cerebras CS-1, and Google TPU.

(a) Computing density (billion operations per mm^2 of silicon).

(b) Computing per watt (billion operations per watt).

(d) Memory density (gigabytes per m^2).

Make good estimates and justify where detailed information is not available.

8.13 The Cerebras CS-1 utilizes a novel wafer-scale computing approach. This enables many "chips" worth of silicon to be connected with a high-quality interconnect on the same wafer.

(a) Compute the bisection bandwidth (bits/second) that can be transmitted across the narrowest part of the machine. How does it compare to a system such as Nvidia's DGX-2? A Google TPU?

(b) With only 48 KB of memory per processing element, the CS-1 is very close to our scaled ENIAC (see Chapter 5) without the increase in memory capacity. How does that proportion affect the speed of the memory?

(c) How does that proportion affect the applications that can be run? Give specific examples.

8.14 MLPerf (http://mlperf.org) is an open competitive benchmarking process for industry machine learning accelerators. Look over the data from the latest benchmarks on the site. Pick one of the categories, such as training or inference.

(a) Which system gives the highest performance? How does the performance compare to that of CPUs? (Note that these CPUs have all been enhanced for higher neural network performance.)

(b) Can you assess which system is the smallest or most energy efficient?

(c) What are the benchmarks they are using for evaluation? Are they representative of your applications?

8.15 We will explore a domain of computing that you identify for acceleration. Find a domain that has significant (long-running) computational challenges.

(a) Describe the domain.

(b) Define a narrower set of datatypes and operations that are useful for that computing domain.

(c) Describe some important computation and data movement patterns for that domain, and how an accelerator could be customized for them.

(d) Are there memory structures that could be customized to increase accelerator performance? Describe them.

(e) Estimate the overall benefit that your accelerator might be able to achieve based on how much it accelerates the domain compared to the surrounding software that calls it.

Credits

Figure 8.2 Image courtesy of NVIDIA; **Figure 8.4** Mehrdad Heydarzadeh, Negin Madani and Mehrdad Nourani, Gearbox Fault Diagnosis Using Power Spectral Analysis, 2016 *IEEE International Workshop on Signal Processing Systems (SiPS)*, 242–247, 2016, doi: 10.1109/SiPS.2016.50; **Figure 8.5** (right) Created by Zinskauf, shared via CC BY-SA 4.0.

9 Computing Performance: Past, Present, and Future

In this chapter we review the major dimensions of computer architecture covered, summarizing the high points and providing an overall perspective. Specifically, we highlight how each has shaped computers and computing. Computer architecture continues to advance, so we discuss its ongoing evolution, including the major technology and architecture trends. In many cases, the promise of computing is great, but as with parallelism and accelerators, increasingly its progress comes with compromises. We highlight the critical emerging constraints. Outlining these provides a strategic perspective on likely vectors of change that form a roadmap for the future.

Beyond the mainstream, there are a number of radical new directions that promise new, divergent capabilities for computing. For many of these, as of yet there is little proof of benefit. We point out the most promising, but only time will tell if they can fulfill their promise. One thing we can be sure of is that any radical departure will require the growth of new layers of software, algorithms, and more to create the ability to compete with traditional computers. We highlight these challenges to provide a realistic perspective.

Finally, it's important to note that computing's impact on society over seven decades is unparalleled, and the progress from mainstream evolution and radical departures will continue and expand computing's extraordinary impact on society in the coming decades.

9.1 Historical Computer Performance

In the decades since the 1950s, when electronic digital computers first came into being, the performance of computers has grown rapidly and steadily, passing a trillion-fold improvement (10^{12}) in the 2010s. The key drivers of this advance have been: (1) miniaturization, (2) instruction-level parallelism (ILP) aka hidden, (3) dynamic locality, and (4) explicit parallelism. The first three pillars enabled computer performance improvement in Phase I, where parallelism was hidden underneath the instruction set interface ISA (Figure 9.1). While the contributions of these three pillars continue, improvement in Phase II has been dominated by multicore and scale-out parallelism.

First, **miniaturization** was perhaps the largest contributor in Phase I, enabled by tremendous progress in microelectronics that took us from discrete transistors (one transistor per chip) to over 50 billion transistors per chip in 2017. This massive

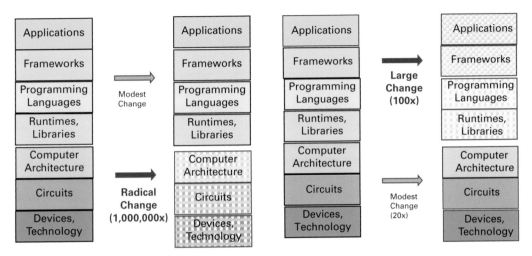

Figure 9.1 Historical scaling of computing stack: Phase I (hidden parallelism) and Phase II (explicit parallelism).

increase allowed a room-sized computer like ENIAC to be shrunk to the size of a few strands of human hair. A simple model of computer clock rate, based on the physical size of computers, captures the improvement of performance due to miniaturization closely. It predicts the clock rate of modern microprocessors within one-thousandth of a percent (a factor of two in a million-fold increase). Enabled by voltage scaling (Dennard scaling), miniaturization was able to finesse the fundamental problem created by shrinking computations: growing power density.

The second important contributor to computer performance is novel architectural techniques that cheat sequential abstraction. That is, they hide parallelism in implementation from programs (software). That is **hidden parallelism**. These techniques leverage the opportunity to execute multiple instructions in parallel without violating the semantics of the sequential state model, enabling the plentiful transistors provided by Moore's Law to be exploited for that parallel execution. Key approaches include multiple-issue, branch prediction, and speculative execution – which all depend on renaming. Together, these techniques enable modern microarchitectures to execute an average of nearly 30 instructions at a time, and at peak as many as 100. This is accomplished while maintaining sequential abstraction – the critical pillar of managing complexity in large software and hardware systems.

Third, despite miniaturization's rapid progress that benefited memory as much as logic, the rapid growth of software and applications in scale, diversity, and complexity has been far faster. Consequently, modern servers have 128 million times larger memories than ENIAC. This makes achieving the needed memory speed and access rates a critical challenge. As a direct consequence, modern computer systems' physical size is dominated by that of memory. A model of memory latency based on physical size captures the impact of this large capacity growth on memory access latency.

It accurately predicts the ratio of memory access latency to processor clock rates at 500:1. This is very close to the ratio we find in computing systems today.

Solving the challenge of slow memory to enable high-speed computing requires successful exploitation of **dynamic locality**. Attempts to address the memory wall and von Neumann bottleneck drove architects to invent address filters (caches) that exploit the idea that a small fraction of the memory can be physically close to the processor (and therefore fast). By dynamically changing the "map" of memory, computers are able to exploit the dynamic locality that most programs exhibit. This dynamic locality arises from structured programming languages and typical application data structures. Successful exploitation of dynamic locality enables computers to achieve remarkable speeds on applications with even terabytes of data mostly stored in slow memory. A consequence of the filter (cache) technique is that smaller computations (less data) continue to be the fastest, but high speed can also be achieved for applications with data needs that are **dynamically** small. In today's computers, multi-level cache hierarchies effectively span the 400-fold latency gap from processors to main memory.

Finally, while parallel computers have been studied since the 1960s [3], the difficulty associated with parallel programming meant that it was relegated to shared server workloads and extreme scientific computing. With the end of Dennard scaling and the advent of multicore processors around 2006, **explicit parallelism** has come to the fore. We have seen that CPUs can incorporate dozens of cores; mainstream products in 2020 have as many as 64 cores in a server CPU and 128 cores in a server node. In these systems, for applications to sustain the continued rapid growth in performance they have come to expect, they must adopt parallel programming, creating threads or data parallelism. This has been a major and ongoing effort in software. Fortunately, this is possible for many large applications; for others, scalable increases in throughput suffice.

Beyond multicore server nodes, there is parallelism in supercomputers and cloud datacenters. These systems include tens of thousands of nodes, which collectively have one-million-fold hardware parallelism. Connecting such large ensembles of computers is challenging. Despite aggressive networking, the physical size of these datacenters means that communication latencies are large (10 microseconds) and bandwidths are limited; consequently, successful parallelism requires much larger parallel tasks (grain size). To cope with these challenges, cloud applications have created major new software architectures (three-tier web, map–reduce, microservices, and serverless) with plentiful coarse-grained parallelism. As a result, many cloud applications have ample coarse-grained parallelism, and scale to a full datacenter and even beyond!

9.2   Future Computer Performance: Opportunities for Performance Increase

9.2.1   Hardware Scaling and Opportunities

While there is little question that Dennard scaling ended around 2005, the miniaturization of electronics has continued, largely in accord with Moore's Law. These repeated

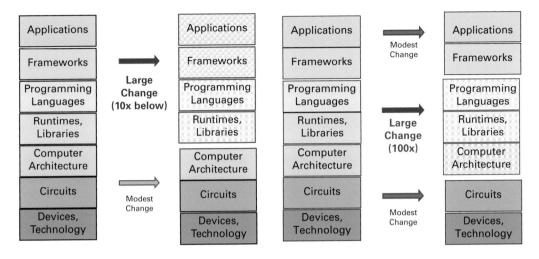

Phase III: Age of Parallelism (2020+) Impact of Accelerators (2018+)

Figure 9.2 In the future, parallel scaling will continue, with the largest benefits coming from software changes to exploit it (left). Acceleration causes a mid-stack disruption in narrow areas, delivering a large bump in specialized performance.

doublings of transistors per chip have produced state-of-the-art CPUs and GPUs with 50 billion transistors in 2020.

In the coming decade, the microelectronics industry expects to continue increasing transistor density (Moore's Law), add three-dimensional packaging, and more sophisticated packages and denser interconnect substrates. Performance increases of 20 percent single-thread and 40 percent annual capacity growth (by parallelism) are expected to continue the advance we have experienced over the past decade. This scenario is depicted as the Continuing Age of Parallelism in Figure 9.2 (left). For example, the chief technology officer of Taiwan Semiconductor Corporation (TSMC), which manufactures chips for Apple, Nvidia, Qualcomm, AMD, and others, gave a talk at Hot Chips 2019 suggesting density will continue to increase for the next 10 years. The next year, a leading technologist from Intel came to Hot Chips 2020 and suggested that perhaps 50 times higher transistor density can be achieved, corresponding to perhaps six more doublings. However, no prediction was made for how long it would take to achieve these advances. Perhaps much longer than the 10–12 years that Moore's Law would predict. These advances will drive a continued slow but steady progress in the computing capabilities of multicore CPUs.

A major obstacle is growing power density. That is, how can we reduce the power consumption in proportion with the density increase. This is the same challenge that Dennard scaling solved, but for which there has been no good solution since 2005. A few things help. For example, better interconnects through photonics and finer pitches may reduce power per transmitted bit by perhaps 10–100 times. These power limits suggest that continuing the single thread and the capacity increase may be optimistic. Some believe that a new kind of transistor, dramatically more power efficient, is required. As part of this, we expect that parallelism in the largest systems will continue to increase the capacity of each building block (CPU, server), and the entire system.

The growing interest in accelerators reflects this situation. With the difficulties of parallel programming in achieving higher performance, some consider the price of maintaining general purpose performance too costly. For a range of domains, too many traditional CPUs are required to meet rapidly increasing application demands. For those with narrow computational needs, many are choosing to build not only accelerator architectures, but also customized tools that ease programming difficulties. Adopting accelerators affects the middle of the stack, as shown in Impact of Accelerators in Figure 9.2 (right), leaving the top and the bottom unchanged. However, each such change addresses only a fraction of the application space. On could imagine perhaps dozens of versions of the middle three layers. Perhaps one for each major type of accelerator. Examples of such narrow spaces include media, machine learning, blockchain (e.g. Bitcoin), molecular dynamics, high-frequency market matching, image processing, signal processing, and more. In narrow domains accelerators can deliver performance increases of 10 times, 100 times, and perhaps more. It remains to be seen if these gains are one-time gains or can be further advanced with subsequent innovation, and what their software consequences are. We are headed for a two-tier world with many applications running on general purpose systems that continue to scale to greater parallelism and capacity, but diving into accelerators for critical sub-pieces in a rich, heterogeneous composition.

9.2.2   Resulting Programming and Software Challenges

Since 2005, nearly all software for computing devices from mobile to the cloud has been parallel. Starting with baby steps to dualcore and quadcore systems, we are now passing 64-core CPUs, and the scale of parallelism in the cloud regularly exceeds 10,000.[1] In the coming decade, continued growth of both transistor density and cloud scale is expected to drive even higher levels of parallelism. With a 50-fold increase in density, a straight extrapolation would suggest single-chip parallelism of 500-fold, and one-billion-fold in the cloud. This growing hardware parallelism will continue the pressure on software to find new ways to expose and manage parallelism in order to tap higher levels of performance. We expect to find ever-larger application uses to fill these future systems' vast computing capabilities.

Further, with continued slower increases in single-thread performance, more and more applications will turn to accelerators for specialized high performance. The proliferation of accelerators will be a significant and growing challenge for programming in terms of difficulty and portability. To meet the challenges of accelerator programming, many programmers are turning to specialized **domain-specific languages** (DSLs) that more easily express special operations and the high degrees of

---

[1] In the world's fastest supercomputers, the degree of parallelism now regularly exceeds 10 million!

parallelism needed. The proliferation of such DSLs will be one challenge for programmers and software portability across increasingly different hardware systems. Further, the software architecture implications for large applications are significant. If they incorporate multiple domain-specific languages to achieve performance, the code fragmentation becomes significant. Functionality will become increasingly difficult to refactor across module boundaries, requiring major reprogramming across DSLs for software architecture changes. Further, the use of multiple hardware accelerators that each have their own memories and memory hierarchies not only increases programming difficult, but also incurs increasing data-movement costs. This cost is created by the presence of the accelerators. This will be a challenging and creative decade for software indeed! We need new inventions from a new generation of computer scientists to invent new programming models to meet these challenges. Finally, software will be asked to deal with new computing models, driven by fundamental changes to underlying hardware, as discussed below.

Principle 9.1: Technology Advances Continue in Core Capabilities, Producing a Continued Improvement in Computing Capability

Microelectronics miniaturization and voltage scaling have provided a bounty of computer hardware (transistors) that computer architects have used to create remarkable increases in computing performance. These trends continue, taking new directions with parallelism, accelerators, and more, fueling the expanding role and impact of computing in society.

9.3 New Computing Models

There is a groundswell of interest in new computing models – that is, those that depart from digital binary computation, and traditional programming ideas. These are large changes indeed! We explore several of the most promising. Each of these approaches formulates a fundamentally new computing model and framework (and hence mathematical structure), and as a result requires a new foundation, hardware base, and programming approaches. One example, **higher-level architecture**, shifts from low-level instructions to higher-level primitives such as mathematical operation on objects (abstract data types) or entire loops in a single hardware primitive. Another example, **quantum computing**, shifts from binary digits (bits) to a new kind of non-deterministic element, qubits (quantum bits), that are coupled together. And yet another, **neuromorphic computing**, follows the long-standing thread of connectionists or neural networks, where computation is structured based on a biologically inspired primitive such as neurons and synapses. For each of these, change is required from the top to the bottom (or perhaps from the bottom to the top!) in the software and hardware computing stack, as shown in Figure 9.3. For any to become a major computing model, much less supplant the mainstream instruction-based digital computers, there is a long way to go!

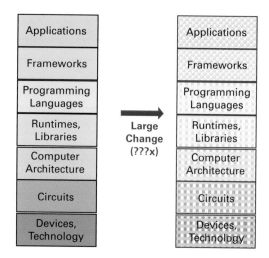

Impact of New Model/Technology (2025+)

Figure 9.3 New technologies or computing models such as quantum computing require new stacks to create rich applications. They need to show a substantial benefit to justify such investment.

9.3.1   Higher-Level Architecture

Many students, upon learning how machine-level instructions work in computers, are astonished at how many instructions must be executed to get even the simplest task done. Accessing an array or structure takes multiple instructions; even the simplest loop takes many instructions, and procedure calls require an entire "calling protocol." One approach to increase the power of computers involves designing instructions that achieve much more computation work. The trick is how to design them for both this greater capability, but also for easy implementation. One emerging group of examples is SIMD/vector instructions that can eliminate looping and indexing overheads, often reducing instruction counts for arithmetic loops by a large factor [77, 91]. This group has added more and more instructions over the past two decades, increasing both the variety of operations and the length of the SIMD vectors, which in the x86 architecture started at 64 bits in 1997 and has now grown to 512 bits (eight times growth). Operations began as simple byte-oriented media operations, but have grown as complex as scans, reductions, and even matrix multiply. Another class of higher-level architectures is specialized domains. Specialized instructions such as AES-NI [33] for cryptography can replace hundreds of traditional x86 instructions with a single special instruction. These instructions not only make AES cryptography much faster, they also dramatically reduce the power required. Other directions for higher-level architecture include optimizing procedure calls, memory management, and even interprocessor communication and synchronization. The lattermost of these has become increasingly important with increasing core counts in multicore CPUs.

9.3.2   Quantum Computing

Another novel computing direction that has garnered much excitement in recent years is quantum computing. This fundamentally different paradim shifts from deterministic bits to non-deterministic quantum bits (qubits). Such bits are much more powerful, similar to the difference in power between a deterministic Turing machine and a non-deterministic Turing machine. These non-deterministic bits can represent a multitude of states, and they are coupled with each other – using quantum physics – allowing them to represent and compute on an exponential number of states. This is radically different from our digital computing systems that isolate bits so that they will not corrupt each other, and continue to hold their values. This classical engineering approach, called a lumped element model by electrical engineers, allows parts of the system to be isolated, separately engineered and made reliable, and then composed into a larger, more complex system.

A quantum computer utilizes the power of entanglement, maintaining the coupling across qubits as a way to increase their ability to represent state and propagate information. This is the source of the computational advantage compared to conventional computers. However, it is also the source of their greatest challenges – the construction of quantum computers. It has taken many years for engineers to design and build quantum computers of just a few qubits. As recently as 1998, a 2-qubit quantum computer was state-of-the-art. It took until 2006 to reach a dozen qubits. But these were all academic science projects. In the past few years, we have begun to see commercial demonstrations, including a 2018 Intel demonstration of a 49-qubit machine and a 2019 IBM demonstration of a 53-qubit machine. Now, before you get too excited, these qubits are not reliable and decohere in just a few minutes, and thus a fraction of them need to be sacrificed to error correction. So, for a quantum programmer, the number of qubits is somewhat less. Leading quantum researchers have set a goal of 100 reliable qubits as the next major step in computational capability. That goal is some years away.

9.3.3   Neuromorphic Computing

Since the earliest days of digital computers, the connectionist or neural networks advocates have pursued a different, biologically inspired approach. In this approach, rather than code, memory, and data structures, the computation structures are layers of neurons with biological properties, often encoding information in sequences of spiking voltages and two-way communication (feedback). These systems should not be confused with the deep neural networks (DNNs) discussed in Chapter 8, which are based entirely on digital computing and traditional electronics. No, these neuromorphic computers seek to emulate biological neurons, their style of information encoding, their learning patterns, and more.

While the approach of neuromorphic computing has failed to keep pace with the development of digital computers, there has been a rise in interest recently for two reasons. First, neuroscience has begun to make real inroads into the structure of the human brain, and the learning, thought, and memory processes that are supported in it. As these mysteries are decoded, scientists have proposed that electronic circuits could be used as analogs to mimic the same structures. This led to the European Brain Project, as well as two major commercial efforts to build spiking neural network computing systems [12, 42, 75]. Building an electronic circuit that is faster than a biological neuron is not difficult, they typically operate at a few kilohertz. However, building an electronic circuit that does the same work with equal energy is quite challenging, so much effort has been expended on creating neural computers that are extremely low-power and can emulate the vast, rich connections of the human brain. No doubt it's clear that this approach is likely to require an equal revolution in the software and hardware stack if it is ever to be a real alternative to today's digital computers.

> **Principle 9.2: Novel Computing Models Promise Exciting New Futures for Computing!**
>
> *New computing models continue to develop and grow in importance. They require the creation of new programming approaches and models of how to deploy and improve applications. However, they each bring new types of capabilities and continue to enrich computing, and expanding the role and impact of computing in society in new directions.*

9.4   Summary

Computer architecture has an extraordinary past and a great future, enabling powerful computing applications in nearly every corner of society. Over the past 75 years, there has been dramatic improvements in computing hardware, combining the benefits of microelectronics miniaturization (Moore) and voltage scaling (Dennard) with architecture innovations including ILP and renaming, and further fueled by speculative execution and branch prediction. Caches have been a key invention supporting the dramatic increases in application memory needs, enabling high-speed and energy-efficient computation.

In the past 15 years the character of progress has shifted, with dramatic increases in parallelism and the attendant software challenges of parallel programming and scale-out. We have seen the rise of acceleration as an important means of energy-efficient, high-performance computing. Despite that change in character, computing hardware has fueled the rise of both smartphones and cloud computing. We expect these improvements to continue, with major trends including increased parallel-scale, acceleration for specific domains, and new programming systems. With potential disruptions from quantum and neuromorphic computing, these are exciting times indeed!

9.5   Digging Deeper

Throughout the book we have cited articles documenting the rapid progress of computing performance – tied to the mechanisms that delivered the improvements [8, 116]. Others take more of a users, view, and thus have documented simply the increased performance [21, 38]. These articles show the dramatic impact of size scaling from a room to a single chip, and the radical shrinking and scaling due to Moore's Law. A 2019 talk by the TSMC CTO, Philip Wong, projects 10 more years of density scaling [113]. In contrast, a report by the US National Academies points out the challenges, and proposes several radical paths forward, including customization, domain-specific programming, and fundamentally new hardware technologies [70]. Examples of specialized computing are now abundant, including molecular dynamics [84], machine learning [36, 52], media processing and more.

Most computer architects study with an empirical approach, and to learn more in that vein a popular reference is *Computer Architecture: A Quantitative Approach* [40]. Leading research can be found in research conferences such as the ACM/IEEE International Symposium on Computer Architecture [47], and more radical subjects in the IEEE International Conference on Rebooting Computing [18, 45].

9.6   Problems

9.1 One of the limitations of accelerators is they apply to only part of a computation.
(a) Explain how this limits the performance benefit achievable via Amdahl's law (defined in Problem 8.3).
(b) Explain how this affects the ability to change a large software system that calls the accelerator in several places. (Hint: consider how the data structures must be organized to present data to the accelerator.)
(c) Now consider a cloud system with accelerators attached to individual cloud nodes (as is typical for GPUs). Explain how an application might organize its data across nodes for presentation to a set of accelerators spread across cloud nodes. How does this constrain application data structures?

9.2 One of the limitations of accelerators is that they apply to only part of a computation, and freeze interfaces to the application.
(a) Explain how this affects the ability to change a large software system that calls the accelerator in several places. (Hint: consider how the data structures must be organized to present data to the accelerator.)
(b) Suppose we replaced the current accelerator with one that performed the same task, but required the data structures at the interface to be radically different. How would you deal with this as a software engineer?

(c)   What effect would the required software change have on performance? (That is, the software impact, separate from the improvement from the new accelerator.)

9.3   Consider GPUs (Section 8.2), the Google TPU (Section 8.3.1), and the Cerebras machine. Do a little internet research to learn how applications use these systems. For each, explain how it does (or does not) fit the model for accelerators described in Figure 9.2. (Hint: consider the breadth of applications and the software/DSL approaches.)

9.4   Neuromorphic computing aspires to build computation based on the biological spiking neuron structure. This building block is considerably more complicated than that used for deep learning, which includes only a single transmitted value and a nonlinear function (called ReLu). There have been several ambitious projects to build specialized architectures that can efficiently implement spiking neuron structures approaching the complexity of biological neural networks in rats, and even humans.
(a)   Study the SpiNNaker project, a part of the EU's Human Brain Project, which sought to implement large-scale spiking neural networks. Describe the architecture and its key approaches to better support large numbers of spiking neurons cheaply. How much did these innovations increase performance? Reduce cost? Could this approach be extended further?
(b)   What are the capabilities created by these projects? Explain in terms of the number of neurons and processing rates. What kind of biological organism does this correspond to? Could we simulate a human brain? How much power would it cost? What is the financial cost?
(c)   Do a little digging on the Internet and in the literature. What do we understand about how to program these systems of spiking neurons?

9.5   Neuromorphic computing aspires to build computation based on the biological spiking neuron structure. This building block is considerably more complicated than that used for deep learning, which includes only a single transmitted value and a nonlinear function (called ReLu). There have been several ambitious projects to build specialized architectures that can efficiently implement spiking neuron structures approaching the complexity of biological neural networks in rats, and even humans.
(a)   Study the TrueNorth project, a part of DARPA's neural computing initiative that sought to implement large-scale spiking neural networks. Describe the architecture and its key approaches to better support large numbers of spiking neurons cheaply. How much did these innovations increase performance? Reduce cost? Could this approach be extended further?
(b)   What are the capabilities created by these projects? Explain in terms of the number of neurons and processing rates. What kind of biological organism does this correspond to? Could we simulate a human brain? How much power would it cost? What is the financial cost?
(c)   Do a little digging on the web and into the literature. What do we understand about how to program these systems of spiking neurons?

9.6   Quantum computing posits a new model of computing based on quantum bits (or qubits), and attributes its power to the coupling between qubits. This non-modularity is a significant problem for scaling (no scale-out). The feasibility of quantum hardware is further complicated by the fact that many of the systems, such as the D-Wave, operate at cryogenic temperatures.

(a) Discuss how the notion of qubits which do not take on discrete values changes the nature of hardware and circuits. For example, is the programming style likely to be more like logic variables, for which we find a solution to rather than traditional sequential circuits? The sequential circuits produced imperative, procedural programs, and the sequential abstraction. What might arise from qubits?

(b) Quantum computations proceed via entanglement among a set of qubits, which accounts for their tremendous computational power. This is the opposite of the modularity that engineers of conventional systems use to separate different concerns and solve them one at a time. What implications does entanglement have for the creation of larger quantum computations?

9.7 Quantum computing posits a new model of computing based on quantum bits (or qubits), and attributes its power to the coupling between qubits. This non-modularity is a significant problem for scaling (no scale-out). The feasibility of quantum hardware is further complicated by the fact that many of the systems, such as the D-Wave, operate at cryogenic temperatures.

(a) What might a notion of cloud datacenter scale-out look like in quantum computing?

(b) What might a notion of geo-distributed datacenters look like in quantum computing?

9.8 Quantum computing posits a new model of computing based on quantum bits (or qubits), and attributes its power to the coupling between qubits. This non-modularity is a significant problem for scaling (no scale-out). The feasibility of quantum hardware is further complicated by the fact that many of the systems, such as the D-Wave, operate at cryogenic temperatures.

(a) One critical challenge is that most quantum systems operate at cryogenic temperatures (about $-273\,°C$, or $-460\,°F$). Given the challenges with power and energy in conventional computers, what challenges does this pose for useful hybrids of the two?

(b) One of the challenges in quantum computing is to have memory that lasts more than a few minutes. If you had to build programs that did not last more than a few minutes, how might you do it?

(c) If you had to build systems whose information did not persist (in the quantum part!) for more than a few minutes, how might you do it?

9.9 Consider a possible path for the future of computing. Assume that no major new computing models emerge. This produces a continued path of slow general purpose computing improvement, and proliferating accelerators.

(a) What kind of performance increase is likely?

(b) What are the implications for the future of software?

(c) What are the implications for the use of acceleration?

(d) With this rate of performance increase, what are the implications for applications?

9.10 Consider a possible path for the future of computing. Assume that major neuromorphic computing is a success.

(a) What applications are most amenable? How will training/learning as a new major programming model affect computing systems? Software development?

(b) What are the implications for the future of software?

(c) What are the implications for use of acceleration?

(d) With this rate of performance increase, what are the implications for applications?

9.11 Consider a possible path for the future of computing. Assume that major quantum computing is a success.

(a) What applications are most amenable? How will quantum programming as a major programming model affect computing systems? Software development?

(b) What are the implications for the future of software?

(c) What are the implications for use of acceleration?

(d) With this rate of performance increase, what are the implications for applications?

Appendix   RISC-V Instruction Set Reference Card

Free & Open ⚡ RISC-V Reference Card ①

Base Integer Instructions: RV32I, RV64I, and RV128I

Category	Name	Fmt	RV32I Base	+RV{64,128}
Loads	Load Byte	I	LB rd,rs1,imm	
	Load Halfword	I	LH rd,rs1,imm	
	Load Word	I	LW rd,rs1,imm	L{D|Q} rd,rs1,imm
	Load Byte Unsigned	I	LBU rd,rs1,imm	
	Load Half Unsigned	I	LHU rd,rs1,imm	L{W|D}U rd,rs1,imm
Stores	Store Byte	S	SB rs1,rs2,imm	
	Store Halfword	S	SH rs1,rs2,imm	
	Store Word	S	SW rs1,rs2,imm	S{D|Q} rs1,rs2,imm
Shifts	Shift Left	R	SLL rd,rs1,rs2	SLL{W|D} rd,rs1,rs2
	Shift Left Immediate	I	SLLI rd,rs1,shamt	SLLI{W|D} rd,rs1,shamt
	Shift Right	R	SRL rd,rs1,rs2	SRL{W|D} rd,rs1,rs2
	Shift Right Immediate	I	SRLI rd,rs1,shamt	SRLI{W|D} rd,rs1,shamt
	Shift Right Arithmetic	R	SRA rd,rs1,rs2	SRA{W|D} rd,rs1,rs2
	Shift Right Arith Imm	I	SRAI rd,rs1,shamt	SRAI{W|D} rd,rs1,shamt
Arithmetic	ADD	R	ADD rd,rs1,rs2	ADD{W|D} rd,rs1,rs2
	ADD Immediate	I	ADDI rd,rs1,imm	ADDI{W|D} rd,rs1,imm
	SUBtract	R	SUB rd,rs1,rs2	SUB{W|D} rd,rs1,rs2
	Load Upper Imm	U	LUI rd,imm	
	Add Upper Imm to PC	U	AUIPC rd,imm	
Logical	XOR	R	XOR rd,rs1,rs2	
	XOR Immediate	I	XORI rd,rs1,imm	
	OR	R	OR rd,rs1,rs2	
	OR Immediate	I	ORI rd,rs1,imm	
	AND	R	AND rd,rs1,rs2	
	AND Immediate	I	ANDI rd,rs1,imm	
Compare	Set <	R	SLT rd,rs1,rs2	
	Set < Immediate	I	SLTI rd,rs1,imm	
	Set < Unsigned	R	SLTU rd,rs1,rs2	
	Set < Imm Unsigned	I	SLTIU rd,rs1,imm	
Branches	Branch =	SB	BEQ rs1,rs2,imm	
	Branch ≠	SB	BNE rs1,rs2,imm	
	Branch <	SB	BLT rs1,rs2,imm	
	Branch ≥	SB	BGE rs1,rs2,imm	
	Branch < Unsigned	SB	BLTU rs1,rs2,imm	
	Branch ≥ Unsigned	SB	BGEU rs1,rs2,imm	
Jump & Link	J&L	UJ	JAL rd,imm	
	Jump & Link Register	UJ	JALR rd,rs1,imm	
Synch	Synch thread	I	FENCE	
	Synch Instr & Data	I	FENCE.I	
System	System CALL	I	SCALL	
	System BREAK	I	SBREAK	
Counters	ReaD CYCLE	I	RDCYCLE rd	
	ReaD CYCLE upper Half	I	RDCYCLEH rd	
	ReaD TIME	I	RDTIME rd	
	ReaD TIME upper Half	I	RDTIMEH rd	
	ReaD INSTR RETired	I	RDINSTRET rd	
	ReaD INSTR upper Half	I	RDINSTRETH rd	

RV Privileged Instructions

Category	Name	RV mnemonic
CSR Access	Atomic R/W	CSRRW rd,csr,rs1
	Atomic Read & Set Bit	CSRRS rd,csr,rs1
	Atomic Read & Clear Bit	CSRRC rd,csr,rs1
	Atomic R/W Imm	CSRRWI rd,csr,imm
	Atomic Read & Set Bit Imm	CSRRSI rd,csr,imm
	Atomic Read & Clear Bit Imm	CSRRCI rd,csr,imm
Change Level	Env. Call	ECALL
	Environment Breakpoint	EBREAK
	Environment Return	ERET
Trap Redirect	to Supervisor	MRTS
	Redirect Trap to Hypervisor	MRTH
	Hypervisor Trap to Supervisor	HRTS
Interrupt	Wait for Interrupt	WFI
MMU	Supervisor FENCE	SFENCE.VM rs1

Optional Compressed (16-bit) Instruction Extension: RVC

Category	Name	Fmt	RVC	RVI equivalent
Loads	Load Word	CL	C.LW rd',rs1',imm	LW rd',rs1',imm*4
	Load Word SP	CI	C.LWSP rd,imm	LW rd,sp,imm*4
	Load Double	CL	C.LD rd',rs1',imm	LD rd',rs1',imm*8
	Load Double SP	CI	C.LDSP rd,imm	LD rd,sp,imm*8
	Load Quad	CL	C.LQ rd',rs1',imm	LQ rd',rs1',imm*16
	Load Quad SP	CI	C.LQSP rd,imm	LQ rd,sp,imm*16
Stores	Store Word	CS	C.SW rs1',rs2',imm	SW rs1',rs2',imm*4
	Store Word SP	CSS	C.SWSP rs2,imm	SW rs2,sp,imm*4
	Store Double	CS	C.SD rs1',rs2',imm	SD rs1',rs2',imm*8
	Store Double SP	CSS	C.SDSP rs2,imm	SD rs2,sp,imm*8
	Store Quad	CS	C.SQ rs1',rs2',imm	SQ rs1',rs2',imm*16
	Store Quad SP	CSS	C.SQSP rs2,imm	SQ rs2,sp,imm*16
Arithmetic	ADD	CR	C.ADD rd,rs1	ADD rd,rd,rs1
	ADD Word	CR	C.ADDW rd,rs1	ADDW rd,rd,rs1
	ADD Immediate	CI	C.ADDI rd,imm	ADDI rd,rd,imm
	ADD Word Imm	CI	C.ADDIW rd,imm	ADDIW rd,rd,imm
	ADD SP Imm * 16	CI	C.ADDI16SP x0,imm	ADDI sp,sp,imm*16
	ADD SP Imm * 4	CIW	C.ADDI4SPN rd',imm	ADDI rd',sp,imm*4
	Load Immediate	CI	C.LI rd,imm	ADDI rd,x0,imm
	Load Upper Imm	CI	C.LUI rd,imm	LUI rd,imm
	MoVe	CR	C.MV rd,rs1	ADD rd,rs1,x0
	SUB	CR	C.SUB rd,rs1	SUB rd,rd,rs1
Shifts	Shift Left Imm	CI	C.SLLI rd,imm	SLLI rd,rd,imm
Branches	Branch=0	CB	C.BEQZ rs1',imm	BEQ rs1',x0,imm
	Branch≠0	CB	C.BNEZ rs1',imm	BNE rs1',x0,imm
Jump	Jump	CJ	C.J imm	JAL x0,imm
	Jump Register	CR	C.JR rd,rs1	JALR x0,rs1,0
Jump & Link	J&L	CJ	C.JAL imm	JAL ra,imm
	Jump & Link Register	CR	C.JALR rs1	JALR ra,rs1,0
System	Env. BREAK	CI	C.EBREAK	EBREAK

32-bit Instruction Formats

	31	30	25 24	21 20	19	15 14	12 11	8	7	6	0
R		funct7		rs2	rs1	funct3		rd		opcode	
I		imm[11:0]			rs1	funct3		rd		opcode	
S		imm[11:5]		rs2	rs1	funct3	imm[4:0]			opcode	
SB	imm[12]	imm[10:5]		rs2	rs1	funct3	imm[4:1]	imm[11]		opcode	
U			imm[31:12]					rd		opcode	
UJ	imm[20]	imm[10:1]		imm[11]	imm[19:12]			rd		opcode	

16-bit (RVC) Instruction Formats

	15 14 13	12	11 10 9 8 7	6 5 4 3 2	1 0
CR	funct4		rd/rs1	rs2	op
CI	funct3	imm	rd/rs1	imm	op
CSS	funct3		imm	rs2	op
CIW	funct3		imm	rd'	op
CL	funct3		imm	rs1'	imm	rd'	op
CS	funct3		imm	rs1'	imm	rs2'	op
CB	funct3		offset	rs1'	offset	op
CJ	funct3		jump target		op

RISC-V Integer Base (RV32I/64I/128I), privileged, and optional compressed extension (RVC). Registers x1–x31 and the pc are 32 bits wide in RV32I, 64 in RV64I, and 128 in RV128I (x0=0). RV64I/128I add 10 instructions for the wider formats. The RVI base of <50 classic integer RISC instructions is required. Every 16-bit RVC instruction matches an existing 32-bit RVI instruction. See risc.org.

Free & Open ⚡ RISC-V Reference Card (riscv.org) ②

Optional Multiply-Divide Instruction Extension: RVM

Category	Name	Fmt	RV32M (Multiply-Divide)		+RV{64,128}	
Multiply	MULtiply	R	MUL	rd,rs1,rs2	MUL{W|D}	rd,rs1,rs2
	MULtiply upper Half	R	MULH	rd,rs1,rs2		
	MULtiply Half Sign/Uns	R	MULHSU	rd,rs1,rs2		
	MULtiply upper Half Uns	R	MULHU	rd,rs1,rs2		
Divide	DIVide	R	DIV	rd,rs1,rs2	DIV{W|D}	rd,rs1,rs2
	DIVide Unsigned	R	DIVU	rd,rs1,rs2		
Remainder	REMainder	R	REM	rd,rs1,rs2	REM{W|D}	rd,rs1,rs2
	REMainder Unsigned	R	REMU	rd,rs1,rs2	REMU{W|D}	rd,rs1,rs2

Optional Atomic Instruction Extension: RVA

Category	Name	Fmt	RV32A (Atomic)		+RV{64,128}	
Load	Load Reserved	R	LR.W	rd,rs1	LR.{D|Q}	rd,rs1
Store	Store Conditional	R	SC.W	rd,rs1,rs2	SC.{D|Q}	rd,rs1,rs2
Swap	SWAP	R	AMOSWAP.W	rd,rs1,rs2	AMOSWAP.{D|Q}	rd,rs1,rs2
Add	ADD	R	AMOADD.W	rd,rs1,rs2	AMOADD.{D|Q}	rd,rs1,rs2
Logical	XOR	R	AMOXOR.W	rd,rs1,rs2	AMOXOR.{D|Q}	rd,rs1,rs2
	AND	R	AMOAND.W	rd,rs1,rs2	AMOAND.{D|Q}	rd,rs1,rs2
	OR	R	AMOOR.W	rd,rs1,rs2	AMOOR.{D|Q}	rd,rs1,rs2
Min/Max	MINimum	R	AMOMIN.W	rd,rs1,rs2	AMOMIN.{D|Q}	rd,rs1,rs2
	MAXimum	R	AMOMAX.W	rd,rs1,rs2	AMOMAX.{D|Q}	rd,rs1,rs2
	MINimum Unsigned	R	AMOMINU.W	rd,rs1,rs2	AMOMINU.{D|Q}	rd,rs1,rs2
	MAXimum Unsigned	R	AMOMAXU.W	rd,rs1,rs2	AMOMAXU.{D|Q}	rd,rs1,rs2

Three Optional Floating-Point Instruction Extensions: RVF, RVD, & RVQ

Category	Name	Fmt	RV32{F|D|Q} (HP/SP,DP,QP Fl Pt)		+RV{64,128}	
Move	Move from Integer	R	FMV.{H|S}.X	rd,rs1	FMV.{D|Q}.X	rd,rs1
	Move to Integer	R	FMV.X.{H|S}	rd,rs1	FMV.X.{D|Q}	rd,rs1
Convert	Convert from Int	R	FCVT.{H|S|D|Q}.W	rd,rs1	FCVT.{H|S|D|Q}.{L|T}	rd,rs1
	Convert from Int Unsigned	R	FCVT.{H|S|D|Q}.WU	rd,rs1	FCVT.{H|S|D|Q}.{L|T}U	rd,rs1
	Convert to Int	R	FCVT.W.{H|S|D|Q}	rd,rs1	FCVT.{L|T}.{H|S|D|Q}	rd,rs1
	Convert to Int Unsigned	R	FCVT.WU.{H|S|D|Q}	rd,rs1	FCVT.{L|T}U.{H|S|D|Q}	rd,rs1

Category	Name	Fmt	Instruction	Operands
Load	Load	I	FL{W,D,Q}	rd,rs1,imm
Store	Store	S	FS{W,D,Q}	rs1,rs2,imm
Arithmetic	ADD	R	FADD.{S|D|Q}	rd,rs1,rs2
	SUBtract	R	FSUB.{S|D|Q}	rd,rs1,rs2
	MULtiply	R	FMUL.{S|D|Q}	rd,rs1,rs2
	DIVide	R	FDIV.{S|D|Q}	rd,rs1,rs2
	SQuare RooT	R	FSQRT.{S|D|Q}	rd,rs1
Mul-Add	Multiply-ADD	R	FMADD.{S|D|Q}	rd,rs1,rs2,rs3
	Multiply-SUBtract	R	FMSUB.{S|D|Q}	rd,rs1,rs2,rs3
	Negative Multiply-SUBtract	R	FNMSUB.{S|D|Q}	rd,rs1,rs2,rs3
	Negative Multiply-ADD	R	FNMADD.{S|D|Q}	rd,rs1,rs2,rs3
Sign Inject	SiGN source	R	FSGNJ.{S|D|Q}	rd,rs1,rs2
	Negative SiGN source	R	FSGNJN.{S|D|Q}	rd,rs1,rs2
	Xor SiGN source	R	FSGNJX.{S|D|Q}	rd,rs1,rs2
Min/Max	MINimum	R	FMIN.{S|D|Q}	rd,rs1,rs2
	MAXimum	R	FMAX.{S|D|Q}	rd,rs1,rs2
Compare	Compare Float =	R	FEQ.{S|D|Q}	rd,rs1,rs2
	Compare Float <	R	FLT.{S|D|Q}	rd,rs1,rs2
	Compare Float ≤	R	FLE.{S|D|Q}	rd,rs1,rs2
Categorization	Classify Type	R	FCLASS.{S|D|Q}	rd,rs1
Configuration	Read Status	R	FRCSR	rd
	Read Rounding Mode	R	FRRM	rd
	Read Flags	R	FRFLAGS	rd
	Swap Status Reg	R	FSCSR	rd,rs1
	Swap Rounding Mode	R	FSRM	rd,rs1
	Swap Flags	R	FSFLAGS	rd,rs1
	Swap Rounding Mode Imm	I	FSRMI	rd,imm
	Swap Flags Imm	I	FSFLAGSI	rd,imm

RISC-V Calling Convention

Register	ABI Name	Saver	Description
x0	zero	---	Hard-wired zero
x1	ra	Caller	Return address
x2	sp	Callee	Stack pointer
x3	gp	---	Global pointer
x4	tp	---	Thread pointer
x5-7	t0-2	Caller	Temporaries
x8	s0/fp	Callee	Saved register/frame pointer
x9	s1	Callee	Saved register
x10-11	a0-1	Caller	Function arguments/return values
x12-17	a2-7	Caller	Function arguments
x18-27	s2-11	Callee	Saved registers
x28-31	t3-t6	Caller	Temporaries
f0-7	ft0-7	Caller	FP temporaries
f8-9	fs0-1	Callee	FP saved registers
f10-11	fa0-1	Caller	FP arguments/return values
f12-17	fa2-7	Caller	FP arguments
f18-27	fs2-11	Callee	FP saved registers
f28-31	ft8-11	Caller	FP temporaries

RISC-V calling convention and five optional extensions: 10 multiply–divide instructions (RV32M); 11 optional atomic instructions (RV32A); and 25 floating-point instructions each for single-, double-, and quadruple-precision (RV32F, RV32D, RV32Q). The latter add registers f0–f31, whose width matches the widest precision, and a floating-point control and status register fcsr. Each larger address adds some instructions: 4 for RVM, 11 for RVA, and 6 each for RVF/D/Q. Using regex notation, { } means set, so L{D|Q} is both LD and LQ. See risc.org. (8/21/15 revision)

References

[1] Grant Ayers, Nayana Prasad Nagendra, David I. August, et al. AsmDB: understanding and mitigating front-end stalls in warehouse-scale computers. In *Proceedings of the 46th International Symposium on Computer Architecture*, New York, NY, 2019. Association for Computing Machinery.

[2] John W. Backus, Friedrich L Bauer, Julien Green, et al. Report on the algorithmic language ALGOL 60. *Numerische Mathematik*, 2(1):106–136, 1960.

[3] George H. Barnes, Richard M. Brown, Maso Kato, et al. The Illiac IV computer. *IEEE Transactions on Computers*, 100(8):746–757, 1968.

[4] Luiz Andre Barroso. Warehouse-scale computing. In *Proceedings of the 2010 ACM SIGMOD International Conference on Management of Data*, New York, NY, 2010. Association for Computing Machinery.

[5] Dileep Bhandarkar. RISC versus CISC: a tale of two chips. *SIGARCH Computer Architecture News*, 25(1):112, 1997.

[6] Dileep Bhandarkar and Douglas W. Clark. Performance from architecture: comparing a RISC and a CISC with similar hardware organization. In *Proceedings of the Fourth International Conference on Architectural Support for Programming Languages and Operating Systems*, New York, NY, 1991. Association for Computing Machinery.

[7] Mark Bohr. A 30 year retrospective on Dennard's Mosfet scaling paper. In *IEEE Solid-State Circuits Society Newsletter*, 12(1):11–13.

[8] Shekhar Borkar and Andrew A. Chien. The future of microprocessors. *Communications of the ACM*, 54(5):67–77, 2011.

[9] James Bornholt, Randolph Lopez, Douglas M. Carmean, et al. A DNA-based archival storage system. *SIGARCH Computer Architecture News*, 44(2):637–649, 2016.

[10] David Brock, editor. *Understanding Moore's Law: Four Decades of Innovation*. Chemical Heritage Foundation, 2006.

[11] Nanette Brown, Yuanfang Cai, Yuepu Guo, et al. Managing technical debt in software-reliant systems. In *Proceedings of the FSE/SDP Workshop on Future of Software Engineering Research*, New York, NY, 2010. Association for Computing Machinery.

[12] Andrew S. Cassidy, Rodrigo Alvarez-Icaza, Filipp Akopyan, et al. Real-time scalable cortical computing at 46 giga-synaptic ops/watt with 100 times speedup in time-to-solution and 100,000 times reduction in energy-to-solution. In *Proceedings of the International Conference for High Performance Computing, Networking, Storage and Analysis*, New Orleans, LA, 2014. IEEE Press.

[13] Yu-Hsin Chen, Joel Emer, and Vivienne Sze. Eyeriss: a spatial architecture for energy-efficient dataflow for convolutional neural networks. In *Proceedings of the 43rd International Symposium on Computer Architecture*, Seoul, Republic of Korea, 2016. IEEE Press.

[14] Andrew A. Chien. Pervasive parallel computing: an historic opportunity for innovation in programming and architecture. In *Proceedings of the 12th ACM SIGPLAN Symposium on Principles and Practice of Parallel Programming*, New York, NY, 2007. Association for Computing Machinery.

[15] Andrew A. Chien, Tung Thanh-Hoang, Dilip Vasudevan, Yuanwei Fang, and Amirali Shambayati. 10 × 10: a case study in highly-programmable and energy-efficient heterogeneous federated architecture. *SIGARCH Computer Architecture News*, 43(3):2–9, 2015.

[16] Computer History Museum. Intel x86 and the microprocessor wars. www.computerhistory.org/revolution/digital-logic/12/330.

[17] Computer History Museum. EDSAC computer employs delay line storage. www.computerhistory.org/storageengine/edsac-computer-employs-delay-line-storage/, 1948.

[18] Thomas M. Conte, Elie Track, and Erik DeBenedictis. Rebooting computing: new strategies for technology scaling. *IEEE Computer*, 48(12):10–13, 2015.

[19] David Culler, Jaswinder Pal Singh, and Anoop Gupta. *Parallel Computer Architecture: A Hardware–Software Approach*. Morgan Kaufmann, 1997.

[20] Ole-Johan Dahl and Kristen Nygaard. Simula: an ALGOL-based simulation language. *Communications of the ACM*, 9(9):671–678, 1966.

[21] Andrew Danowitz, Kyle Kelley, James Mao, John P. Stevenson, and Mark Horowitz. CPU DB: recording microprocessor history. *Communications of the ACM*, 55(4):55–63, 2012.

[22] Jeffrey Dean and Sanjay Ghemawat. Mapreduce: a flexible data processing tool. *Communications of the ACM*, 53(1):72–77, 2010.

[23] Robert H. Dennard, Fritz Gaensslen, Hwa-Nien Yu, et al. Design of ion-implanted MOSFET's with very small physical dimensions. *IEEE Journal of Solid-State Circuits*, SC-9(5):256–268, 1974.

[24] Edsger W. Dijkstra. Guarded commands, non-determinacy and a calculus for the derivation of programs. In *Proceedings of the International Conference on Reliable Software*, New York, NY, 1975. Association for Computing Machinery.

[25] Chen Ding and Yutao Zhong. Predicting whole-program locality through reuse distance analysis. In *Proceedings of the ACM SIGPLAN 2003 Conference on Programming Language Design and Implementation*, New York, NY, 2003. Association for Computing Machinery.

[26] John Presper Eckert Jr. and John W. Mauchly. Electronic numerical integrator and computer. US Patent, February 1964. United States Patent Office, US Patent 3,120,606, filed 1947-06-26, issued 1964-02-04; invalidated 1973-10-19 after court ruling on Honeywell v. Sperry Rand.

[27] Hadi Esmaeilzadeh, Emily Blem, Renee St. Amant, Karthikeyan Sankaralingam, and Doug Burger. Dark silicon and the end of multicore scaling. In *Proceedings of the 38th Annual International Symposium on Computer Architecture*, New York, NY, 2011. Association for Computing Machinery.

[28] Joseph A. Fisher, John R. Ellis, John C. Ruttenberg, and Alexandru Nicolau. Parallel processing: a smart compiler and a dumb machine. In *Proceedings of the 1984 SIGPLAN Symposium on Compiler Construction*, New York, NY, 1984. Association for Computing Machinery.

[29] Richard Feynman. Waveguides. In *Feynman's Lectures on Physics, Volume II*. Addison-Wesley, 1977.

[30] Michael R. Garey and David S. Johnson. *Computers and Intractability; A Guide to the Theory of NP-Completeness.* W. H. Freeman and Co., 1990.

[31] Sanjay Ghemawat, Howard Gobioff, and Shun-Tak Leung. The Google file system. *SIGOPS Operating Systems Review*, 37(5):29–43, 2003.

[32] Adele Goldberg and David Robson. *Smalltalk-80: The Language and Its Implementation.* Addison-Wesley, 1983.

[33] Shay Gueron. Intel advanced encryption standard (AES) new instructions set. Intel Corporation, 2010.

[34] Erico Marui Guizzo. The essential message: Claude Shannon and the making of information theory. Technical report, Massachusetts Institute of Technology, 2003.

[35] Linley Gwennap. Microprocessor report: insightful analysis of microprocessor technology. The Linley Group, 1987.

[36] Linley Gwennap. Alibaba takes AI performance lead. *Microprocessor Report*, November 2019.

[37] Song Han, Xingyu Liu, Huizi Mao, et al. EIE: efficient inference engine on compressed deep neural network. In *Proceedings of the 43rd International Symposium on Computer Architecture*, Seoul, Republic of Korea, 2016. IEEE Press.

[38] Michael T. Heath. A tale of two laws. *The International Journal of High Performance Computing Applications*, 29(3):320–330, 2015.

[39] Jing Xia-Xiping Zhou Heng Liao, and Jiajin Tu. Davinci: a scalable architecture for neural network computing. *Hot Chips 31*, July 2019.

[40] John Hennessy and David Patterson. *Computer Architecture: A Quantitative Approach*, 6th ed. Morgan-Kaufmann, 2017.

[41] Geoff Hinton and Yann LeCun. 2018 Alan M. Turing award lecture. https://amturing.acm.org/vp/hinton_4791679.cfm, 2019.

[42] Human Brain Project. http://humanbrainproject.eu.

[43] IEEE. Fifth workshop on serverless computing. www.serverlesscomputing.org/wosc5.

[44] IEEE Computer Society. An wang: a computer pioneer. https://history.computer.org/pioneers/wang.html.

[45] IEEE. *International Conference on Rebooting Computing.* IEEE. https://rebootingcomputing.ieee.org/.

[46] IEEE. Hot chips: a symposium on high performance chips. In *Proceedings of Hot Chips.* IEEE, 1989 to present. https://hotchips.org/.

[47] IEEE/ACM. *International Symposium on Computer Architecture.* IEEE/ACM, 1973–2020. www.iscaconf.org/.

[48] Intel. Intel architecture instruction set extensions programming reference. http://software.intel.com.

[49] Ciji Isen, Lizy K. John, and Eugene John. A tale of two processors: revisiting the RISC–CISC debate. In *Proceedings of the 2009 SPEC Benchmark Workshop on Computer Performance Evaluation and Benchmarking*, Berlin, 2009. Springer-Verlag.

[50] Bruce Jacob, David Wang, and Spencer Ng. *Memory Systems: Cache, DRAM, Disk.* Morgan-Kaufmann, 2007.

[51] Khronos OpenCL Working Group SYCL Subgroup. SYCL provisional specification. Khronos OpenCL Working Group, September 2014.

[52] Norman P. Jouppi, Cliff Young, Nishant Patel, et al. In-datacenter performance analysis of a tensor processing unit. In *Proceedings of the 44th Annual International Symposium on Computer Architecture*, Toronto, ON, 2017. IEEE.

[53] Paul Kocher, Jann Horn, Anders Fogh, et al. Spectre attacks: exploiting speculative execution. In *40th IEEE Symposium on Security and Privacy (S&P'19)*, San Francisco, CA, 2019. IEEE.

[54] Paul Kocher, Jann Horn, Anders Fogh, et al. Spectre attacks: exploiting speculative execution. *Communications of the ACM*, 63(7):93–101, 2020.

[55] Peter Kogge. *Architecture of Pipelined Computers*. Hemisphere Publishing Corporation, 1981.

[56] Yann Lecun, Yoshua Bengio, and Geoffrey Hinton. Deep learning. *Nature*, 521:436–444, 2015.

[57] Shang Li, Dhiraj Reddy, and Bruce Jacob. A performance & power comparison of modern high-speed DRAM architectures. In *Proceedings of the International Symposium on Memory Systems*, New York, NY, 2018. Association for Computing Machinery.

[58] A. Limaye and T. Adegbija. A workload characterization of the SPEC CPU2017 benchmark suite. In *2018 IEEE International Symposium on Performance Analysis of Systems and Software*, Belfast, UK, 2018.

[59] Erik Lindholm, John Nickolls, Stuart F. Oberman, and John Montrym. NVIDIA Tesla: a unified graphics and computing architecture. *IEEE Micro*, 28(2):39–55, 2008.

[60] Moritz Lipp, Michael Schwarz, Daniel Gruss, et al. Meltdown: reading kernel memory from user space. *Communications of the ACM*, 63(6):46–56, 2020.

[61] Barbara Liskov, Alan Snyder, Russell Atkinson, and Craig Schaffert. Abstraction mechanisms in CLU. *Communications of the ACM*, 20(8):564–576, 1977.

[62] John D. McCalpin. Trends in system cost and performance balances and implications for the future of HPC. In *Proceedings of the 2nd International Workshop on Hardware–Software Co-Design for High Performance Computing*, New York, NY, 2015. Association for Computing Machinery.

[63] J. McCarthy. A revised version of maplist. Technical report, MIT AI Laboratory, 1958.

[64] Sally A. McKee. Reflections on the memory wall. In *Proceedings of the 1st Conference on Computing Frontiers*, New York, NY, 2004. Association for Computing Machinery.

[65] Meltdown and spectre. https://meltdownattack.com, 2018.

[66] Sunil Mirapuri, Michael Woodacre, and Nader Vasseghi. The MIPS E4000 processor. *IEEE Micro*, 12(2):10–22, 1992.

[67] Mlperf: fair and useful benchmarks for measuring training and inference performance of ML hardware, software, and services. https://mlperf.org.

[68] Gordon Moore. Cramming more components onto integrated circuits. *Electronics Magazine*, 1965. https://en.wikipedia.org/wiki/Moore%27s_law.

[69] National Research Council. *Embedded, Everywhere: A Research Agenda for Networked Systems of Embedded Computers*. National Academies Press, 2001.

[70] National Research Council. *The Future of Computing Performance: Game Over or Next Level?* National Academies Press, 2011.

[71] Netflix. Microservices tech blog. https://netflixtechblog.com/tagged/microservices.

[72] John Nickolls, Ian Buck, Michael Garland, and Kevin Skadron. Scalable parallel programming with CUDA. In *ACM SIGGRAPH 2008 Classes*, New York, NY, 2008. Association for Computing Machinery.

[73] John Nickolls and William J. Dally. The GPU computing era. *IEEE Micro*, 30(2):56–69, 2010.

[74] David Patterson and Andrew Waterman. *The RISC-V Reader: An Open Architecture Atlas*. Strawberry Canyon, 2017.

[75] Luis A. Plana, David Clark, Simon Davidson, et al. SpiNNaker: eesign and implementation of a GALS multicore system-on-chip. *Journal of Emerging Technologies in Computer Systems*, 7(4):1–8, 2011.

[76] Steve Pryzbylski. *Cache and Memory Hierarchy Design: A Performance-Directed Approach*. Morgan-Kaufmann, 1990.

[77] James Reinders. Avx-512 instructions. Intel Corporation, 2013.

[78] Kamil Rocki, Dirk Van Essendelft, Ilya Sharapov, et al. Fast stencil-code computation on a wafer-scale processor. In *Proceedings of the International Conference for High Performance Computing, Networking, Storage and Analysis*, Atlanta, GA, 2020. IEEE Press.

[79] Olga Russakovsky, Jia Deng, Hao Su, et al. Imagenet large scale visual recognition challenge. *International Journal of Computer Vision*, 115(3):211–252, 2015.

[80] Richard M. Russell. The Cray-1 computer system. *Communications of the ACM*, 21(1):63–72, 1978.

[81] R. K. Sato and P. N. Swarztrauber. Benchmarking the connection machine 2. In *Proceedings of the 1988 ACM/IEEE Conference on Supercomputing*, Washington, DC, 1988. IEEE Computer Society Press.

[82] M.S. Schlansker and B.R. Rau. EPIC: an architecture for instruction-level parallel processors. Technical Report HPL-1999-111, Hewlett-Packard Laboratories, 2000.

[83] Claude E. Shannon. A mathematical theory of communication. *Bell System Technical Journal*, 27:379–423, 623–656, 1948.

[84] David E. Shaw, J. P. Grossman, Joseph A. Bank, et al. Anton 2: raising the bar for performance and programmability in a special-purpose molecular dynamics supercomputer. In *Proceedings of the International Conference for High Performance Computing, Networking, Storage and Analysis*, New Orleans, LA, 2014. IEEE Press.

[85] Anand Shimpi. Anandtech: Hardware news and tech reviews since 1997. www.anandtech.com.

[86] Arjun Singh, Joon Ong, Amit Agarwal, et al. Jupiter rising: a decade of CLOS topologies and centralized control in Google's datacenter network. In *Proceedings of the 2015 ACM Conference on Special Interest Group on Data Communication*, New York, NY, 2015. Association for Computing Machinery.

[87] Arjun Singh, Joon Ong, Amit Agarwal, et al. Jupiter rising: a decade of CLOS topologies and centralized control in Google's datacenter network. *Computer Communication Review*, 45(4):183–197, 2015.

[88] James E. Smith. A study of branch prediction strategies. In *Proceedings of the 8th Annual Symposium on Computer Architecture*, Washington, DC, 1981. IEEE Computer Society Press.

[89] Gurindar S. Sohi, Scott E. Breach, and T. N. Vijaykumar. Multiscalar processors. In *Proceedings of the 22nd Annual International Symposium on Computer Architecture*, New York, NY, 1995. Association for Computing Machinery.

[90] Jimmy Soni and Rob Goodman. *A Mind at Play: How Claude Shannon Invented the Information Age*. Simon and Schuster, 2017.

[91] N. Stephens, S. Biles, M. Boettcher, et al. The arm scalable vector extension. *IEEE Micro*, 37(2):26–39, 2017.

[92] William D. Strecker. Transient behavior of cache memories. *ACM Transactions of Computer Systems*, 1(4):281–293, 1983.

[93] Shan Tang. AI chip (ICs and IPs). https://github.com/basicmi/AI-Chip, 2019.

[94] Arnold Thackray, David Brock, and Rachel Jones. *Moore's Law: The Life of Gordon Moore, Silicon Valley's Quiet Revolutionary*. Basic Books, 2015.

[95] Today's Engineer. Magnetic-core memory. https://ethw.org/Magnetic-Core_Memory, 2003.

[96] R. M. Tomasulo. An efficient algorithm for exploiting multiple arithmetic units. *IBM Journal of Research and Development*, 11(1):25–33, 1967.

[97] Y. Turakhia, G. Bejerano, and W. J. Dally. Darwin: a genomics coprocessor. *IEEE Micro*, 39(3):29–37, 2019.

[98] US Department of Energy. The Exascale Compute Project. www.exascaleproject.org.

[99] US National Science Foundation. Exploiting parallelism and scalability (XPS), 2016.

[100] Ashish Vaswani, Noam Shazeer, Niki Parmar, et al. Attention is all you need. In *31st Conference on Neural Information Processing Systems*, Long Beach, CA, 2018.

[101] Daniel Waddington, Mark Kunitomi, Clem Dickey, et al. Evaluation of Intel 3D-Xpoint NVDimm technology for memory-intensive genomic workloads. In *Proceedings of the International Symposium on Memory Systems*, New York, NY, 2019. Association for Computing Machinery.

[102] W. Warner. Great moments in microprocessor history. www.ibm.com/developerworks/library/pa-microhist/index.html, 2004.

[103] Andrew Waterman and Krste Asanovic. The RISC-V instruction set manual volume I: unprivileged ISA 2020. http://riscv.org/, 2020.

[104] Martin H. Welk. The ENIAC story Ordnance. American Ordnance Association, 1961.

[105] Wikipedia. Consistency model. https://en.wikipedia.org/wiki/Consistency_model.

[106] Wikipedia. Maspar computer corporation. https://en.wikipedia.org/wiki/MasPar.

[107] Wikipedia. Pollack's rule. https://en.wikipedia.org/wiki/Pollack%27s_rule.

[108] Wikipedia. Silicon graphics. https://en.wikipedia.org/wiki/Silicon_Graphics.

[109] Wikipedia. Intel Skylake server information. https://en.wikichip.org/wiki/intel/microarchitectures/skylake_(server).

[110] Wikipedia. Intel XE. https://en.wikipedia.org/wiki/Intel_Xe.

[111] Wikipedia. OpenMP. https://en.wikipedia.org/wiki/OpenMP.

[112] Wikipedia. Apple A11: neural processor. https://en.wikipedia.org/wiki/Apple_A11, 2017.

[113] Philip Wong. What will the next node offer us? Keynote at Hot Chips 31, August 2019. www.hotchips.org/hc31-keynotes-available-to-all.

[114] Wm. A. Wulf and Sally A. McKee. Hitting the memory wall: implications of the obvious. *SIGARCH Computer Architecture News*, 23(1):20–24, 1995.

[115] Tse-Yu Yeh and Yale N. Patt. A comparison of dynamic branch predictors that use two levels of branch history. In *Proceedings of the 20th Annual International Symposium on Computer Architecture*, New York, NY, 1993. Association for Computing Machinery.

[116] Albert Yu. The future of microprocessors. *IEEE Micro*, 16:46–53, 1996.

[117] Matei Zaharia, Mosharaf Chowdhury, Michael J Franklin, et al. Spark: Cluster computing with working sets. In *Proceedings of the 2nd USENIX Conference on Hot Topics in Cloud Computing*, Berkeley, CA, 2010.

[118] Yutao Zhong, Xipeng Shen, and Chen Ding. Program locality analysis using reuse distance. *ACM Transactions on Programming Languages and Systems*, 31(6), 2009.

[119] Alexey Andreyev, Xu Wang, and Alex Eckert, Reinventing Facebook's data center network, Facebook engineering blog. March 14, 2019.

Index